READING IN THE CONTENT AREAS
Strategies for Teachers

READING IN THE CONTENT AREAS
Strategies for Teachers

DELVA DAINES
Brigham Young University

Scott, Foresman and Company
Glenview, Illinois

Dallas, Tex.　　　Oakland, N.J.　　　Palo Alto, Cal.　　　Tucker, Ga.　　　London, England

Library of Congress Cataloging in Publication Data

DAINES, DELVA, 1919-
 Reading in the content areas.

 Includes bibliographies and index.
 1. Reading. 2. Reading comprehension. 3. Reading—Ability testing. I. Title
LB1050.D24   428.4'07'11   81-13601
ISBN 0-673-16025-4   AACR2

ISBN: 0-673-16025-4

Copyright © 1982 Scott, Foresman and Company.
All rights reserved.

1 2 3 4 5 6 7 8-KPF-88 87 86 85 84 83 82 81

Printed in the United States of America

This book is dedicated to my parents,
daughter, friends, and students—all of whom
made possible the writing of it.

CONTENTS

ACKNOWLEDGMENTS

My sincere appreciation is extended to James Bell and Peggy Roland for suggestions on improving the manuscript and to Jeffrey Baldwin and Sharon Black for their assistance in writing Chapter 2. I am grateful to Chris Jennison for his confidence in the text and his encouragement to complete it. I would like to thank Stuart Heimdal for the illustrations, drawn specifically for this book, and Joy Maughan for typing the manuscript. I also want to salute the many teachers and students whose encouragement and inspiration helped make this book possible.

D. D.

Learning to read content materials is a continuous process for students as they progress through the elementary and secondary grades and even after they leave their formal schooling. A teacher's task is to develop in students the interests and skills necessary to comprehend and learn from textual materials. This book contains information and ideas for instructing students in processing content materials. It is designed to perform two major functions:

1. To provide the basic principles, concepts, and procedures for preservice teachers to use in teaching reading in the content areas.
2. To serve as a reference source for graduate students, teachers, reading specialists, and administrators.

The purpose of teaching reading in the content areas is to provide students with the skills necessary to process information with greater understanding and retention, and to provide them with strategies for acquiring knowledge independent of the teacher. *Reading in the Content Areas* presents to the teacher instructional principles and strategies to use in helping students to increase their comprehension of text information. Although the many examples throughout the book are for the middle and secondary school levels, the ideas are applicable in the lower grades and in all subject matter areas. Having studied the principles and the examples, teachers can design their own ideas.

Effective teachers in the content areas include reading skills as part of their everyday teaching of subject matter. Students need to learn the processes for absorbing textual information to achieve a better understanding of subject matter, and the best place to teach reading and thinking skills to students is in the subject classes. Learning from textual materials is a process that continues to develop throughout life as people gain new vocabulary, concepts, and general knowledge in various content areas.

Features of This Book

Each of the nine chapters deals with different principles and reading strategies that can be used to help students learn important concepts contained in textual materials. Each chapter also offers features designed to aid the reader:

> overview
> marginal notes
> summary
> reinforcement activities
> references and bibliography

Overviews. Overviews briefly summarize the important concepts presented in the chapters. They immediately precede the first page of each chapter.

Marginal Notes. Marginal notes, in the form of questions, are provided throughout the text to accentuate important ideas. Questions read before and after a given section of text will direct the kind of information remembered and facilitate the recall and retention of that information. They are in the margins next to the material from which a response can be formed.

Summaries.   Chapter summaries contain, in capsule form, a brief restatement of the chapter contents, showing the relationship between elements within the chapter. They are located at the end of the chapter before the reinforcement activities.

Reinforcement Activities.   The reinforcement activities suggest learning experiences that will enable the reader to implement the concepts and procedures found in each chapter, they also supply models upon which to base instructional strategies. These activities indicate how the chapter content can be used in an instructional setting. They are located at the end of each chapter between the chapter summary and the references and bibliographies.

References and Bibliographies.   The references and bibliographies list relevant literature at the end of each chapter. Each section contains only sources pertinent to that chapter.

The references list alphabetically the literature cited in a chapter, the bibliographies give additional literature deemed relevant to the topic of the chapter but not specifically cited therein. The references cited in a chapter are not included in the bibliography.

Index.   The index includes the names of all authors cited in the references enumerated at the end of each chapter, and important concepts and topics discussed in the text.

How to Use This Book

This book was written to be used as a textbook in a college course or for inservice purposes by teachers, reading specialists, and administrators. Information and ideas that can be integrated with instruction in content are presented. Two plans for using the text are suggested, the plan to follow depends upon the reader's purpose. Readers who are interested in the information for recall or retention might follow the suggestions in Plan A. Readers who will be using the text for reference might follow Plan B.

Plan A.   Follow the steps below to process information for recall or retention.

1. Read the chapters in order, as they appear in the book.
2. Preview each chapter before reading it, by:
   a. Reading the overviews.
   b. Reading the section headings.
   c. Reading the marginal questions.
   d. Reading the summary.
3. Read the marginal questions before and after each section is read.
4. Read section by section for a thorough understanding of the information and for details, while making diagrammatic notes.
5. Review the chapter information for the purpose of remembering important ideas.
6. Complete the reinforcement activities.

Plan B.   Follow the steps below to use the text as a reference work.

1. Examine the table of contents and the overviews for each chapter to obtain a general picture of the whole book or of each chapter.
2. Consult the index to locate specific information about a predetermined topic or subject.
3. Consult the references or bibliographies if you are seeking specific information about the sources or studies referred to in each chapter.

Reading to learn from textual materials is a continual process based on the foundation provided in the school setting. Content area teachers should not teach reading skills in isolation. Instead, if they are to teach reading successfully, they will fuse instruction in the reading skills with the content of the course being taught.

1 READING AND COMPREHENSION

OVERVIEW

Comprehension ought to be the end result of all reading, but too often teachers fail to provide their students with the kind of guidance that will enable them to read effectively. To be able to do that, a teacher must (1) understand what is meant by reading comprehension, and (2) realize what is involved in achieving comprehension.

What is reading
comprehension?

COMPREHENSION is the ultimate goal and hopefully the end result of reading. In fact, reading without understanding cannot be called reading, because reading, by definition, involves deriving meaning from the written word. It necessitates the recognition of graphic symbols and syntactic patterns that both stimulate the recall of meanings drawn from past experience and aid in the constructing of new or extended meanings through the manipulation of ideas. These meanings are organized into thought processes according to the purposes of the reader. Reading, then, is a process, and information from content materials is more easily understood when it is learned as a process rather than an undisciplined collection of facts.

READING FOR MEANING

The processes of comprehending what one reads go on internally, in the mental operations that occur while one is reading. Although they cannot be observed or evaluated directly, the degree of comprehension can be inferred from the way a student responds to what he has read. Several students can read the same passage and yet comprehend the information in different ways, even to the point of not comprehending at all.

Smith (1978, Ch. 5) suggests that obtaining meaning from reading results from a student's interaction with his perceptions of graphic symbols that represent language and meaning, his memory of past experiences and knowledge, and his ability to predict the incoming message conveyed by the written materials. It is a search for relationships between what a reader knows and the new information being processed.

What factors influence
comprehension?

Meaning is not inherent in graphic symbols; rather it exists in the minds of the writer and the reader and in the meaning they together attribute to such symbols. Symbols (or words) and the way in which they are combined must be used by the writer and the reader in the same way for communication to occur. Reading is a process of selecting the graphic cues that signal meaning and extracting the intended meaning from these cues. As Goodman (1976) has noted, the efficient reader uses only as much information as necessary to obtain the meaning. Goodman classifies the information used into three types: graphic, syntactic, and semantic. The graphic information is supplied by the writer, and the reader supplies the other two structures. As a reader reads, he is also employing his knowledge of syntactic rules (patterns for combining words into sentences) as well as semantic rules, which enable him to derive meaning from the written word.

Background experience is an essential factor in enabling a student to explore and interact with his environment and to establish a sense of predictability as he deals with the world of ideas (Ausubel 1968, Karlin 1977, and Smith 1978). The background experience of a student directly affects the quality and quantity of his ideas, and these ideas affect every kind of communication. During the reading process, the incoming information, gleaned from graphic and grammar cues, is molded by the reader's prior knowledge and by his organization of that knowledge. For example, a student must have some prior knowledge of the topic and its related vocabulary to arrive at an understanding consistent with the author's meaning. Comprehension, then, involves relating the new and the known during the reading process (Pearson, Hansen, and Gordon 1979, and Anderson and Freebody 1979).

The process of making predictions while reading, which involves eliminating any unlikely alternatives and interpretations, is as much a part of reading as it is of everyday living. Prediction requires the use of prior knowledge relevant to daily events. The knowledge and experience a student brings to what he reads will determine in part how well he can make accurate predictions and comprehend the material.

Reading comprehension is a communication process. It involves reconstructing an author's message by using one's prior knowledge, especially the knowledge of language. Thought and language become one when a student reads with understanding; however, the process of comprehension is not dependent solely upon the student's understanding of words and the way they are used. Decoding skills, the ability to reason in verbal and nonverbal terms, having a purpose for reading, and the characteristics of the text contribute as well.

As is evident, many factors influence students' comprehension of what they read. Some of the more essential elements may be summarized as follows:

1. Word recognition skills influence comprehension.
2. The reader must be able to employ the same level of abstraction in using words as has the writer.
3. Comprehension is largely dependent on the ability to reason in verbal and nonverbal terms.
4. The purpose for which a student reads has considerable influence on comprehension.
5. The teacher's guidance influences how the student understands particular assignments.
6. The ability to read at different rates seems to influence reading comprehension.
7. Questions asked by the teacher and student influence what is comprehended.
8. The length and difficulty of the material contribute to the understanding of its content.
9. Memory plays an important role in reading with comprehension.
10. Study skills enable a student to use information effectively.
11. Vocabulary acquisition and the ability to form concepts are essential skills for reading with understanding.
12. Interest in the material being read adds to comprehension.

Students, then, comprehend and retain textual information by using their general knowledge, semantic understanding, and reasoning abilities. As they read a written message, the students enlarge upon existing knowledge or produce new knowledge by grouping together and organizing the information they perceive (Pezdek 1980). Textual material that the student organizes is more likely to be remembered than when it is dispersed. This ability to learn from textual materials improves as the student matures in general mental ability. Since individual differences in general mental ability increase with age and as students progress through school, the range of reading achievement likewise increases (Anderson, Spiro, and Montague 1977, Kintsch 1974, and Taylor 1980).

Being intent on understanding and remembering textual material improves a student's comprehension. Students generate responses when they have a purpose for reading (Marks, Doctorow, and Wittrock 1974, and Singer 1976). Having this purpose enables students to store in memory certain information that is retrieved when recalling specific ideas, sequence, words, etc. (Pichert and Anderson 1976).

As students interact with their texts, according to their purposes and the structure of the text, they may use a "bottom-up" or "top-down" mode to learn and comprehend. In the bottom-up mode, the students approach their reading in sequence from (1) perceiving the words and forming these sensations into words, (2) organizing words into phrases and sentences, utilizing their syntactic understanding, (3) associating meaning through concepts or schemas for assimilating the incoming information, and (4) using reading, the process to reason and to store meaning. In the top-down mode, students use an abstract knowledge schema to direct their attention to print materials or stimuli in a selective manner. The information either confirms or disconfirms the reader's expectations (Rumelhart 1977).

SUMMARY

Reading is the assimilation of meaning that results from the interaction between the graphic and grammar cues offered by the material and the reader's background of experiences and prediction of the written material's message. Background experiences, syntax, and semantics are essential parts of information processing. The comprehension processes are mental operations that occur while an individual is reading.

The achievement of students is increased when comprehension skills instruction is integrated with instruction in content. Guided reading and instruction should be provided for students when they first encounter textbooks and materials that are unfamiliar. This procedure helps to assure the students' comprehension of new vocabulary and concepts, and to give them confidence in approaching new reading tasks.

Reinforcement Activity

Examine and explain your definition of reading comprehension. Tell how it will influence or change your approach to teaching in the content area.

References

ANDERSON, RICHARD C., SPIRO, RAND, and MONTAGUE, W. E., eds. *Schooling and Acquisition of Knowledge*. Hillsdale, New Jersey: Lawrence Erlbaum Associates, 1977.

ANDERSON, R. C., and FREEBODY, P. *Vocabulary Knowledge*. Technical Report No. 136, University of Illinois at Urbana-Champaign: Center for the Study of Reading, 1979.

AUSUBEL, DAVID P. *Educational Psychology—A Cognitive View*. New York: Holt, Rinehart and Winston, 1968.

GOODMAN, KENNETH S. "Reading: A Psycholinguistic Guessing Game." In *Theoretical Models and Processes of Reading*, edited by Harry Singer and Robert Ruddell. 2nd ed. Newark, Delaware: International Reading Association, 1976, 497–508.

KARLIN, ROBERT. *Teaching Reading in High School: Improving Reading in Content Areas*. Indianapolis: Bobbs-Merrill Co., Inc., 1977.

KINTSCH, WALTER. *The Representation of Meaning in Memory*. Hillsdale, New Jersey: Lawrence Erlbaum Associates, 1974.

MARKS, C. B., DOCTOROW, M. J., and WITTROCK, M. C. "Word Frequency and Reading Comprehension." *Journal of Educational Psychology* 67 (1974): 259–262.

PEARSON, P. D., HANSEN, J., and GORDON, C. "The Effect of Background Knowledge on Young Children's Comprehension of Explicit and Implicit Informa-

tion." *Journal of Reading Behavior* 11 (1979): 201–209.

PEZDEK, KATHY. "Arguments for a Constructive Approach to Comprehension and Memory." In *Reading and Understanding*, edited by Frank B. Murray. Newark, Delaware: International Reading Association, 1980, 40–73.

PICHERT, J. W., and ANDERSON, R. C. *Taking Different Perspectives on a Story*. Technical Report No. 14. University of Illinois at Urbana-Champaign: Center for the Study of Reading, 1976.

RUMELHART, D. E. "Understanding and Summarizing Brief Stories." In *Basic Processes in Reading: Perception and Comprehension*, edited by D. La Berge and S. J. Samuels. Hillsdale, New Jersey: Lawrence Erlbaum Associates, 1977.

SINGER, HARRY. "Conceptualization in Learning to Read." In *Theoretical Models and Processes of Reading*, edited by Harry Singer and Robert B. Ruddell. 2nd ed. Newark, Delaware: International Reading Association, 1976, 302–319.

SMITH, FRANK. *Understanding Reading: A Psycholinguistic Analysis of Reading and Learning to Read*. New York: Holt, Rinehart and Winston, Inc., 1978.

TAYLOR, BARBARA M. "Children's Memory for Expository Text after Reading." *Reading Research Quarterly* 15 (1980): 399–411.

Bibliography

BORMUTH, JOHN R. "An Operational Definition of Comprehension Instruction." In *Psycholinguistics and the Teaching of Reading*, edited by K. S. Goodman and J. T. Fleming. Newark, Delaware: International Reading Association, 1969, 48–60.

DAVIS, FREDERICK B. "Psychometric Research on Com-

prehension in Reading." *Reading Research Quarterly* 7 (1972): 628–678.

GOODMAN, KENNETH S. *The Psycholinguistic Nature of the Reading Process*. Detroit, Michigan: Wayne State University, 1968, 15–26.

HARKER, JOHN W. "Implications from Models of Reading

Comprehension." In *Teachers, Tangibles, Techniques: Comprehension of Content in Reading*, edited by Bonnie Smith Schulwitz. Newark, Delaware: International Reading Association, 1975, 2–9.

KOLERS, P. A. "Reading Is Only Incidentally Visual." In *Psycholinguistics and the Teaching of Reading*, edited by K. S. Goodman and J. T. Fleming. Newark, Delaware: International Reading Association, 1969, 8–16.

LANTAFF, ROGER E. "Two Factors Affecting Text Recall." In *Reading: Disciplined Inquiry in Process and Practice*, edited by P. David Pearson and Jane Hansen. Clemson, South Carolina:Twenty-seventh Yearbook of the National Reading Conference, 1978, 93–98.

MEYER, B. F., BRANDT, D. M., and BLUTH, G. J. "Use of Top-Level Structure in Text: Key for Reading Comprehension of Ninth-Grade Students." *Reading Research Quarterly* 16 (1980): 72–103.

OLSHAVSKY, JILL E. "Comprehension Profiles of Good and Poor Readers across Materials of Increasing Difficulty." In *Reading: Disciplined Inquiry in Process and Practice*, edited by P. David Pearson and Jane Hansen. Clemson, South Carolina: Twenty-seventh Yearbook of the National Reading Conference, 1978, 73–76.

PEARSON, P. DAVID and JOHNSON, DALE D. *Teaching Reading Comprehension*. New York: Holt, Rinehart and Winston, 1978.

SCHWARTZ, ROBERT M. "Levels of Processing: The Strategic Demands of Reading Comprehension." *Reading Research Quarterly* 15 (1980): 433–450.

SMITH, FRANK. "The Role of Prediction in Reading." *Elementary English* 52 (1975): 305–311.

STEFFENSEN, MARGARET S., JOAG-DEV, CHITRA, and ANDERSON, RICHARD C. "A Cross-Cultural Perspective on Reading Comprehension." *Reading Research Quarterly* 15 (1979): 10–29.

WATERHOUSE, LYNN H. "The Implications of Theories of Language and Thought for Reading." In *Language Awareness and Reading*, edited by Frank B. Murray. Newark, Delaware: International Reading Association, 1980, 1–22.

WHEAT, THOMAS E., and EDMOND, ROSE M. "The Concept of Comprehension: An Analysis." *Journal of Reading* 18 (1975): 523–526.

2 COMPREHENSION AND THE CONTENT AREAS

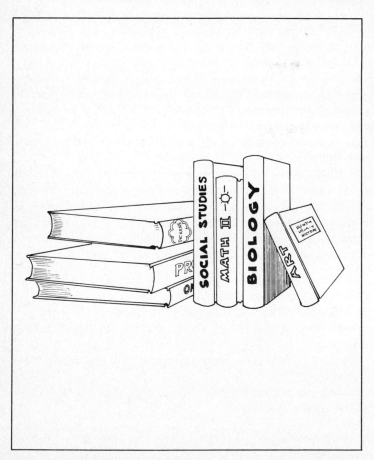

OVERVIEW
In order to help students develop comprehension skills, teachers must understand what those skills are and be able to give students specific direction appropriate to the content area. This chapter analyzes the skills needed to comprehend written material and illustrates how such teaching can be integrated with teaching the various content areas.

How can comprehension skills be taught?

SOME OF THE BEST opportunities for teaching reading skills—often called reading, thinking, or reasoning processes—occur in teaching how to improve comprehension when reading in content areas such as social studies, science, mathematics, etc. While learning the multiple reading processes, students are also absorbing and understanding content. This productive relationship between reading comprehension instruction and developing a mastery of the content areas centers on the process of reading for content. Teachers should stress instruction in comprehending while reading in the content areas.

Research shows that general reading ability alone is often insufficient to ensure comprehension of content area materials. According to Otto (1977), the teaching of relevant reading skills sharpens the process of developing reading comprehension. Students' achievements in content areas improve when instruction in the reading process is integrated into content instruction (Artley 1944, Herber and Sanders 1969). Rupley (1976, 1977) and Rupley and Blair (1978) indicate that the ability of students to read well is directly influenced by the instruction they receive from teachers. If reading is to become functional in the lives of students, formal instruction in developing comprehension skills should begin as soon as children start using written materials.

The reading and thinking skills students use to structure information as they read content materials vary from subject to subject. An important role of the teacher, therefore, is to provide instruction in the processes necessary to meet these diverse reading needs, as well as in the purposes for reading. A teacher should also be prepared to provide materials that match the different reading levels of the students. (The spread from the high to low achievers frequently is one-and-one-half to twice the number of the grade level. Thus, in the fifth grade, there may be more than an eight-year difference between the best and poorest readers [Goodlad, 1966].)

Durkin (1978–1979) conducted a study in grades three through six to learn if comprehension instruction is provided in the reading of social studies and, if so, the amount of time allotted to it. Classroom observations yielded eight categories for classifying teacher behavior in relation to comprehension instruction: instruction, review of instruction, application, assignment, help with assignment, preparation for reading, assessment, and prediction. Major findings indicated:

1. Almost no comprehension instruction was found.
2. Fact questions served for assessing comprehension.
3. Considerable time was spent on giving, completing, and checking assignments.
4. Large amounts of time were spent on transitional and noninstructional activities.
5. Social studies was not viewed as a time to help students with comprehending written discourse.

Hodges (1980) and Durkin suggest that the data of this study do not explain how those students considered to be good readers acquire their ability to comprehend. Hodges offers three reasons: maturation; transfer of instruction from other areas, such as listening comprehension; and comprehension instruction.

There are specific reading skills or thinking processes that students can use to increase their comprehension of subject materials. These processes stem from the mind forming patterns of concepts concerning objects, events, processes, and relationships. Teachers should be very clear about the specific reading processes they wish students to respond to or develop. Some skills, such as analysis, are common to many subjects, whereas an ability to detect propaganda is needed in only a few subjects. The various reading skills must be taught along with instruction in the content areas, since students increase their comprehension by using these processes.

The identification of the reading skills necessary for comprehension has been an objective of research for many years (Bloom et al. 1956; Bloom, Hastings, and Madaus 1971; Davis 1968, 1972; Otto 1977; and White 1973). Various taxonomies have sought to describe hierarchical levels of thinking and to identify distinguishable comprehension skills. The research findings of Peters and Peters (1976) seem to verify the existence of separate skills. Many skills-management systems subscribe to the skills approach. These approaches are based on the supposition that reading comprehension can be divided into subskills, which are needed to help students learn content.

The combined approach of using the psycholinguistic views of language and cognition and the subskills of the reading process in assisting students to increase their comprehension of textual materials is recommended. Some of the specific comprehension skills or thinking processes that are necessary for students to learn text are presented in the remainder of this chapter; strategies to teach many of these skills are presented in the following chapters. Now, a general overview of the reading skills used to process text materials in the content areas of social studies, science, mathematics, English and the language arts, general business, bookkeeping and accounting, art, music, physical education, health, homemaking, and industrial arts.

What reading skills are needed for comprehension?

SOCIAL STUDIES

Reading in the social studies includes subject areas such as geography, history, civics, anthropology, economics, sociology, and psychology. These subjects are taught as either separate or integrated courses, using either single or multiple textbooks. The texts or units of study serve as a guide in determining the topics and the sequence in which they are studied.

The writing style of most social studies textbooks is expository. Authors use the expository style of writing to convey information and explain facts and ideas. At times, narration is used to introduce or elaborate on an event or to tell about a famous person. Definitional paragraphs are frquent. Social science textbooks are usually loaded with complex concepts, and the vocab-

How does one read the social sciences?

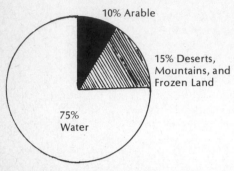

A Graphic Representation of
the Earth's Surface

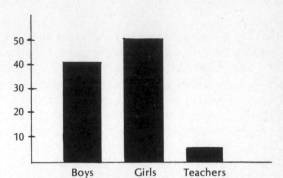

A Comparison of the Number of Boys, Girls, and
Teachers in the First Grade Classrooms

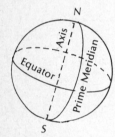

International
Dateline

ulary may be highly specialized. Some aspects of social studies are controversial, and occasionally issues are presented in an emotional way.

The major source for reading about social studies is the textbook. Graphic materials, major reference books, magazines, journals, newspapers, trade and other nonfiction books can be used to obtain additional information. Pictures, maps, charts, tables, graphs, and diagrams are abundant in social studies materials, although the extent to which graphics are used varies from text to text, and even within texts. Often the reader is referred to a graphic to obtain specific information, such as the location of a city or a river, before he continues reading; or a reader may be directed to study the details on a graph and to relate the information to another concept before proceeding further in the textbook.

The interpretation of social studies materials is highly dependent upon the students' abilities to comprehend a specific group of concepts. The teacher should emphasize retaining major concepts instead of many unrelated facts. Students should also be expected to gain enough specific information to expound on or defend key concepts.

The vocabulary used to present the various concepts may include technical terms, multisyllabic words, and common words used in new and different ways. For example:

board	democracy	regulatory
commission	equality	restrictive
congress	family	rights
constitution	nature	values

What thinking skills are basic to understanding the social sciences?

When reading social studies materials, students will find that some ideas and information are stated explicitly, whereas other information must be inferred. Students will need to react to ideas, make associations, research

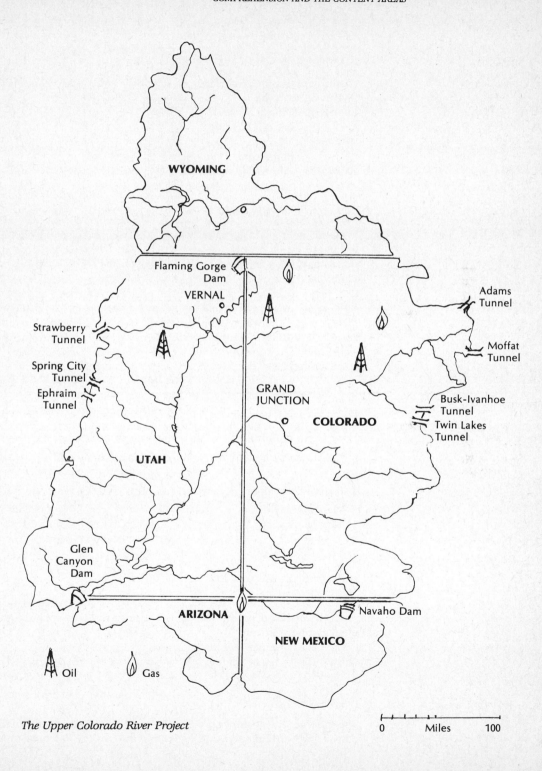

The Upper Colorado River Project

information, and solve problems. A few of the reading processes basic to understanding social studies materials are:

1. *Sequencing important chronological events.*

   The major events that influenced immigration to the United States between 1860 and 1920 were:
   1860–1880: Settling the West
                      Railroad building
   1880–1900: Famine in Ireland
                      Militarism in Germany
   1900–1920: Industrial development
                      Demand for unskilled labor

2. *Conceptualizing time and space.*

   In the 1950s the world appeared neat and orderly, but danger lurked because of the powers of Washington and Moscow. In the 1960s the power blocs confronted the nationalism of underdeveloped countries claiming "sovereignty," and Moscow and Peking bitterly denounced each other, while in the USA, under the disguise of benevolence, militarism emerged. The 1970s saw even greater overcrowding and hunger among people in the most crowded parts of the world. Washington and Peking resumed a relationship that was unsteady in the face of the continued Sino-Soviet schism. A world crisis arising in the Middle East around hostages, energy supplies, and ideology spilled over into the 1980s.

3. *Differentiating fact from opinion.*

   The following statements of opinion were converted to statements of fact.

Opinion	Fact
a. Taxes increase every year.	a. Taxes increased 15% last year, but remained the same this year.
b. It is cold enough to freeze water.	b. It was 39 degrees today.
c. The schools have money to maintain the same programs.	c. The school population has increased 3.5% and state school funds will be decreased by 2.5% next year.

4. *Identifying cause and effect relationships.*

   When a company has to pay for the repair of too many damaged cars, it raises the amount of money it charges its customers for protection by increasing their insurance rates.
   Effect: The insurance rates are increased.
   Cause: The company has to pay for the repair of too many damaged cars.

5. *Detecting propaganda.*

   The MX system is a strategic disaster. It will lead to major environmental destruction, social disorder, depletion of water resources, increased risk of cancer, and an economic drain on the United States treasury. (This is a card-stacking technique since other points of view are not recognized or presented.)

Other reading and thinking processes necessary for understanding social studies concepts include the following:

6. *Comparing ideas.*
7. *Classifying ideas.*
8. *Predicting outcomes.*
9. *Analyzing multiple events.*
10. *Interpreting rudimentary information.*
11. *Organizing and summarizing information.*
12. *Making and defending judgments.*

SCIENCE

Reading materials in the biological and physical sciences include biology, botany, zoology, physical science, chemistry, physics, and geology. The writing style of science materials is expository and is integrated with directions and mathematical equations as well as charts, graphs, and diagrams. The vocabulary includes many technical terms and special uses of common words. The writers of science textbooks introduce many new concepts and words that result in higher readability levels. The lack of sequence and the overlap of science content between grade levels adds to the problem of concept acquisition and vocabulary development.

How does one read science materials?

Examples of highly specialized technical terms used in science textbooks, articles, and magazines are:

amphibian	electron	piston
bryophytes	molecule	radioactivity
capillary	nonparastic	rarefaction
cartilage	photosynthesis	sporophyte

Graphic materials are an integral part of science textbooks and are used to help explain concepts, theories, and processes, and to demonstrate procedures. Thus, it is vital that students receive direct instruction in utilizing graphics in the study of science. Examples of graphics are shown on pages 14–15.

Reading science materials requires that students follow, understand, and retain a great amount of detail related to abstractions and theories. Students are expected to become proficient in using many comprehension or thinking processes essential to understanding science concepts, including:

What thinking skills are basic to understanding science?

1. *Identifying the meaning of and explaining the significance of symbols and formulas.*

   a. When substances are expressed in terms of chemical symbols, identifying the meaning of each symbol, explaining the signifi-

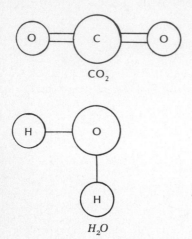

CO₂

H₂O

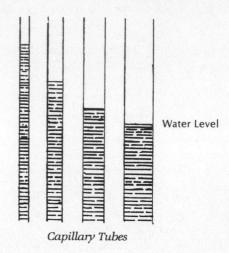

Water Level

Capillary Tubes

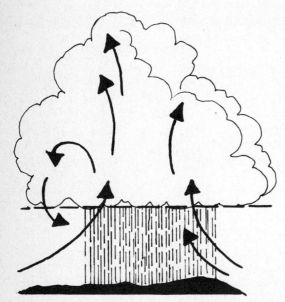

Conventional Rainfall

Orographic Rainfall

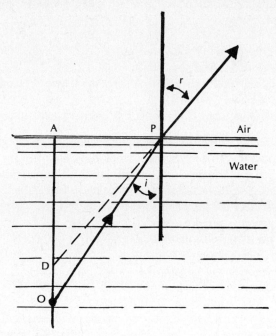

*Apparent Depth of a
Submerged Object*

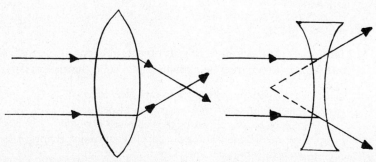

*Deviation of Parallel Light
Rays by Lenses*

cance of their arrangement, and identifying the substances are essential skills in being able to apply symbols, formulas, and abbreviations.

H₂O

H represents a hydrogen atom

O represents an oxygen atom

The subscript **2** indicates that there are 2 hydrogen atoms for each oxygen atom.

The arrangement of symbols represents the substance of water.

b. The ideal gas law is used in several scientific disciplines. Knowing the meaning of each symbol (including appropriate units) in the mathematical expression of this law and understanding the significance of their arrangement are necessary skills.

PV = nRT

P represents pressure exerted by the gas

V represents volume of the gas

n represents amount of gas

R represents gas constant

T represents temperature of the gas

= means "equals" or "is equivalent to"

Symbols written in sequence with no mathematical symbol separating them are to be multiplied. Thus **nRT** means, "multiply the amount of gas by the gas constant and then multiply that result by the temperature of the gas."

The units of pressure, volume, amount, and temperature must correspond to the value of the gas constant used. If the gas constant $0.08206 \frac{\text{liter–atom}}{\text{mole–K}}$ is used, then pressure must be expressed in atmosphere, volume in liters, amount in moles, and temperature in kelvin.

2. *Classifying objects.*

a. Many scientific disciplines classify objects in terms of their physical state. A substance may be classified as a solid, liquid, or gas.

    solid: has a definite volume and shape (ice, iron)
    liquid: has a definite volume but no definite shape.
            (Shape is determined by the container.) (water)
    gas: has no definite volume or shape. (Volume and shape are determined by the container.) (steam, chlorine)

b. Each of the chemical elements may be classified as a metal or a nonmetal depending upon its chemical properties.

    metal: iron, chromium, mercury
    nonmetal: sulphur, phosphorous

3. *Noticing and describing conditions and pertinent details.*

Experiments may be rendered useless by neglecting to describe important conditions or by failing to collect pertinent data.

a. The value of a chemical analysis of a certain rock is lessened considerably if the site where the rock was found is not recorded.

b. The cost of a box of soap is most relevant only if the amount of soap in the box is known.

c. The effect of plunging one's hand into a pot of water will be dramatically altered, depending on the temperature of the water.

4. *Applying data to solve a problem.*

Knowing what data are necessary to solve a problem is very important. Consider this question: How many grams of oxygen are required to react with 10 grams of iron to form red iron oxide?

To solve this problem, one must know the stoichiometric relationship available from a balanced chemical equation ($4Fe + 3O_2 \rightarrow 2\ Fe_2O_3$) and the atomic weights of iron and oxygen. Data regarding temperature, pressure, purity of the iron or oxygen, color of the iron oxide, or phase of the moon are not necessary to the solution of the problem. If, however, the *volume* of oxygen were needed, then the problem could not be solved with the data given, for temperature and pressure of the oxygen are also required.

Other reading or thinking processes necessary to understanding science concepts include the following:

5. *Following precise directions.*
6. *Sequencing information.*
7. *Comparing similarities and dissimilarities.*
8. *Hypothesizing solutions to problems.*
9. *Collecting, organizing, and listing data.*
10. *Interpreting data.*
11. *Determining and explaining relationships.*
12. *Making and defending decisions.*

There is so much information available in the science areas that students need to learn how to organize their study of textbooks and other instructional materials. Instruction in applying study skills is an important part of this organization for learning. The ability to read carefully and critically is essential for the comprehension of the biological and physical sciences.

MATHEMATICS

Mathematics textbooks make great demands on the reading skills of students. Page after page presents specialized and rigorous analytical exposition, graphics, examples, and computation problems. The writing style used for

How is reading math specialized?

mathematics includes definitions, classifications, explanations, equations, formulas, abbreviations, and problems. There are more ideas per line and per page in a math book than in any other type of writing. The mathematical material is concise and abstract and is interlaced with complex relationships. These many patterns necessitate that students develop diverse reading skills.

Vocabulary development is most important in mathematics. Technical terms, such as *isosceles*, *sine*, and *cosine*, are used to convey concepts that are precise and complex. Precision is essential in the study of math. Words with similar meanings are not functional since the meanings have to be exact in mathematical computations. Common words like *cone*, *set*, and *square* are used with different meanings in this subject area. Some words, such as *add*, *subtract*, or *divide* are process signals. *Before, decrease*, and *of* are words that signify to the readers that directions are being given for procedures they are to follow. Learning and using numerical symbols and signs that represent basic concepts, such as $+$, $\times$, $-$, $\div$, $>$, $<$, are essential in reading mathematics textbooks.

Comprehension or reading processes fundamental to understanding mathematics textbooks include:

What thinking processes are basic to understanding mathematics?

1. *Translating verbal symbols into mathematical symbols and formulas.*

   "The ratio of twice the number and seven is the same as five times the number decreased by three."

   The mathematical equation for this statement would be $\dfrac{2X}{7} = 5X - 3$. (This may be a true mathematical statement or a false mathematical statement for all numbers.)

2. *Identifying the meaning of symbols and abbreviations.*

   "2X means 2 times the same number."

   $\sqrt{}$ is the symbol for square root.

   $\dfrac{6}{4}$ means 4 divided into 6.

   3^4 means 4 factors of 3 or 3 multiplied by itself 4 times.

3. *Selecting appropriate processes to analyze and solve problems.*

   "Bill purchased 3 ties and a $4.00 belt. The total cost was $13.00. How much did each tie cost?"
   To analyze this problem, one would follow these steps:

   a. Let X equal the price of each tie.

   b. $\underbrace{\text{The cost of the 3 ties}}_{3X} + \underbrace{\text{the cost of the belt}}_{4} \underset{\downarrow}{=} \underbrace{\text{the total cost}}_{13}$

   c. $3X + 4 = 13$ is the equation.

    d. Solve: $3X = 13 - 4$

$$3X = \frac{9}{3}$$

$$X = 3$$

    e. Each tie cost $3.00.

4. *Differentiating between significant and insignificant facts.*

"Jerry and Mary purchased an economical car, which cost $3,000.00 with a monthly payment of $196.66 for 18 months, to travel 2,000 miles to visit family. They traveled 50 miles per hour, averaging 30 miles to the gallon of gasoline. How much driving time did it take them to reach their destination?" Significant facts:

Distance traveled: 2,000 miles

Rate of travel: 50 miles per hour

$$(Formula):\ D = RT \text{ or } T = \frac{D}{R}$$

$$T = \frac{2,000}{50}$$

$$(Answer):\ T = 40 \text{ hours}$$

Insignificant facts:

The cost of the car, the monthly payments on the car, and the gasoline mileage are unimportant facts for solving this problem.

Other reading or thinking processes fundamental to understanding mathematics textbooks include:

5. *Following the directions precisely and sequentially.*
6. *Explaining an overview of a problem.*
7. *Translating formulas into significant relationships.*
8. *Utilizing tables of square roots, common logarithms of numbers, etc.*

When students receive direct instruction in the highly specialized mathematical reading skills, their comprehension of the concepts improves. These improved comprehension skills increase their ability to solve mathematical word problems. Examples of graphics are shown.

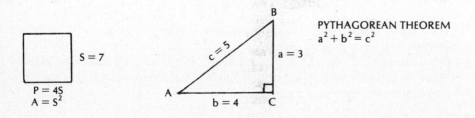

$S = 7$

$P = 4S$
$A = S^2$

$c = 5$, $a = 3$, $b = 4$

PYTHAGOREAN THEOREM
$a^2 + b^2 = c^2$

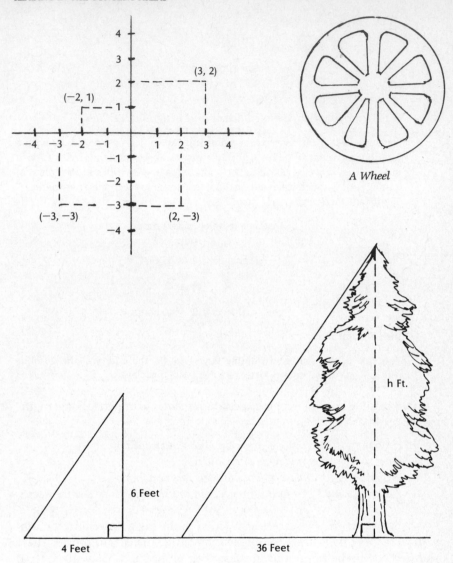

A Wheel

ENGLISH AND THE LANGUAGE ARTS

Teachers of English and language arts have a variety of subjects to teach—literature, speech, drama, grammar, written composition. In addition to printed materials, they utilize all kinds of nonprint and media materials. These teachers are also expected to help students develop an appreciation of and continuing interest in literature.

Reading literature requires the use of many diverse skills if one is to gain appreciation and comprehension of a selection. The emotional maturity and general reading skills of the readers will influence their appreciation and understanding of what is read. Vocabulary development is important, since words provide clues to the meaning of the materials. Literature allows for identification between the readers and fictional characters and often contributes to solving personal problems. Then, too, the same selection or passage may stimulate different reactions at different times as readers develop an understanding of themselves and those around them. These factors become even more essential when all students are not expected to read the identical selection at the same time.

The reading processes considered essential to understanding literature are:

What thinking processes are basic to understanding literature?

1. *Focusing on the author's meaning.*

   One of the most important factors in comprehending and enjoying the richness of literature is the ability to unfold the layers of meaning that lie beneath the surface of an essay, a story, a novel, or a poem. For kindergarten and first grade children, a detective analogy might be used to urge them to look for clues to detect the real meaning behind some of Aesop's fables, the simpler parables of Jesus, or the illustrative stories from Zen.

   At the third or fourth grade level, children may be ready to look for meanings in a more advanced work such as C. S. Lewis's extended Christian allegory, *The Chronicles of Narnia.*

   Children who have been trained in the early grades to look for deeper meanings are prepared, when they reach a secondary level, to consider Ralph, Simon, Jack, Piggy, and Roger of *Lord of the Flies* not merely as participants in an exciting adventure, but as representatives of human nature at its primitive level. *The Scarlet Letter* becomes not merely a search for the guilty, but a study in the deeper effects of that guilt. Advanced students may be ready to work with the many-faceted symbols and implications of Tolkien's *Lord of the Rings.*

   Lifelong habits of reading for depth of meaning can thus be established in the early grades and carried through each level to prepare the student eventually to interpret and comprehend the richest and most complex works of our literature.

   Closely related processes also essential to this type of understanding include:

   a. Being alert to shades of meaning.

   b. Recognizing subplots to the central theme.

   c. Evaluating and looking objectively at the ideas of the author.

2. *Analyzing characters and their motives, events, and problems.*

   The film *The Wizard of Oz* had been shown on television, and the following morning the playground at St. George's preschool in Austin, Texas, was filled with the shrieks and squeals of a five-year-old "wicked witch" chasing a four-year-old Dorothy, Scarecrow, Tin Man, and Toto through the barrels and up and down the jungle gyms.

Children have a natural tendency to identify with characters in a story and to act out in play not only the story itself but projected "future adventures" of the characters that they enjoy. Teachers can work with this natural tendency, to help young children learn to look more closely at the characters in the stories they read and to consider their motives and the events and problems in which they are involved.

Kindergarten children respond well to a "what if" situation. "What if Curious George (a monkey, hero of a series of books by H. L. Rey) were to visit our school? He got ink all over the house trying to fill a fountain pen. What would happen if he got into our art supplies?" Questions like these help the children to think about specific incidents from the books that show what George does, to draw inferences about his character (thoughtless curiosity, impulsive action, childlike innocence about possible consequences to his action), and to consider how the same traits and motives might cause the character to respond to other situations. "If George ate a puzzle piece in one of the books, he would probably want to taste our puzzles too. He might even try to eat our blocks—or our Lincoln logs." Through an imaginative discussion of a mischievous monkey, children are learning processes of observation and inference that will help them in the more complex character analysis they will encounter in advanced reading throughout their education.

Secondary students with some early experience in imaginative character analysis are more capable of understanding abstract problems, conflicts, and motivations. They are ready to wonder whether, if they had experienced the treatment Heathcliff did as a child in *Wuthering Heights*, they would have responded with the intensity of emotion and vindictiveness that he did as an adult when fate gave him power over those who had manipulated him. They are ready to look in themselves for some of the feelings, impulses, and desires represented by the extremes of Ralph and Jack in Golding's *Lord of the Flies*. They are ready to see Anne Frank as an intimate friend, responding to parents, pressures, and problems in the same way that they might respond. They are ready to notice what aspects of her personality caused her to respond to pressures differently from her sister Margot and her friend Peter.

The understanding of character is important to the comprehension and appreciation of most literature and drama. This understanding can begin as an imaginative game in the early grades, and should continue with meaningful examination of problems during the secondary years.

3. *Drawing inferences from characters, settings, and events.*

Just before the morning recess, the teacher had read aloud the first chapters of Lewis Carroll's *Alice's Adventures in Wonderland*. When the children returned from the playground, they found at their places small paper cups filled with a mysterious purple liquid. Beside each cup was a sign, "Drink Me." "You have in front of you the same magic liquid that Alice found," their teacher instructed them. "When you drink it, you will become exactly three inches high. How are things going to look to you? What are you going to think? What are you going to do?" She told the children to drink the liquid and then take a sheet of paper and write about the way the world looked to them and the adventures that they were going to have. The result was one of the most meaningful creative writing experiences that the children had ever had. For many of them it was the beginning of a fascination with Alice that was to last for several years. To participate with Alice in the experience of being small, the children had to draw inferences about Alice's personality and about their own. They had to think about the setting and the events of the story; and they had to make changes, adaptations, and imaginative projections in creating their own "Wonderlands."

Children in the elementary grades can draw particularly meaningful inferences from some of the books of history and biography that are written on the children's level. *Abe Lincoln Gets His Chance* allows the child to draw inferences not only about Abe as he is portrayed in the story, but also about other children who grew up enduring a life of hard work and frequent loss on the American Frontier. More advanced children may be urged to draw inferences about those qualities in Abe's personality that led him to persist and achieve in the face of circumstances that would have forced many to abandon all hope of educating themselves or rising above a discouraging early environment.

Students on a secondary level often find Walter Van Tilberg Clark's *The Ox Bow Incident* to be an exciting "horse opera," but students who have had experiences in drawing inferences are ready to look beyond the stereotyped saloon, drunken brawl, and hastily formed lynching party. They are ready to notice that the residents of Bridger's Wells are not the kind of individuals ordinarily found in a John Wayne or Clint Eastwood movie. There is a difference between the formalistic, Bible-quoting Christianity of the town's minister as he throws a few empty clichés at the mob and then retreats in his cowardice, and the genuine, empathetic Christianity of the black former slave Sparks as he relinquishes a coat that would have protected him from the blizzard and later as he risks public condemnation to offer some words of comfort to the "rustlers" who are about to be killed. Sensitive students will notice the contrast; they can learn to draw the intended inferences from it. Davies is a man with very intense convictions but without the strength to stand up for them in the face of powerful mob opposition. Which is correct, his rationalization at the time of the crisis that he can do nothing, or his self-condemnation afterward as he tortures himself with the thought that possibly he could have? Again, alert students can draw meaningful inferences from this dilemma. Students enrolled in history as well as English courses will be able to draw inferences from the frightening parallel between the leadership style of Colonel Tetley—as he leads his mob to irrational vengeance and the hanging of innocent men—and that of Adolf Hitler as he was leading his country to irrational hatred and the killing of thousands of innocent Jews at the very time that the novel was written.

Again, the simple patterns of inferences established with Alice or with Abraham Lincoln in the early grades can give way to complex and mature inferences as students are challenged by deeper and more sophisticated works of literature.

4. *Identifying characteristics of good writing.*

A teacher must be very careful not to spoil the spontaneous enjoyment of reading by over-insistence on what "good writing" is according to mature literary considerations. From the earliest grades, however, a teacher can work subtly to promote an awareness of *why* certain books continue to interest and delight the children.

The youngest kindergarten children can recognize that Dr. Seuss books are "fun to say." Concepts such as rhythm and rhyme can be introduced inductively while the children are still chuckling with delight over Dr. Seuss's *One Fish Two Fish Red Fish Blue Fish* or laughing over the escapades of *Yertle the Turtle* or *Horton Hatches the Egg.*

Elementary school children will listen spellbound to a reading of Poe's "The Raven." While they are fascinated with the various sound patterns and images of the poem, the teacher can explain to them, using Poe's own words if the essay is available, how those sounds were selected and arranged to create the particular effect that Poe desired. If the children show interest, the teacher can continue by using some of Poe's short stories—"The Tell Tale Heart" and "The Masque of the Red Death," for example—to demonstrate the descriptive power of language and detail.

Secondary students can begin to understand more sophisticated concepts such as point of view, plot structure, major themes, methods of character development, and symbolism. These concepts should be introduced inductively rather than prescriptively, and should not be emphasized to the extent that the students' enjoyment of reading is impaired. Attention to Twain's skillful character development should not detract from the exciting adventure of *Huckleberry Finn.* Huck's problem with his conscience should not detract from the excitement of riding the raft down the river; it should help the students to perceive Huck as a very human boy with some of the same fears and questions that they themselves may have at the same age. Students can understand how this kind of detail can help them to identify with Huck and make his adventures more realistic for them. Similarly, study of the symbolism in Tolkien's *The Hobbit* should add richness to the fantasy, not destroy a student's enjoyment of it.

Other reading or thinking processes vital to understanding literature include:

5. *Interpreting the relationship of details.*
6. *Appreciating the mood and style of the author.*
7. *Responding to form, rhyme, and overtones.*
8. *Dealing with various literary devices and forms such as metaphors, sonnets, etc.*
9. *Recognizing the plot, climax, and final solution to the story.*
10. *Evaluating and looking objectively at the author's ideas.*

SPEECH AND DRAMA

What thinking processes are basic to speech and drama?

Students' comprehension and appreciation of drama and speech are increased when they understand the setting and characters of a play, and learn to make inferences about the action and dialogue of the characters. The thinking processes necessary for comprehending drama and speech are:

1. *Understanding the action and setting.*

Many high school students find it difficult to appreciate Shakespeare's *Julius Caesar* because the setting is so distant and the actions and motivations of the characters may seem contrived and unreal. A teacher can help to increase comprehension and appreciation by providing a background in which the culture that forms the setting of the play can be more easily understood. Slides or films can provide a visual background that will make the setting seem more natural, more real. Discussions of Roman life, customs, and religion may help students grasp the significance of the soothsayer's predictions, the unusual signs that are seen in the heavens, and Calpurnia's dream, as well as the motivating effect that these events have on the characters in the play. If the idealism of a Brutus or the opportunism of an Antony seems contrived to the students, a discussion of the historical characters—including possibly reading the accounts of these men from Plutarch's *Lives*, the source that Shakespeare himself used in developing their characterizations—might help to make their actions seem more consistent. In addition to the need for better historical background, many students might need help in finding personal significance in the actions and characterizations of a play that takes place at a point in history that seems so remote from their world. A comparison of some of the language and oratory of modern political propaganda with that represented in the play might make the manipulations of Cassius and Antony seem more realistic and more relevant, despite the fact that they are cast in the context and the language of an earlier time.

2. *Using auditory and visual imagination.*

Students need to be aware that drama is written to be performed, not merely to be read. Effective drama depends on auditory and visual stimulation, and students cannot comprehend and appreciate it without an awareness of the auditory and visual elements which are an integral part of the effect that an author intends. If a filmed performance of the play to be studied is available— for example Zeffirelli's imaginative treatment of *Romeo and Juliet*—the students will begin to sense the merging of the audiovisual and the literary aspects of the play. Pictures or slides of a performance will contribute to this aspect of comprehension if a film cannot be used. Incidental music written to accompany a play—for example Grieg's music for Ibsen's *Peer Gynt* or Mendelssohn's music for *A Midsummer Night's Dream*—can add much to a student's awareness of the moods and tones that are created by auditory elements. Teachers often use a model of Shakespeare's Globe Theater to give students a sense of the movement that is involved in a visual presentation. The availability of aids to auditory and visual imagination will vary with the play being studied, but the teacher should be aware of the need to provide as much stimulation in these areas as possible.

3. *Making inferences from the dialogue.*

In Robert Bolt's *A Man for All Seasons*, Sir Thomas More stands on trial for his life, accused of treason because he will not compromise his principles at the demand of the King. Richard Rich, a witness called against him, is a man who habitually sacrifices honor and integrity for political favor. More, seeing that Rich wears a medallion indicating that he holds a high political office, asks what office is held. Upon being told that Richard Rich is the Attorney General for Wales, he responds, "Richard, it profits a man nothing to give his soul for the whole world. . . . But for Wales!"

A lecture to Rich on the questionable morals of his life of political opportunism would have been tedious at this point in the play. Yet the contrast between the two men, which forms the crux of the play, needs to be emphasized at this dramatic point in the trial. Bolt does it through skillful allusion and implication. The impact and drama are heightened by the audience's participation in the discovering of the inference. If students are not sensitive to this kind of implication and capable of participating in the inference required, much of the richness of drama will be lost to them. Drama portrays action and interaction, with little opportunity for narrative interruption or comment. An audience is constantly involved in forming inferences from what it hears and observes; making it necessary for an audience to form inferences as they react to the dialogue is an important dramatist's tool.

4. *Inferring character traits, feelings, and motives.*

Gibson's play, *The Miracle Worker,* allows the student to observe closely the motivations, manifestations, and results of one woman's determination. Annie Sullivan's background of pain, fear, deprivation, and loss is shown in brief flashbacks and in one vivid description as she details to Captain and Mrs. Keller the terrors of the asylum in which she has lived. Given her stubbornness and her desperate refusal to accept the possibility of failure, the student must infer the extent of her suffering and the enormity of the consequences to herself as well as to her blind-deaf pupil, Helen, if she should fail in her attempt to establish communication with the child. The implications are rich and dramatic, and the teacher must guide the student in becoming sensitive to them. Through a succession of frustrating impediments, including a continual clash of wills between Annie and the parents and Annie and the child, the student observes Annie's unflagging determination and infers her toughness, born unquestionably of the terrors glimpsed in her past. It is not until the last few moments of the play that Annie expresses her feelings for the child, yet the alert student can learn to infer—from Annie's total preoccupation with her pupil, the continual personal frustration and humiliation that she endures, her intense reaction against the Kellers' mention of putting Helen into an asylum, her complete surrender of personal comfort, dignity, and the respect and approval of others—that her feelings of love are active, deep, and motivating. Indeed, they pervade her words and actions throughout the play. Annie Sullivan's character traits, feelings, and motives are not stated directly in the play, but for the student who learns to infer them from her actions, responses, and speeches as the drama unfolds, they are striking and memorable. Much of the effective drama that is based on character must be inferred in this same way.

Background material provided by the teacher may aid the students' drawing of inferences. In studying *The Miracle Worker,* for example, the teacher might have students read passages from the letters of Annie Sullivan describing the particular incidents that are portrayed in the drama, and possibly also the account of that time period in Helen Keller's autobiography, *Story of My Life.* With a more complete knowledge of the actual events surrounding the climax depicted in the play, the student can ask why the author selected the incidents that he did, and which personality traits of Annie and of Helen are emphasized by this selection. Reading the more realistic portrayals of James Keller and Captain Keller, the student may be led to ask why the author of the play would exaggerate these characters as he does? How does this exaggeration aid in the portrayal of Annie, her motivations, her personality, and her desires?

All drama is rich in implication. The ability to make inferences, particularly in the area of character, is essential to its enjoyment and comprehension.

Other reading processes necessary for comprehending dialogue and drama include:

5. *Being aware of specific stage directions.*
6. *Noting the author's organization and purpose for writing.*
7. *Visualizing various actions going on at the same time.*
8. *Understanding specialized vocabulary.*
9. *Interpreting figurative language.*
10. *Evaluating what is read.*

Understanding figurative language is especially important when reading poetry. Syntax may be irregular, the verb is often difficult to identify, and language is generally very abstract. Taking time to help students overcome these problems inherent in reading poetry will greatly increase their reading comprehension.

Students also need to be shown that in novels, autobiographies, or biographies the plot deals with human nature, and the focus is on human motives and emotions. Students should be encouraged to seek out and understand the author's prejudices, biases, and attitudes.

Grammar textbooks are used as guides in grammar lessons and composition. These textbooks are usually expository and include many definitional paragraphs. Typographical aids are used to center attention on the definitions, details, examples, and exercises, and students should be made aware of them.

GENERAL BUSINESS, BOOKKEEPING AND ACCOUNTING

Mathematics is an important part of the business field. Refer to the basic thinking processes needed to read mathematics in addition to the general reading processes listed below.

What reading skills are basic to understanding business education materials?

1. *Interpreting signs and symbols.*

Bookkeeping Symbols

<1700>   This symbol represents a negative balance of $1700.00

1500   The double lines beneath a figure represent the final total in
‗‗‗‗   a computation.

"T"   (forms) represent balance sheets.

2. *Solving problems.*

From all information given to you concerning Jerry White's income in 1980, figure Jerry's income tax using Form 1040A.

3. *Following directions with precision.*

Using Income Tax Form 1040, fill in the following information only:

a. Place your IRS label at the top of the page as directed on the form. If you do not have your IRS label, print or type the required information onto the form.

b. Indicate your filing status by checking only one box.

c. Determine your exemptions, check appropriate box or boxes, and enter your total number of exemptions where specified on the form.

4. *Differentiating between significant and insignificant facts.*

After skimming the 1980 Federal Income Tax Booklet, Nancy Miller listed all *taxes* she paid in 1980 that she felt she could deduct in preparing her income tax return. These taxes include the following items:

a. State and local income taxes withheld from her salary

b. FICA

c. Taxes on gasoline

d. Real estate taxes

e. Car inspection fees

f. Personal property taxes

Significant facts: Miller can deduct the following taxes only: a, d, and f.

Insignificant facts: Miller cannot deduct the following: b, c, or e. The fact that she paid these taxes is insignificant for income tax purposes. A careful reading of the section on taxes in the booklet would have informed her of these facts.

In addition to the thinking processes listed above, other general reading or thinking processes include:

5. *Interpreting graphics, diagrams, and charts.*
6. *Interpreting requirements of documents and charts.*
7. *Locating main ideas.*
8. *Listing or recalling details.*
9. *Locating information.*
10. *Interpreting symbol systems.*

The study of other content areas does not involve as much textbook reading because the students are involved more in developing motor skills. Although the time spent reading textbooks and other printed materials is less than in some subjects, the students are expected to read and learn new information, to extend ideas, to follow directions, to read symbols, to locate information, to write research papers, to extend word power, and to apply what they read. The understanding and utilization of technical language is basic to concept acquisition, to the communication of ideas, and to the application of specialized skills. A list of reading skills basic to improving reading comprehension in subjects that emphasize motor skills follows.

ART

As students participate in art activities they often must read various kinds of information. Processes important in reading instructional materials in art are:

What reading skills are basic to understanding works on art?

1. *Interpreting diagrams and charts.*
   Using the color wheel, identify the complementary colors of red, yellow, and blue.

2. *Interpreting moods and feelings.*

   The lines used in a drawing set the mood and feeling of the finished product. Horizontal lines suggest sadness, death, loneliness; vertical lines represent victory, boldness, strength.

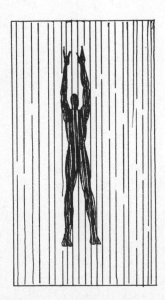

Examine the drawing on page 29 and notice the two boxes—the victor standing erect (vertical), the loser lying face down (horizontal).

3. *Following directions accurately and sequentially.*

A Woodcut: Relief Printing Process.
Materials: wood (block), pocket knife or gouge, brayer, bench hook, pencil, paper, and spoon.

Procedures:

a. Work out design or drawing with a pencil on the block of wood.

b. Cut design out of the block of wood with knife or gouge.

c. Ink the woodcut completely with the brayer.

d. Set paper squarely on the woodcut, and rub the back of the paper with the back of the spoon in circular movements.

e. Peel the paper from the woodcut.

4. *Identifying different art styles or movements.*

Having read about, studied, and discussed the characteristics of realism, naturalism, surrealism, and romanticism as they apply to art (paintings), identify the art style of each painting as its appears on the screen. (Slide presentation)

Important thinking processes in reading instructional materials in art may also include the following:

5. *Differentiating between essential and nonessential ideas and information.*
6. *Utilizing details.*
7. *Locating reference materials.*
8. *Transferring specialized information into more abstract ideas.*
9. *Stating related ideas.*
10. *Creating design and new media.*

MUSIC

Music activities require students to read various kinds of materials, often highly specialized. Important thinking processes in reading such instructional materials are:

What reading skills are basic to reading about music?

1. *Recognizing and applying symbols rapidly.*

Kindergarten and first grade children can learn to recognize basic rhythm symbols such as the quarter note, the half note, the rest, and the most common time signatures—2/4, 3/4, and 4/4. These symbols may be interpreted with simple "rhythm band" instruments: sticks, bells, tambourines, drums, and rattles. Rapid recognition and interpretation can be reinforced through practice in the form of games, parades, or concerts that will help to keep motivation high.

Children at the third or fourth grade level are ready to add melody symbols—the tones of the musical scale. Children can learn to play a simple instrument like a soprano recorder to bring symbols into musical reality. Folk songs, melodies from popular songs, and show tunes are usually well accepted for this kind of activity.

Secondary students are ready to add symbols and concepts of harmony and dynamics. Part singing in choirs or small ensembles will provide practice and reinforcement for this symbol recognition. Students who are interested may wish to go into guitar, autoharp, or simple piano accompaniment.

2. *Interpreting moods, feelings, and tones.*

Children are by nature responsive to moods, feelings, and tones in music. Kindergarten children almost always enjoy "story" music like Prokofiev's "Peter and the Wolf" or Dukas's "The Sorcerer's Apprentice," where each shift or nuance in the music represents an aspect of the story.

Elementary school children will usually enjoy the distinctive moods and tones of Moussorgsky's "Night on Bald Mountain," Sibelius's "Valse Triste," or Mendelssohn's "Fingal's Cave Overture." Most have no trouble drawing elaborate interpretations of these selections. In a relaxed small-group atmosphere, many—boys as well as girls— will enjoy dancing or acting out their interpretations. The vivid musical imagery of Tchaikovsky's "Nutcracker" or Grieg's "In the Hall of the Mountain King" is also appealing to children in this age group.

The vivid tone colors of "program music" (music that has a story or picture behind it) may help the secondary music teacher to break down the prejudice that many junior high and high school students have for any music that is not the popular idiom of the teen culture. The sensuous beauty of Smetana's "The Moldau" is enhanced for young people by the ease with which they can interpret the smooth flowing of the river, the robustness of the peasant wedding, the ethereal quietness of the evening scene, the sudden blusteriness of the storm. The shimmering impressionism of Debussy's "Afternoon of a Faun" is less explicit and more suggestive, but the reading of the Mallarmé poem on which the composition is based will again enable the student to interpret in a way that is almost visual.

3. *Recognizing different styles of music.*

Beethoven was one of the early composers to write in the romantic spirit and style of music, and time has proven him one of the greatest. The romantic spirit was one of individualism, emotionalism, and freedom. Beethoven greatly admired Napoleon, who he felt was a liberator of men, and he dedicated his "Eroica" symphony to him; when Napoleon had himself crowned emperor, Beethoven tore up his dedication. On one occasion Beethoven declared that the man who could truly understand his music would be forever free. Knowing these facts and incidents in Beethoven's life makes the tempestuousness of the first movement of the Fifth Symphony or of the first movement of the "Pathétique" Sonata both fitting and memorable. It represents more than an abstract style of music; it represents a man who exemplified freedom and individualism in his life and in his personality, as well as in his music. The student also might be aware that at the height of his career Beethoven discovered that he was losing his hearing, to him the most precious of all of his senses. His suffering was deep and intensely personal. The haunting lyricism of many of his slow movements—particularly the well known second movement of the "Pathétique" Sonata—reflects the depth of his suffering. The exalted Ninth Symphony reflects the triumph of genius and spirit over the physical handicap as the master learned that he could compose—and even conduct—hearing the music in his mind and soul. At the first performance of that symphony, one of the musicians gently turned the composer-conductor around so that he could see the thunderous ovation that he could not hear. Knowing something about the man makes the tone and style meaningful.

Kindergarten and primary-grade children are really too young and inexperienced to think of "style" or "movement" in music. They enjoy the selection because it moves or excites them. But they can respond to a story about a man showing his feelings in the music he wrote. They can recognize "angry" feelings or "gentle" ones.

Secondary students are ready to add the term "romanticism" to describe the music of Beethoven, but the stories and anecdotes still help to make that term meaningful. They are ready to listen to the lush lyricism of Liszt and Mendelssohn, to see how it also is embraced in romantic individualism and emotionalism, and to note how these composers differed in their personalities and in their musical styles from Beethoven. The baroque, classical, and realistic styles of music can also be presented not merely in terms of abstract characteristics, but in terms of people and events whose lives shaped those styles. Then, as the students read materials containing these terms, they have a rich background of understandings and associations to build their comprehension of the material.

4. *Associating related ideas.*

Young children who are not yet overly self-conscious about their feelings or inhibited in expressing their ideas respond easily and naturally to the concept that moods and feelings can be expressed in many different ways. They can hear a lively tune by Schubert, look at a design made with bright colors, and listen to a poem like Stevenson's "How Do You Like to Go up in a Swing" and realize that all are ways of expressing bright, happy feelings. They respond to the idea that they too can express this kind of feeling by singing a song, drawing a picture, or telling a story. Relating the expression of ideas on a simple level comes easily to them, because they are not terribly worried about it.

Secondary students can be more sophisticated about relating ideas. Having learned about the romantic spirit as it is reflected in Beethoven's music, they can relate Beethoven's vehement independence and worship of freedom to Byron's. Mendelssohn's lyricism can be seen to have similarities to that expressed in the poems of Shelley or the paintings of Constable. Liszt's lushness seems to have a counterpart in the poetry of Keats. The super-romanticism that becomes impressionism was expressed first in America by Edgar Allan Poe, then taken up in Europe by painters like Monet and Renoir and by composers like Debussy and Ravel. Here is an influence that students can find explicitly stated in the letters of the artists themselves.

Since so much of the study of the humanities centers around periods and styles, students comprehension of their reading in these fields will increase if they can relate similar impulses, feelings, and ideas as they are expressed in different media and in different forms.

Other thinking processes important in reading specialized materials in the field of music are:

5. *Memorizing selections.*
6. *Syllabicating words.*
7. *Matching notes and words on a musical score.*
8. *Interpreting diagrams.*
9. *Following directions.*

PHYSICAL EDUCATION AND HEALTH

Reading in physical education and health uses many of the following processes:

1. *Following directions accurately and sequentially.*

   To stop arterial bleeding, one should follow these steps:

   a. Determine the extent of the wound by the amount of bleeding. (If it is arterial, blood will spurt out; if it is from a large vein, the blood will flow.)

   b. If the wound is in a limb, elevate it.

   c. Use the largest compress possible—a large towel, a piece of clothing, etc.

   d. Apply the compress directly on the opening of the wound, pressing down with the palm of the hand.

   e. Use direct pressure for 3 to 4 minutes.

   f. Release pressure to determine whether or not there has been any clotting. (Spurting will stop.)

   g. Repeat the process, using a new compress if the first one has become saturated, until the bleeding has been either stopped or curtailed.

   h. The patient, if he can be moved, should be transported to a physician for further care.

What reading skills are basic to physical education and health materials?

Nine Players

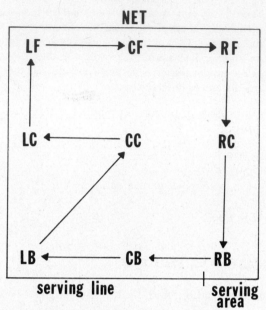

Volleyball Team Rotation

2. *Following and interpreting diagrams.*

   Back Row: Right Back, Center Back, Left Back
   Center Row: Right Center, Center Center, Left Center
   Front Row: Right Forward, Center Forward, Left Forward

3. *Interpreting signals.*

   Basketball players must be able to interpret official signals from the referee. Examples include the following:

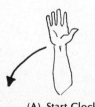

(A) Start Clock

(B) Stop Clock

(C) Jump Ball

(D) Holding

Referee Signals

4. *Following a sequence in developing a specific skill.*

Handspring Vault

a. Gymnast places Reuther board body length from horse.

b. Gymnast has a normal two-foot takeoff with body extended in flight.

c. Heels rise, legs remain extended, and arms extend upon leaving the board.

d. Arms, upon contact with the horse, remain extended, shoulders flex and block to allow push from the horse.

e. Gymnast attempts continued flight with extended body and arms.

f. Gymnast arrives on mat with two feet stance, knees flexed, hips tucked, and arms extended overhead.

Handspring Vault

Reading in physical education and health requires using many of these thinking processes:

5. *Interpreting symbols.*
6. *Recalling details.*
7. *Locating reference materials.*
8. *Identifying main ideas.*
9. *Identifying related ideas.*
10. *Condensing information into limited space.*

HOMEMAKING

What reading skills are basic
to homemaking materials?

Reading in the various fields of homemaking arts necessitates a diversity of thinking processes. They include:

1. *Following directions accurately and sequentially.*

Butterscotch Chocolate Chewies

Add the following ingredients *together* and *follow* the stated baking directions.

1 pkg. yellow cake mix

2 c. brown sugar

4 tsp. melted margarine

4 tbsp. honey

4 eggs

12 oz. pkg. chocolate chips

2 c. chopped walnuts

Combine all ingredients *in order listed* and *stir* until *just* blended. *Spread* with a spatula into a *well-greased* 9 × 13 inch pan. Bake in 350 degree *preheated* oven for *30 minutes.* Allow to cool. Cut into 1½ in. squares.

2. *Interpreting graphs, charts, diagrams, and patterns.*

Here is an easy set of directions for cooking a hot cereal. Read and interpret the information given on the chart.

Servings	1	2	4
Water	1 cup	2 cups	4 cups
Salt	¼ tsp.	½ tsp.	1 tsp.
Oats	½ cup	1 cup	2 cups

From the information given, fill in the chart below for 3 servings of that cereal.

Servings	(3)
Water	(3 cups)
Salt	(¾ tsp.)
Oats	(1½ cups)

3. *Identifying meanings of abbreviations.*

Identify the following abbreviations, which deal with weights or amounts used in preparing recipes.

9 g.	(9 grams)
⅛ tsp.	(⅛ teaspoon)

2 lb. 10 oz.	(2 pounds 10 ounces)
3 tbsp.	(3 tablespoons)
15 mg.	(15 milligrams)
1 qt.	(1 quart)
1 pt.	(1 pint)
1 doz.	(1 dozen)

4. *Identifying and understanding the meanings of significant details.*

A   = Center of arm—place at shoulder seam
B   = Front
C   = Back
D   = Match sides
E   = Place on straight grain of fabric
F   = Casing line

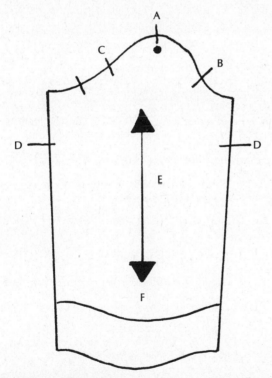

A Pattern for a Sleeve

The successful attachment of a sleeve to a garment depends on one's ability to identify and correctly interpret the meanings of significant details of the pattern.

Reading in the various fields of homemaking arts also includes:

5. *Interpreting symbols and codes.*
6. *Interpreting labels.*
7. *Locating main ideas.*
8. *Locating related or supporting ideas.*
9. *Condensing information into limited space.*

INDUSTRIAL ARTS

Students use many motor skills in industrial arts activities, but they also need to master the following reading processes:

What reading skills are basic to industrial arts materials?

1. *Identifying and explaining the uses of tools, machinery, etc.*

   Read the assigned pages, and then identify and explain the use of each of the following basic hand and power tools as used in the specific project construction.

Bandsaw	Hand drill
Disc sander	Jigsaw
Drill press	

2. *Demonstrating an understanding of the basic safety and construction procedures in a workshop situation.*

   Using basic safety and construction procedures, construct a basic core (standard) project from the basic plans provided in the text.

3. *Interpreting drawings, diagrams, patterns, and charts.*

   Given an isometric drawing, demonstrate your understanding of the design by providing the following dimensions of it:

   height:
   length:
   width:

4. *Demonstrating a knowledge of industrial career awareness.*

   List as many types of employment as you can that might require drafting skills.

Other thinking processes in industrial arts include:

5. *Locating information.*
6. *Following directions accurately and sequentially.*
7. *Interpreting graphs and tables.*
8. *Following formulas and the explanation of them.*
9. *Locating main ideas.*
10. *Associating related ideas.*

SUMMARY

As should be evident by now, reading is a dynamic, ever changing process that must be adapted to what is being read. Different materials require different strategies, and teachers must teach these strategies to their students. In addition to teaching the kinds of strategies discussed in this chapter, teachers should help their students to learn to read actively rather than passively. The passive reader sees little more than words on a page; but the active reader, who knows how to interact with the material, will comprehend what he reads in such a way that it will become an integral part of his knowledge.

Reinforcement Activity

Contrast the reading processes you have been teaching with the examples and lists in this chapter. Determine what additional skills you might include in comprehension instruction to accompany your teaching of content.

References

ARTLEY, A. STERL. "A Study of Certain Relationships Existing between General Reading Comprehension and Reading Comprehension in a Specific Subject-Matter Area." *Journal of Educational Research* 37 (1944): 464–473.

BLOOM, BENJAMIN, ed. *Taxonomy of Educational Objectives: Cognitive Domain.* New York: Longmans, Green and Co., 1956.

BLOOM, B. S., HASTINGS, J. T., and MADAUS, G. F. *Handbook for Formative and Summative Evaluation of Student Learning.* New York: McGraw-Hill Book Co., 1971.

DAVIS, FREDERICK B. "Research in Comprehension in Reading." *Reading Research Quarterly* 3 (1968): 449–545.

DAVIS, FREDERICK B. "Psychometric Research on Comprehension in Reading." *Reading Research Quarterly* 7 (1972): 628–678.

DURKIN, DELORES. "What Classroom Observations Reveal about Reading Comprehension Instruction." *Reading Research Quarterly* 14 (1978–79): 481–533.

GOODLAD, JOHN L. *School, Curriculum and the Individual.* New York: John Wiley and Sons, Inc., 1966.

HERBER, HAROLD L., and SAUNDERS, P. L., eds. *Research in Reading in the Content Area: First Year Report.* Syracuse, New York: Reading and Language Arts Center, Syracuse University, 1969.

HODGES, CAROL A. "Commentary: Toward a Broader Definition of Comprehension Instruction." *Reading Research Quarterly* 15 (1980): 299–306.

OTTO, WAYNE. "Design for Developing Comprehension Skills." In *Cognition, Curriculum, and Comprehension*, edited by John T. Gutherie. Newark, Delaware: International Reading Association, 1977, 193–232.

PETERS, CHARLES W., and PETERS, NATHANIEL A. "A Systematic Approach to Predicting Reading Performance at the Secondary Level." In *Reflections and Investigations on Reading* edited by George H. McNinch and Wallace D. Miller, Clemson, South Carolina: Twenty-fifth Yearbook of the National Reading Conference, 1976, 121–128.

RUPLEY, WILLIAM H. "Effective Reading Programs." *The Reading Teacher* 29 (1976): 116–120.

RUPLEY, WILLIAM H. "Teacher Instructional Emphasis and Student Achievement in Reading." *Peabody Journal of Education* 54 (1977): 286–291.

RUPLEY, WILLIAM H., and BLAIR, TIMOTHY R. "Teacher Effectiveness in Reading Instruction." *The Reading Teacher* 31 (1978): 970–973.

WHITE, R. T. "Research into Learning Hierarchies." *Review of Educational Research* 43 (1973): 361–375.

Bibliography

AARON, IRA E. "Reading in Mathematics." *Journal of Reading* 6 (1965): 391–395, 401.

AHRENT, KENNETH, and HASELTON, SHIRLEY S. "Essential Reading Skills in Bookkeeping." *Journal of Reading* 16 (1973): 314–317.

AIKEN, LEWIS R., JR. "Language Factors in Learning Mathematics." *Bureau of Educational Research* 42 (1972): 359–385.

ALBERT, BURTON, JR. "Purple Marbles and Little Red Hula Hoops." *The Reading Teacher* 24 (1971): 647–651.

ALLINGTON, RICHARD L. "Improving Content Area Instruction in the Middle School." *Journal of Reading* 18 (1975): 455–461.

ANDERSON, BERNICE. "Business Teacher: Are You Prepared to Teach Reading?" *Business Education Forum* 26 (1971): 3–4.

BALOW, IRVING H. "Reading and Computation Ability as Determinants of Problem Solving." *Arithmetic Teacher* 11 (1964): 18–22.

BJURSTOM, DIXIE POTTER. "Reading as a Secondary School Subject." In *Classroom-Relevant Research in the Language Arts*, coordinated by Harold G. Shane and James Walden. Washington, D.C.: Association for Supervision and Curriculum Development, 1978, 85–106.

BOSANKO, ROBERT J. "They Learn to Read in Auto I. Honest!" *Journal of Reading* 19 (1975): 33–35.

BULLERMAN, MARY, and FRANCO, E. J. "Teach Content Material but Teach Reading Too!" *Journal of Reading* 19 (1975): 19, 21–23.

CARNEY, JOHN J., and LOSINGER, WILLIAM. "Reading and Content in Technical-Vocational Education." *Journal of Reading* 20 (1976): 14–17.

CARRIAR, SHIRLEY M. "Teaching Skills in the Junior High School." *English Journal* 58 (1969): 1357–1361.

CATTERTON, JANE H., ed. *Children and Literature*. Newark, Delaware: International Reading Association, 1970.

DAVIS, LUCIAN. "Reading Skills in World Geography." *Reading Improvement* 7 (1970): 73–79.

EARLE, RICHARD A. *Teaching Reading and Mathematics*. Reading Aid Series. Newark, Delaware: International Reading Association, 1976.

EASP, N. WESLEY. "Observations on Teaching Mathematics." *Journal of Reading* 13 (1970): 529–532.

EDIGER, MARLOW. "Reading in the Elementary School Science Program." *Science Education* 49 (1965): 389–390.

ERICKSON, ROBERT, and THOMAS, ELLEN L. "Art Class Look Collection Promotes Better Reading." *Journal of Reading* 11 (1968): 333–336.

FRANKEL, JILL C. "Reading Skills through Social Studies Content and Student Involvement." *Journal of Reading* 18 (1974): 18, 23–26.

FREDERICK, E. COSTON. "Reading and Vocational Education." In *Fusing Reading Skills and Content*, edited by H. A. Robinson and E. L. Thomas. Newark, Delaware: International Reading Association, 1969, 145–150.

GENTILE, LANCE M. *Using Sports and Physical Education to Strengthen Reading Skills*. Newark, Delaware: International Reading Association, 1980.

GENTILE, LANCE M., and MCMILLAN, MERNA M. "Why Won't Teenagers Read?" *Journal of Reading* 20 (1977): 649–654.

GROFF, PATRICK. "How Do Children Read Biography about Adults?" *The Reading Teacher* 24 (1971): 605–615, 629.

GRUBER, PAULETTE M. "Junior High Boasts Super Stars." *Journal of Reading* 16 (1973): 600–603.

HAEHN, FAYNELLE. "Let's Have A 'Read-in' in Typewriting." In *Fusing Reading Skills and Content*, edited by H. A. Robinson and E. L. Thomas. Newark, Delaware: International Reading Association, 1969, 69–74.

HARKER, W. JOHN. "Teaching Secondary Reading: Review of Sources." *Journal of Reading* 16 (1972): 149–155.

HARRISON, J. MEANS. "Nine Years of Individualized Reading." *Journal of Reading* 20 (1976): 144–149.

Journal of Reading 16, No. 7 (April 1973). This issue is devoted entirely to reading in the content areas.

KENNEDY, LARRY D. "Textbook Usage in the Intermediate-Upper Grades." *The Reading Teacher* 24 (1971): 723–729.

LEES, FRED. "Mathematics and Reading." *Journal of Reading* 19 (1976): 621–626.

MANZO, ANTHONY. "Compass: English—A Demonstration Project." *Journal of Reading* 16 (1973): 539–545.

MCAULAY, J. D. "Social Studies Dependent on Reading." *Education* 82 (1961): 87–89.

MCKAY, J. W. "Developing Reading Skills through Literature." In *Reaching Children and Young People through Literature*, edited by Helen W. Painter. Newark, Delaware: International Reading Association, 1971, 50–57.

MUELDER, RICHARD H. "Reading in a Mathematics Class."

In *Fusing Reading Skills and Content,* edited by H. A. Robinson and E. L. Thomas. Newark, Delaware: International Reading Association, 1969, 75–80.

PAINTER, HELEN W. *Poetry and Children.* Newark, Delaware: International Reading Association, 1970.

PATLAK, SANFORD. "Physical Education and Reading: Questions and Answers." In *Fusing Reading Skills and Content,* edited by H. A. Robinson and E. L. Thomas. Newark, Delaware: International Reading Association, 1969, 81–88.

PIERCEY, DOROTHY. *Reading Activities in the Content Areas: An Idea Book for Middle and Secondary Schools.* Boston: Allyn and Bacon, Inc., 1976.

PRESTON, RALPH C. *New Look at Reading in the Social Studies.* Newark, Delaware: International Reading Association, 1969.

PRIBNOW, JACK R. "Why Johnny Can't 'Read' Word Problems." *School Science and Mathematics* 69 (1969): 591–598.

ROBINSON, H. ALAN, and THOMAS, ELLEN L. *Reading and Study Strategies: The Content Areas.* 2nd ed. Boston: Allyn and Bacon, Inc., 1978.

SHEPHARD, DAVID L. "Teaching Science and Mathematics to the Seriously Retarded Reader in the High School." *The Reading Teacher* 17 (1963): 25–30.

STRANG, RUTH. "Developing Reading Skills in the Content Areas." *High School Journal* 49 (1966): 301–306.

STRANG, RUTH, McCULLOUGH, CONSTANCE, and TRAXLER, ARTHUR E. *The Improvement of Reading.* New York: McGraw-Hill, 1967.

SZYMKOWICZ, DOROTHY. "Home Economics and Reading." In *Fusing Reading Skills and Content,* edited by H. A. Robinson and E. L. Thomas. Newark, Delaware: International Reading Association, 1969, 62–66.

THELAN, JUDITH. *Improving Reading in Science.* Newark, Delaware: International Reading Association, 1976.

TIRRO, FRANK. "Reading Techniques in the Teaching of Music." In *Fusing Reading Skills and Content,* edited by H. A. Robinson and E. L. Thomas. Newark, Delaware: International Reading Association, 1969, 103–107.

WULFFSON, DON L. "Music to Teach Reading." *Journal of Reading* 14 (1970): 179–182.

YOUNG, EDITH M., and RODENBORN, LEO V. "Improving Communication Skills in Vocational Courses." *Journal of Reading* 19 (1976): 373–377.

3 ASSESSING READABILITY

OVERVIEW

The reader must be capable of reading the material assigned. If the material is too difficult, the reader will become frustrated and probably will lose interest. And if the material is too easy, the reader will likely become bored. The teacher, then, needs to be aware of (1) the levels at which the students read, and (2) the level at which the materials are written. To assist the teacher in matching students with the appropriate materials, readability formulas (used to determine the readability level of materials) and measurement analyses (used to determine the level at which students read) will be discussed in the chapter in such a way that teachers in the content areas will be able to use this information to maximize their students' comprehension.

TEACHERS MUST ESTIMATE in the content areas the readability level of textbooks, and determine the ability of students to comprehend these materials. "Matching" students with subject matter can increase their comprehension of text. Formulas are used to estimate the grade level of texts, and cloze tests and group informal reading inventories are considered effective ways to ascertain how well students can comprehend the texts.

The difficulty of reading materials is determined by using readability formulas and by measuring a student's comprehension of texts. Measurement analysis determines a student's comprehension of a specified text selection, by observing errors in word recognition or syntactic and semantic errors or miscues made while reading. The results are a measure of how well the student has read and learned from the text.

A teacher needs to know how to select those materials students can read with a high degree of comprehension. Some of the more commonly recognized factors that influence the readability of materials are:

What factors influence the readability of materials?

The student's prior knowledge.

The student's background of experiences.

The student's interests.

The student's language aptitude.

The student's decoding abilities.

The student's purpose for reading.

The author's style of writing.

The concept load of the written materials.

The abstractness and multiple meanings of words.

The syntactic complexity of sentences.

The physical appearance of the printed text.

Not only do teachers have to consider each of these factors, but they must also recognize the increasing diversity of reading levels between students that comes with each succeeding year of school. Although not all factors that affect readability can be measured, readability formulas, cloze tests, and group informal reading inventories are useful tools in helping teachers provide students with materials they can read with a high degree of comprehension.

READABILITY FORMULAS

Measurement and control of readability have been traced to A.D. 900, when the Talmudists made word and idea counts of written materials to help them distinguish usual from unusual meanings. About 1,000 years later, when Thorndike published *The Teacher's Word Book* in 1921, the way was opened for more precise measures of readability. Using Thorndike's data, Lively and Pressey developed a readability formula in 1923. Since that time, numerous

What are the various types of readability formulas?

formulas have been developed for use with textual materials. Readability formulas are to be used only with prose. Some readability formulas are applicable only to books written for children; others are employed for adolescent and adult books. Some formulas can be used to estimate the reading level of books written for children, youth, and adults, and are not limited to the use of materials written for the primary grades. Several formulas are complex and time consuming to use with manual aids, other formulas are designed to utilize computers. A few formulas are structured to be simple and quickly applied (Klare 1963 and 1974–1975).

How is the difficulty of a passage determined?

The linguistic factors of sentence length and vocabulary are widely used in formulas as indexes for determining the difficulty of a passage. The Dale-Chall Readability Formula (Dale and Chall 1948), the Spache Formula (Spache 1953), and the Harris-Jacobson Readability Formulas (Harris and Sipay 1980) use word lists accompanying their formulas to compare with the words used in the passages being examined. Other formulas rely on word length or on a relationship between word length and sentence length in the predictive analysis. The Flesch Formula (Flesch 1948) emphasizes syllable count. The Fry Readability Formula (Fry 1968, 1969, and 1977), the Fog Formula (Gunning 1968), the Raygor Formula (Raygor 1977), and the SMOG Grading Formula (McLaughlin 1969) use a relationship of word and sentence length to determine readability of materials. Singer (1975) has developed the SEER technique, by which paragraphs of unknown difficulty are matched to paragraphs of known difficulty in order to estimate their readability. The Formula for Measuring Syntactic Complexity, by Botel and Granowsky (1972), is an example of predictive analysis by syntactic components. As an alternative to formulas, Irwin and Davis (1980) have devised a checklist to analyze the readability factors of content area textbooks for specific groups of students.

Readability formulas provide an objective method for measuring components of writing to yield estimates of the reading ease or difficulty of prose materials. The basis for many formulas is that a word is considered easy or difficult according to the number of syllables it contains. Syntactic complexity, as determined by the length of a sentence, is also thought to provide an index of comprehension difficulty. Long, complex sentences are considered harder to understand than shorter, simpler ones, particularly when there is a distance between the subject and verb (Fry and Depierro 1978). Most language elements, such as adjectives, adverbs, and dependent clauses, seem to have a bearing on the difficulty of textbooks. When the factors of word and sentence length are considered in relationship to each other, they help to predict the reading difficulty of prose materials.

Yet the grade level designations of selections and books seem not always to reflect their difficulty. The human variables of interests and understanding of word meanings affect readability (Koenke 1971). Stories of high interest to readers are better understood than low interest stories (Belloni and Jongsma 1978). Picture books may contain many long and involved sentences with phrases like "exquisite flakes," "Doondoggle team," and "meadow rue" (Hunt and Reuter 1978). Such phrases are usually new to children and they may not understand their meaning. Books may vary in difficulty from one part to another, and the grade levels assigned to the books do not assure that a student will be able to read various parts of a book equally well. There is even variance between the grade level designations of some test items taken from reading tests and the assigned plotted grade levels (Daines and Mason 1970). Word meanings and sentence meanings in context, the abstractions and density of ideas, the literary quality and organization of materials, the physical appearance, and a reader's interest and motivation in reading are but a few of the factors that need to be considered in determining the difficulty of materials.

Three formulas that teachers regard as easy and quick to apply to prose materials are the Fry Readability Graph, the Raygor Readability Estimate, and the SMOG Grading.

Fry Readability Graph

The Fry Readability Graph was devised by Edward Fry. The formula estimates the readability of prose materials from grade one into the college levels. It is established on the predictive analysis of sentence length and word difficulty based on the number of syllables. In the first publication of the Fry Graph, proper nouns were not counted. Fry has reversed this omission, and proper nouns are now included in the word count because they are considered to contribute to the difficulty of the materials (Fry 1968, 1969, and 1977). Fry's formula is actually a graph. The curved line in the graph represents the smoothed mean of the plots of sample passages. When a large number of passages with a wide range of readability are plotted on the graph, they tend to fall somewhere near this curved line. The grade lines are perpendicular to the curved line, and the grade levels are designated between the perpendicular lines. The grade levels are predicted when the calculations of analyzing the linguistic variables of word and sentence difficulty are interpolated on the graph. (See graph on page 46.)

Fry's instructions for predicting the grade level of materials are:

1. Randomly select three sample passages from near the beginning, middle, and end of a book. Count exactly one hundred words from each sample, beginning with the first word of a sentence. Be sure to count proper nouns, initializations, and numerals. A word is a symbol or group of symbols bounded by a blank space on either side. Thus, *1980*, *&*, and *IRA* are all words.

2. Count the total number of sentences in each one-hundred word passage and estimate the number of sentences to the nearest tenth of a sentence. Average these numbers.

3. Count the total number of syllables in each one-hundred word sam-

What criteria does the Fry formula use?

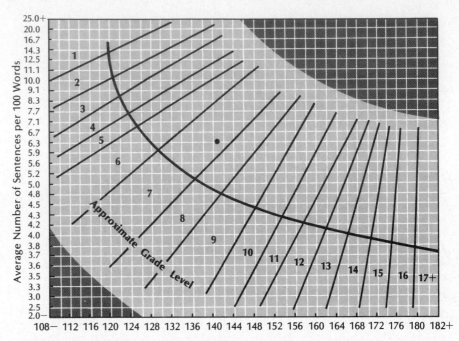

Fry Readability Graph

Edward Fry, "Fry's Readability Graph: Classifications, Validity, and Extension to Level 17." *Journal of Reading* 21, No. 3 (December 1977), p. 249. (Reproduction permitted by the author and the International Reading Association)

ple. Every syllable has a vowel sound. When counting syllables, go by the speech sounds. For example, *hopped* is a one-syllable word, while *counted* consists of two syllables. One syllable is counted for each symbol in numerals and initializations: when pronounced, *IRA* has three syllables, *1980* has four syllables, and *&* has one syllable. Total the results on a hand calculator, or place a mark above every syllable over one in each word, and add 100 to the total count of marks. Average the total number of syllables for the three one-hundred word samples.

4. Enter on the graph the average sentence length and the average number of syllables. Plot a dot where the two lines intersect. This point indicates the approximate grade level of the materials.

5. If a great deal of variability is found in the syllable or sentence count, more samples should be incorporated into the sample.

6. If short articles from magazines, newspapers, and other sources are used, steps two, three, and four should be followed. One representative one-hundred word sample is sufficient. If the article is long, two or even three randomly selected passages will provide a more

valid estimate of readability. Sums of averages are figured to plot the estimated grade level of the article only when two or more passages are sampled.

Compute the readability level of the following short passage to become familiar with the Fry Graph.

> The home of George Washington at Mount Vernon is a national shrine for Americans. It is located on the west bank of the Potomac River, in Virginia, about 15 miles from Washington, D.C. The white house faces the river from a bluff two hundred feet high. There is a tiled veranda, whose roof is supported by eight columns, that runs the full width of the mansion. West of the house is a row of out-buildings used as farm quarters. Between the house and the wharf is a plain brick tomb that holds the remains of Washington and his wife, Martha.

The answers are as follows:

1. The number of sentences in the one-hundred word passage is 5.9.
2. There are 134 syllables.
3. The estimated grade level is seven on the Fry Graph.

Readability formulas are sometimes used by teachers to write and rewrite expository materials for students who have difficulty in reading. To modify materials, concept load or idea density may be reduced, vocabulary simplified, and sentences shortened. Pearson (1974–75), on the other hand, found that grammatical complexity is often an aid rather than an interference to understanding and recall of ideas, and McCracken (1959) has suggested that simplifying vocabulary and sentence length can result in decreased comprehension; Smith (1971) also has indicated that simplifying syntax can adversely affect reading comprehension. However, Palmer (1974) contends that short and simple base clauses should not be completely rejected as unimportant factors in readability measures. He cites two reasons: first, a base clause reflects on the memory span of readability; second, a base clause does not represent a whole sentence, and modification around and within a base clause does have an effect on a reader's comprehension since the main clause serves as the base for meaning. Shaffer (1977) also indicates that comprehension is improved when both word difficulty and sentence length are simplified. Although different viewpoints exist concerning the use of readability formulas they should not be used to simplify content texts, as such simplification represents a downward adaptation of the curriculum.

Why are readability formulas not used to simplify content texts?

Raygor Readability Estimate

The Raygor Readability Estimate also is easy and quick to apply. Raygor (1977) devised a formula to estimate the readability of books used in the middle and secondary schools. The difficulty of a book is determined by

How is the Raygor Formula used?

sentence and word length. Word difficulty is determined by counting words of six or more letters. This process is considered faster and more accurate than counting syllables in words. The estimated grade level is plotted on a graph similar to the Fry graph. (See the graph below.)

Baldwin and Kaufman (1979) conducted a study to determine if the Raygor and Fry graphs produce similar readability levels of the same books, whether the Raygor or the Fry graph is faster to use, and if the Raygor graph has greater computational accuracy than the Fry graph. Both the Raygor and Fry formulas were applied to 100 books by preservice and inservice teachers. The Raygor and Fry readability graphs yielded corresponding scores. In only six percent of the passages assessed did the results differ by more than one grade. The Raygor graph took less time to use than the Fry graph. There was no overall difference between the two graphs in computational accuracy. Thus, the factors of simplicity and less time were not considered a disadvantage in using the Raygor graph.

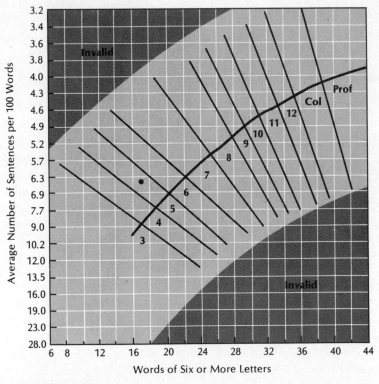

Raygor Readability Graph

R. Scott Baldwin and Rhonda K. Kaufman, "A Concurrent Validity Study of the Raygor Readability Estimate." *Journal of Reading* 23, No. 2 (November 1979), p. 151. (International Reading Association)

The directions for estimating the grade level of books using the Raygor Readability Estimate are as follows:

1. Select sample passages at the beginning, middle, and end of a selection or book. Count exactly 100 words for each of the three samples. Count proper nouns, but not numerals.
2. Count the number of sentences in each passages, estimating the length to the nearest tenth.
3. Count words of six or more letters.
4. Average the sentence length and word length of the three samples. Plot the averages on the graph.

Use the following short passage to become familiar with the Raygor graph.

> The home of George Washington at Mount Vernon is a national shrine for Americans. It is located on the west bank of the Potomac River, in Virginia, about 15 miles from Washington, D.C. The white house faces the river from a bluff two hundred feet high. There is a tiled veranda, whose roof is supported by eight columns, that runs the full width of the mansion. West of the house is a row of out-buildings used as farm quarters. Between the house and the wharf is a plain brick tomb that holds the remains of Washington and his wife, Martha.

The answers are:

1. The number of sentences in the one-hundred passage is 5.9.
2. There are twenty-one words of six or more letters.
3. The estimated grade level is between the sixth and seventh grade on the Raygor graph.

SMOG Grading

McLaughlin (1969) devised a readability formula to be used with materials fourth grade and above that is considered less complex and time consuming than other formulas. He approached the interrelationship of the linguistic variables of sentence and word difficulty in a way that is different than other formulas. The SMOG formula requires the count of polysyllabic words in three ten sentence samples. The assumption is that shorter sentences usually present less possibility for many polysyllabic words to be included in a selection. The difficulty of a passage is determined by the number of words with three or more syllables in it.

How is the SMOG formula different from the Fry and Raygor formulas?

Soon after the publication of the Fry and SMOG formulas, Pauk (1969) published the results of a study in which the Dale-Chall, Fry, and SMOG formulas were compared. He found some agreement between the grade levels obtained through applying the Dale-Chall and Fry formulas to the same passages. The SMOG formula produced higher grade levels.

Concern over the SMOG scores being consistently higher than those of Dale-Chall and Fry led to a study by Muir (1978). Three decreasing constants—two, one, and zero—were compared with the constant three used in the formula. The most likely predictor was the constant *one* when it was substituted for the original constant *three* in the SMOG formula. It produced the same grade level as Dale-Chall in five of the six cases.

Vaughn, Jr. (1976) conducted a study to verify the findings reported by Pauk. The Dale-Chall, Fry, and SMOG formulas were applied to the same passage of eighty-seven articles. By using the Spearman rank correlations (rho) among the scores yielded by the formulas, Vaughn found:

1. The Dale-Chall and Fry scores usually agree.
2. SMOG scores are usually two grades higher than those of Fry and Dale-Chall.
3. SMOG is highly correlated with the Dale-Chall and Fry formulas.
4. The Dale-Chall formula and Fry's graph are based on a prediction criterion of 50 to 75 percent comprehension.
5. The SMOG formula is based on a predictive criterion of 90 to 100 percent comprehension.

The apparent inconsistencies, according to Vaughn, are the result of variance in what the formulas predict. They are explained by examining predictive validity, or a formula's consistent prediction of the difficulty level of reading materials. The Dale-Chall and Fry formulas are based on a prediction criterion of 50 to 75 percent comprehension. If the Dale-Chall and Fry formulas yield a readability score of six for a book, students reading on that level, however determined, are expected to read that material with 50 to 75 percent accuracy. In comparison, the SMOG formula is based on a predictive criterion of 90 to 100 percent comprehension. For example, when the SMOG formula yields a readability score of six for a book, students reading on a sixth grade level will read the material with 90 to 100 percent accuracy, according to the formula's prediction. Thus, the Fry formula suggests a reading level somewhere between the frustration and instructional levels whereas the SMOG criterion score predicts a reading ability equivalent to reading at the independent level.

Since a readability score is only an estimate of the difficulty of a reading passage, it would be inappropriate to assume that students are always able to understand material with 90 to 100 percent accuracy, or that teacher guidance is unnecessary. Too many variables influence reading in the content areas. Furthermore, the SMOG formula will predict the grade level of a passage correctly within about one and a half grades, and the Fry formula range of accuracy is one grade.

Instructions for using the SMOG grading formula are few and simple to follow and compute.

1. Count ten consecutive sentences near the beginning of the chapter or

text, ten sentences near the middle, and ten near the end. (Any string of words ending with a terminal punctuation mark should be counted as a sentence.)

2. Count every word of three or more syllables in the thirty selected sentences. Any string of letters or numerals beginning and ending with a space or punctuation mark should be counted if you can distinguish at least three syllables when you read it aloud in context. Count a polysyllabic word each time it is repeated.

3. Estimate the square root of the number of polysyllabic words counted, which is done by taking the square root of the nearest perfect square. For example, if the count were 89, the nearest perfect square would be 81, which yields a square root of 9. If the count lies roughly between two perfect squares, choose the lower number. For instance, if the count is 57, take the square root of 49, rather than that of 64.

4. Add three to the approximate square root. This result gives the SMOG grade, which is the reading grade that a student must have reached if he is to comprehend fully the text assessed.

Read the following short passage, and apply the SMOG formula.

> In 1776, the colonists took care of most of their own needs. They produced food, shelter, and clothing. The work was hard, and the hours were long. People were concerned about the harvest of crops and the weaving of cloth. What was produced was consumed.
>
> Individual self-sufficiency was a characteristic of the economy of 1776. People produced goods for their survival or for barter. Most of the workers were farmers. Today this has changed. The economy has become more complex, and production is more specialized. We rely on others to produce what we need. We pay for those needs with our wages and other income.

The answers are:

1. The number of three or more syllable words in the first ten consecutive sentences is eleven.
2. The nearest square root of eleven is three.
3. Three added to three provides the SMOG grade of 6 for the passage.

CLOZE PROCEDURE

Wilson Taylor (1953) first introduced the *cloze procedure* as a new and better tool for measuring the readability of English prose. Cloze is considered a measure of readability, whereas readability formulas predict it. The cloze procedure is applied to a reading passage in which words are systematically deleted and the words are to be replaced by the reader. It is customary to use the cloze procedure as a measure of readability only with students in the fourth grade and above; the reading and writing skills of primary grade

How does the cloze procedure differ from formulas in determining readability?

children may prevent them from using the cloze procedure for this purpose, unless it is modified by fewer word deletions, by reducing the number of words in a passage, or by providing a choice of words to replace the deleted word. Most research has focused on cloze as a measure of readability, reading comprehension, and language variables. However, many writers and researchers also have recommended that the cloze procedure serve as a teaching device. This section will discuss how to use the cloze procedure to measure readability.

When the cloze procedure is used to measure readability, the reader's success in supplying the deleted words is an index to his ability to comprehend the reading matter. The procedure is related to a reader's ability to deal with the relationship between words and ideas (Horton 1974–1975). The closer the patterns of language structure approximate a reader's language aptitude, the better he tends to comprehend the passage. Poor readers apparently do not take advantage of the language structure used in printed materials (Schneyer 1965). Furthermore, low-achieving students better comprehend material they consider highly interesting than that which they rate as having low interest.

Other factors affecting readability are semantics and syntax. The understanding of sentences is mainly a function of meaning and, to a lesser degree, of grammar. It is thought that an unknown word is easier to understand in a "good" contextual setting (Danks 1969). Stoodt (1972), Hittleman (1973), and Pikulski and Pikulski (1977) have shown that irrelevant or extraneous details and examples included in printed materials confuse readers. Smith (1971) conducted a study in which four levels of written language served as a basis for creating readability levels. He concluded that syntax does make a difference in reading difficulty. There seems to be a correspondence between readers' level of syntactic maturity and the syntactic level of the material they read best. Components considered to influence readability are concept loads within different syntactical transformations and in comparison to a reader's knowledge in a subject area, and the ease with which readers identify and use the syntactic context of a passage. Hittleman (1973) suggests that psycholinguistic formulas for readability need to include the relationships between the characteristics of a reader, author, and topic.

A reader's familiarity with a topic or subject area increases his ability to predict content words in a cloze test more often than function words. More content words in a passage facilitates a reader's inferences for content words, but limits the prediction of function words. The prediction of function words seems to be dependent upon words on either side of the deletions, and readers pay less attention to context in making such predictions. Easy materials have a greater number of function words than more difficult materials. Furthermore, content words are more difficult to predict and are related to a reader's knowledge of the subject. Cloze tests measure reading as information processing and they are congruent with psycholinguistic theories of reading comprehension, according to Rankin and Thomas (1980).

The cloze test is easy to prepare, administer, and score. It is a relatively accurate and practical procedure to use in the classroom, particularly by teachers of the content areas. Students should have the opportunity to become acquainted with the technique by working on short passages, to prevent the feeling of frustration when a cloze test is administered to help match students with a textbook they can comprehend. A more accurate assessment of reading ability may be achieved by using multiple cloze selections (Vaughn, Jr. and Meredith 1978).

In the cloze procedure, words are deleted from a passage by an objectively specified process. Words at regular intervals, or nouns, verbs, or adjectives may be deleted. The deletion of words at spaced intervals correlates with general comprehension (Bormuth 1963). The deletion of every fifth word seems to be the most common pattern, although teachers of young children and bilingual students often begin by deleting words at longer intervals, such as every eighth, ninth, or tenth word.

Since its introduction by Taylor, the cloze procedure has been the subject of numerous investigations—too many to survey in this discussion. Many of these studies determined criteria for establishing a student's instructional level, since instruction is more effective if teachers use materials that provide neither too much nor too little challenge. The cloze procedure requires the reader to determine the exact word that has been deleted and replace it. Thus, criteria for converting cloze scores to equivalent reading levels need to be followed if proper placement in materials and comprehension of the materials are to be achieved. A student will probably learn best from materials that he reads with ease and comprehension. This is known as the independent level. He also can learn from a book written at his instructional level. This is the level at which he can read with understanding when given sufficient guidance by the teacher. A student should not be assigned a book that is so difficult for him that he will become frustrated.

The most researched aspect of the cloze procedure has been its scoring and interpretation. The cloze placement table developed by Rakes and McWilliams (1979) enables a teacher to compute with little effort and time the percentage levels and functional reading levels of students. Criteria for establishing reading levels from cloze test percentage scores, as determined by several researchers, are shown in Table 1. The categories for reading at the independent, instruction and frustration levels, with which the cloze scores were equated, were taken from the work of Betts (1946).

The steps for preparing and scoring cloze tests have become fairly standardized for grades four and higher:

1. Select a passage the students have not previously read. It should be approximately three hundred consecutive words in length. (Students are not to use the book when completing the test.)
2. Start with the fifth word in the second sentence and delete every fifth word until there are fifty deletions, including contractions, hyphen-

TABLE 1
Criteria for Converting Cloze Scores to Reading Levels

Researcher	Independent Level	Instruction Level	Frustration Level
Bormuth (1967)	50% and above	38–49%	37% or less
Rankin and Culhane (1969)	61% and above	41–60%	40% or less
Ransom (1968)	50% and above	30–49%	29% or less
Jones and Pikulski (1974)	46% and above	30–45%	29% or less
Zintz (1975)	51% and above	41–50%	40% or less

ated words, and numerals, such as 1776. Apostrophes are deleted along with the words in which they appear. Punctuation and hyphens are to be retained. The first and last sentences are to remain intact.

3. Type the passage for duplication. Double space between lines, and for each deleted word type a line 15 spaces long. The spaces should be uniform in length regardless of the length of the deleted word.
4. Provide students with instructions and a few sample tests before giving them the actual cloze tests. The directions might include: "In this selection you are to write the word that was omitted in the blank space, after you have read through the passage once. Write only one word in each blank and try to fill each blank with the exact word used by the author. If you skip blanks, return and fill them in later. Wrong spellings do not count against you."
5. Collect and score the papers. The exact words of the author that were deleted must be used by the students. If there are 50 word deletions, each correct answer receives two percentage points.
6. Select criteria, such as Bormuth's or Jones's, to determine the reading level of each student as it relates to the prose material from which the sample was taken.

An abbreviated sample cloze test follows.

BATTLEGROUND

No one knew where the Rangers came from, or what they looked like. They had been attacking 1. _____ and her colony planets. 2. _____ had won some battles 3. _____ them. But no Ranger 4. _____ ever been captured. Mars 5. _____ always ready for a 6. _____ war. Then scouts in 7. _____ space reported that thousands 8. _____ Rangers ships were headed 9. _____ Mars. And thousands of 10. _____ ships went out to 11. _____ them. The battleships moved swiftly into position.

Check your answers. They are listed for your convenience. Deleted words are not shown on a student's cloze test.

1. Mars
2. Mars
3. with
4. had
5. was
6. destructive
7. outer
8. of
9. toward
10. Mars
11. stop

The cloze test is sometimes criticized because of the anxiety students develop when presented with a test that contains many blanks to be filled in. A potential solution to this problem was suggested by Page (1975). It differs from the conventional procedure in that the test is administered after students have read the passage aloud in its original form. A strong relationship between conventional and postreading scores was found. According to Ganier (1976) the postreading scores tend to be about ten percent higher. Using the cloze test as a postreading technique is most useful in a diagnostic situation. It is effective when used with an informal inventory or miscue analysis (Carey 1979).

MAZE PROCEDURE

A process to measure or monitor the reading comprehension of readers is the maze, a modified cloze procedure. It is considered an assessment technique, and not a method of teaching. Activities and programs that help improve comprehension will perhaps reflect in a maze score (Guthrie et al. 1974). Teachers of primary grade children and resource teachers of older students can use it where the cloze procedure is less desirable or as an introduction to cloze tasks.

How might you use the maze procedure?

The maze procedure calls for recognizing the correct word in a series of sentences extracted from a selection or book. The text is modified by including "distractors," two alternative words for every fifth word in the passage. No procedure has been defined for choosing or placing the distractors. Selecting distractors at about the same level of reading as the correct word might increase the reliability of the process. The closer the distractors are in meaning to the correct word, the more difficult the maze.

Guthrie considers the optimal teaching range to be between 60 and 75 percent accuracy on the maze. If a reader performs at 85 percent or better for three or four administrations of sample pages, the material is probably at the reader's independent level, which indicates the student's need for more difficult material. If the scores fall below 50 percent, the material is considered frustrating for the reader, and less difficult material might be needed. It is important not to overestimate the skills of readers in cloze and maze tasks, since overplacement seems to occur more often than underplacement (Pikulski and Pikulski 1977).

The directions to follow when using the maze procedure are:

1. Select a passage of approximately one hundred consecutive words that the students have not previously read.
2. The first and last sentences are to remain intact. After the first sentence, add to every fifth word:
   a. an incorrect word that is the same part of speech as the correct word
   b. an incorrect word that is a different part of speech than the correct word

   The order of the three words should be varied.
3. Students are instructed to read the passage silently, and to circle the alternatives they believe to be correct.
4. The percentage of words the students circle correctly indicates their level of comprehension of the passage. For example, if a student answered fifteen of twenty maze items correctly, it could be said that he understood the passage with 75 percent proficiency.
5. Another step might be added. Ask the student to read the words from the passage either in context or isolation. Record the percent of words read accurately. Compare the maze and oral reading scores. If the maze score is lower, about 20 percent or more, comprehension is a problem for the reader.
6. The maze procedure should be used often enough to measure students'comprehension of the materials being read.

An abbreviated sample of a passage using the maze technique is shown below:

bridge
"The train stopped. It was at the station. People left
run

   They   playfully
the train. You hurried to the bus lanes.   They waited
   Cats   stop

   train   Night
for the bus   to take them home. They was late.
   funny   It

The people had worked a long day."

INFORMAL MEASUREMENT PROCEDURES

What are the advantages of using informal measures of assessment?

Informal group tests in the content areas determine the reading levels at which students can be instructed. Such informal testing is essential so that the teacher can make instructional adjustments in the classroom. Students cannot achieve success in the content areas unless they are provided with materials they can read and comprehend. The selection of inappropriate materials can contribute to an inadequate understanding of the subject matter. When students receive instruction from materials that are too easy for them, they are not motivated toward maximum achievement. In contrast, if books are too difficult for students to read and understand, they become frustrated and discouraged. The importance of selecting materials at the appropriate reading levels cannot be overemphasized.

Group reading inventories are adaptations of individual reading inventories. The procedures and criteria for individual informal reading inventories influence the preparation of informal group reading tests. In an individual inventory, a student reads both orally and silently at known levels of increasingly difficult material and responds to questions designed to measure his understanding of what he read. The student continues to read at successively higher levels until he reaches the level at which he no longer performs adequately.

An inventory is designed to determine four reading levels: independent, instructional, frustrational, and listening. The independent level is the highest level at which a student can read without assistance and encounter practically no problems in word recognition or in understanding ideas in the context. The level at which students might best be taught is the instructional level. If a student's reading performance is below the instructional level, the material is too difficult for instructional purposes. This level is known as the frustrational level. There should be a challenge to the reader, but it is preferable to strengthen his reading abilities than to place him in too difficult material and so obstruct his progress. The listening (expectancy) level is the highest level at which a student can comprehend material read aloud to him. Sometimes the listening level suggests that a reader may be able to read better and at a higher level than his performance indicated.

Word-Recognition Errors in Determining Reading Levels

Informal reading inventories, available for classroom use, measure better the assessment of individual reading abilities than standardized instruments (Early 1964 and Powell 1970). The most widely used criteria for identifying reading levels are those suggested by Betts (1946, Ch. 21). The word recognition criterion of one error in every twenty consecutive words, or 95 percent accuracy, as an indication of the instructional level has been generally accepted, although it was based on only a few cases. Some reading specialists have advised caution in using the standard, while others have proposed variations. Yet all criteria are generally thought to yield similar results.

How are word recognition errors determined?

Powell (1970) suggested that only further research will demonstrate whether a few percentage points in the word recognition score can make a difference in determining the instructional level. Powell finds that younger children can tolerate more word perception errors than their older counterparts and still maintain an acceptable comprehension standard in materials at their level. The word recognition criterion for the instructional level appears to be a function of the difficulty of materials and the age-grade of the child. Therefore, Powell suggests that the criterion of 95 percent may be too high for the majority of children in grades one through six. Furthermore, a study by Davis and Ekwall (1976) found that many third through fifth graders began to show signs of frustration when their oral reading errors were in the six to nine percent range. Thus, the error ratios increase in error latitude as the difficulty of the material increases and the age-grade of the sample increases. The criterion now in use is the same for all grade levels, one through twelve. Further research might modify practices in using informal reading inventories at both the elementary and secondary levels.

Oral reading of a single passage at sight seems to provide inadequate evidence of performance to determine the suitability of materials (Lowell 1970). Oral reading at sight yields the poorest performance when there has not been preparation for reading. Betts originally permitted students to read the passages silently before reading them orally. Other specialists permit only an oral reading at sight. However, Betts' criterion is often used to judge the performance. Still other points of difference in procedure among reading specialists are that although they count all word perception errors, some examiners count repetitions in reading as errors and others do not. Oral reading is thought by some to be unreliable as a way of measuring reading performance because of the difficulties related to judging word errors, inflectional endings, and phrasing.

In addition to silent and oral reading, as well as the number and kinds of word errors, other factors that influence reading performance are motivation, personality, and interest in reading. Two selections, of equal difficulty according to readability estimates, can differ greatly in terms of interest to the reader. Nevertheless, informal reading inventories are considered a valuable device for measuring reading levels.

INFORMAL READING INVENTORIES

What are the advantages of using a group informal reading inventory?

Informal reading inventories (IRI) are tests teachers construct to diagnose reading comprehension. The students read successively higher level passages and answer questions designed to measure their understanding—questions being the most common form of evaluating reading comprehension. Informal reading inventories, like the cloze test, are an efficient procedure for assessing the interaction between students and a text, and hence the reading difficulty of a text for those students. The passages chosen for the inventories should be representative of the content materials available for instruction that have not been previously read. Many adaptations of informal inventories can be used as measures of readability in order to match students with books they can read and comprehend.

Test of Comprehension

This modified test of comprehension screens students' reading levels.

1. Select a short passage of several pages from the first one fourth or one third of the text. Ask the students to read it silently.
2. Observe the students while they read, for lip or head movements, pointing to words with their fingers, frowning, smiling, and other overt behaviors that might provide clues as to the ease or difficulty they have during the reading process. Observe the fast and slow readers as they close their books.
3. Provide written or oral short-answer questions for the students to answer.
4. Score the tests. Those readers who receive a score below 70 percent are likely to encounter difficulty in reading and understanding the textbook.

Open Textbook Inventory

Shepherd (1978) presents a variation of the informal reading inventory called the "Open Textbook Reading Assessment." It includes the following steps:

1. Select three passages from a textbook not previously read by students.
2. Write questions at three levels of difficulty (literal, inferential, and generalized) for students to answer by using an open textbook.
3. Provide further testing for students scoring below 70 percent.
4. Ask students to read the passage orally to determine if poor word recognition skills account for the low comprehension scores.
5. Test the students on the technical language from the text passages if the word recognition skills seem adequate, to determine if the causal factor might be low vocabulary ability.

Informal Test of Reading Speed

McCracken (1972) suggests an informal reading test that is simple to administer. It tests reading speed:

1. The student is to silently read a page from a book.
2. The student's reading time is recorded.
3. Comprehension of the information is checked.
4. The student is to reread orally for 30 seconds. Words are pronounced for the reader if he hesitates.
5. The student's oral and silent reading speeds are calculated.

As a general rule, a reader is at the independent level if his silent reading is double his oral reading speed. If his silent and oral reading speeds are about the same, the material is too difficult. Previous instruction in speed reading would invalidate this test. This informal test cannot be used with students reading at or below the first reader level.

Group Informal Reading Inventory

An estimate of the instructional level of each student should be made before constructing a group informal reading inventory. These estimates can be made by observing daily performances in reading assignments and examining test data and records. This information serves as a basis for selecting passages from different level textbooks for use in the inventory. An English IRI might include a poem and narrative passages, a math IRI would include word problems and expository passages, and a science IRI would encompass expository and narrative paragraphs, and so on. The textbooks should be examined for the general and technical vocabulary used, the word recognition problems that some students might encounter, and the thinking skills needed to comprehend the material. These observations should be made from the viewpoint of both the teacher and students. After completing these preliminary steps, follow these procedures:

1. Select representative passages from textbooks at each of the estimated reading levels represented by the students in the class. A passage should consist of approximately sixty to one hundred words at the primary grade levels and should gradually increase to about six hundred or even one thousand words at the senior high level. The passage should have a logical beginning and conclusion.
2. Prepare five to ten questions to measure the students' comprehension. Open ended and content related questions appear to reveal more about a student's ability to formulate main ideas. Try to have a balance of different types of questions pertaining to main ideas, facts, inferences, and the relationship of ideas. Passage dependent questions are important to measure what students comprehend from a specific selection. If questions can be answered without reading a passage, the questions measure prior knowledge, not reading comprehension. Answers to questions can be written or oral.
3. Administer the test to groups consisting of five to ten students. Seek to keep the students relaxed.
4. Prepare and present a very brief introduction to each passage before it is read. Do not include information from the passage to be read or about the answers to the questions.
5. Ask the students to read silently the passage directly from the textbook. As they read, observe overt behaviors that indicate whether they are reading with ease or difficulty.
6. Direct the students to answer questions that have been typed on paper with sufficient space provided for their answers. If students lack the

necessary writing skills, let them discuss answers to the questions. Make certain each student is involved in responding to questions.

7. Repeat the above procedures for each higher reading level until a student scores below 70 percent. The percentage is based on the number of questions scored correctly. It may take more than one session to complete the inventory with some students.

The above procedures can be modified by:

1. Selecting two representative passages at each reading level from the textbook.
2. Letting each student in the group read one of the selections orally so that his reading performance can be observed and recorded. This procedure can be used individually with young students in the elementary school. Errors made during oral reading might be recorded in the following ways.

omissions	Weather stations are to observe . . .
insertions	*black* A cloud . . .
substitutions	*bright* The blazing star . . .
repetitions	The space orbit was . . .
unknown words	*TP* The critique was . . .

3. When a student is reading a passage orally, identify an unknown word after five seconds or when assistance is requested. The reader should not be corrected or instructed during the inventory.
4. The student should reread silently the passage before answering the questions.

Instead of using questions to determine comprehension of the selection, the teacher may lead an open discussion. To facilitate this procedure, the teacher should make an outline of the passage and check the concepts as students discuss what they have read.

A common standard of comprehension is 91 to 100 percent at the independent level, 70 to 90 percent at the instructional level, and 50 percent or below, frustration. A score between 70 and 50 percent suggests that the material is probably too difficult, that further analysis is needed, or that special instructional assistance is needed. An estimate of the listening comprehension or expectancy level may be obtained by using the inventory. The teacher should read the passage aloud, starting at the level where students failed to obtain a comprehension score of 70 percent. Comprehension is checked in the same manner as if they had read the passage, either in writing or by discussion. The procedure continues until the reader fails to meet the comprehension criterion. These scores are indices that can be used to confirm findings on a more thorough analysis of students' reading skills.

Sometimes a word recognition test may help diagnose reader needs in the content areas. A random sampling of ten to fifty words should be used for the inventory. The words should be typed doubled spaced as a word list, or printed on separate cards. The words may be presented by giving the readers a copy of the typed list of words or by flashing the word cards before them. The students take turns pronouncing a different word on the list or cards. Another procedure that might be followed is to select five to ten words from each passage to test word meaning in context. The words should be related to the content of the passage. Criteria are not applicable when words are presented in this informal manner, but approximately 95 percent accuracy is necessary to assume the independent level has been reached.

A rapid and fairly accurate gauge of readability can be obtained by the "finger method." If a student is reading a book and he can place a finger on at least five words on one page that he cannot pronounce or tell the meaning of, the book will usually be at that student's frustration level. Such information indicates a need for a teacher to use instruments that will give a more precise measurement of the student's reading performance.

MISCUE ANALYSIS OF ORAL READING

What is the purpose of miscue analysis?

Miscue analysis is a technique for analyzing a student's ability to reconstruct a written message. A miscue analysis can be made of students' oral reading by assessing those responses that are not an exact reproduction of a written message. It is the quality rather than the quantity of miscues that are important.

Miscue analysis measures how well students are able to use decoding skills, syntactic and semantic context, and prediction to derive meaning from a passage. When students read words different from those on the page, the mistakes are regarded as miscues. Usually the miscues made by efficient readers preserve the basic meaning of the original sentence. An analysis of the oral reading miscues uncovers the reading strategies used by students and their reading strengths and weaknesses.

Miscue analyses are done on the oral reading of an unfamiliar and complete selection. The selection should be difficult enough for the students to make miscues, but not so difficult as to cause frustration. Students are not given aids as they read, so that the teacher can gain insights into the kinds of strategies students use under these conditions. After the oral reading, a series of questions is asked dealing with linguistic information. A qualitative analysis of the miscues provides more significant information than the quantitative data (K. Goodman 1965, 1969, Y. Goodman 1972, and K. Goodman and V. J. Goodman 1980).

Goodman's research (1976, 1976) shows that comprehension consists of grapho-phonic information, syntactic information, and semantic information, and that obtaining meaning is the goal of the proficient reader. In research on miscue analysis, Burke and Goodman (1970) list questions to analyze students' miscues. Goodman and Burke (1972) developed *The Reading Miscue Inventory Manual* for analyzing miscues. Students' miscues are analyzed by asking questions about each miscue: how well the students recognize words in context and use their knowledge of language, and how much the miscues change the intended meanings of the author. Observing miscues that are self corrected also provides useful information.

D'Angelo and Wilson (1979) examined substitutions, insertions, and omissions made in oral reading to determine their usefulness in miscue analysis. Of a total of 595 miscues, 87 percent were substitutions, six percent were insertions, and seven percent were omissions. Insertions and omissions that distorted semantics and syntax were found in less than three percent of miscues analyzed. It was suggested that coding and interpreting insertion and omission miscues be simplified and attention be focused on reading behaviors that may cause difficulties in the reading process.

The number and nature of miscues a student makes in reading expository material may be different from those made in reading narrative passages. The semantic and syntactic clues may not be as useful to the poor reader because of the emphasis on many concepts. An informal and quick technique suggested by Tortelli (1976) for gathering and analyzing the miscues of a student might be used with narrative as well as with content materials. The steps involved are:

1. Have the student read aloud an unfamiliar selection.
2. Record all the student miscues or readings that are not contained in the original text.
3. At the completion of the reading, ask questions about what happened and did not happen in the selection, as a comprehension check.
4. After the student has finished reading, list and analyze the miscues under four headings.

   a. Unexpected readings (different from the text).

   b. Intended readings (words in text).

   c. Language (grammatically correct).

   d. Meaning (the same or different).

An example of this procedure is shown below. Using the information derived from this technique, a teacher can plan ways to strengthen a student's reading strategies.

Deception and Survival

What ~~seems~~ *looks* to be one thing in nature

is often an *big* imposter in disguise.

Deceptions by some plants and insects

allow them to hide from ~~predators~~ *people* and

to increase the chances of procreation.
TP
The chameleon, for example, has the

ability to change the color of its skin in

respect
~~response~~ to both external ~~stimuli~~ *things* and

internal factors.

Comprehension Check

1. What is an imposter?

2. Why do some plants and animals disguise themselves?

3. Does deception increase survival?

4. What is another word for deception?

5. Can camouflage help catch prey?

Unexpected Readings	Intended Readings	Language	Meaning
looks	seems	yes	same
big		insertion	different
people	predators	yes	different
	chameleon	unknown word	
respect	response	no	different
things	stimuli	yes	different

ADJUSTING READING MATERIALS

When it has been determined that a student cannot read a text without problems or frustration, the teacher needs to make adjustments in the procedures and materials the student will use to obtain the information. This is accomplished by one or more of the following:

1. Recording the textual information on a cassette tape.
2. Letting tutors read the text to the student.
3. Locating a text that presents the same topics at a lower reading level.
4. Using a variety of books, print and nonprint materials.

These techniques allow the poor reader to learn the new concepts and to interact with peers and the teacher during the recitation or discussion that follows the processing of textual information. Assistance in learning how to read should be provided to the student at another time.

SUMMARY

A major task in the content areas is to determine the appropriate match between students and subject matter materials so that they can read with a high degree of comprehension. There are different ways of determining the readability of prose. The four approaches examined in this chapter are readability formulas, the cloze procedure, group informal reading inventories, and miscue analysis.

Readability formulas predict the reading ease or difficulty of materials by examining the linguistic factors of word and sentence difficulty. Such formulas are limited to use with prose materials. Formulas cannot determine the concept load or indicate how well a student comprehends the material.

Readability formulas can be used by teachers (1) to predict reading levels of materials for students' use, and (2) to choose material for instructional purposes.

The cloze procedure is a word deletion technique designed to test a student's ability to anticipate meaning from context by supplying the exact words deleted at regular intervals from a written message. The success a student has in supplying the deleted words reflects his ability to comprehend the message and to see relationships among words. The more similar a student's language is to the structure of language used in the written message, the better the reader will comprehend the materials.

The maze technique is less difficult for the students to perform than the cloze procedure, and it is used as a monitoring technique. It is used with primary grade children and poor readers to determine their comprehension of prose.

Informal reading inventories, both individual and group, are classified as nonstandardized tests. Informal reading inventories can be modified for use with groups of students to measure their reading levels in content area materials. The quality and effectiveness of informal reading inventories will vary with a teacher's competence in constructing and administering the tests and using their results.

Both proficient and less proficient readers make miscues. In assessing oral reading it is not the number of miscues or errors that are important, but the quality or kinds of miscues. An informal technique of assesing oral miscues in expository and narrative materials can be used to diagnose the significance of students' miscues.

The importance of providing students with materials they can read with adequate levels of comprehension cannot be overemphasized. Therefore, evaluating the readability of materials is an essential task of a content area teacher.

Reinforcement Activities

1. Select a textbook and apply the Fry, Raygor, and SMOG formulas. Use the following worksheet to record your computations.

Fry Readability

Title of Textbook: _____

	Sentences per 100 words	Syllables per 100 words
First 100-word sample, page ____	_____	_____
Second 100-word sample, page ____	_____	_____
Third 100-word sample, page ____	_____	_____
Totals:	_____	_____
Average:	_____	_____
Estimated grade level:	_____	_____

Raygor Estimate

Title of Textbook: _____

	Sentences per 100 words	Words with 6 letters or more
First 100-word sample, page ____	_____	_____
Second 100-word sample, page ____	_____	_____
Third 100-word sample, page ____	_____	_____
Totals:	_____	_____
Average:	_____	_____
Estimated grade level:	_____	_____

SMOG Grading

Title of Textbook: _____

	Number of words with three or more syllables
First 10 consecutive sentences, pages _____	_____
Second 10 consecutive sentences, pages _____	
Third 10 consecutive sentences, pages _____	
Total:	_____
Nearest perfect square:	_____
Add three to square root:	_____
Estimated SMOG Grading:	_____

2. Prepare cloze tests using the same chapter or unit to which you applied the readability formulas.
   a. Administer a cloze test, including trial cloze tests.
   b. Select the criteria you plan to follow, and score and interpret the cloze test.
   c. Explain how you might use the results in planning the use of the instructional materials, making assignments, etc.

3. Construct, administer, and interpret a group informal reading inventory.

4. Analyze the oral reading miscues of a student. Use a selection from a textbook, and the modified informal way of gathering information and diagnosis of miscues shown in the chapter.

References

BALDWIN, R. SCOTT, and KAUFMAN, RHONDA K. "A Concurrent Validity Study of the Raygor Readability Estimate." *Journal of Reading* 23 (1979): 148–153.

BELLONI, LORETTA F., and JONGSMA, EUGENE A. "The Effects of Interest on Reading Comprehension of Low-Achieving Students." *Journal of Reading* 22 (1978): 106–109.

BETTS, EMMETT A. *Foundations of Reading Instruction.* New York: American Book Company, 1946.

BORMUTH, JOHN. "Cloze as a Measure of Readability." In *Reading as an Intellectual Activity*, edited by J. Allen Figurel. International Reading Association Proceedings, 1963, 131–134.

BORMUTH, JOHN. "Comparable Cloze and Multiple Choice Comprehension Test Scores." *Journal of Reading* 10 (1967): 291–299.

BOTEL, MORTON, and GRANOWSKY, ALVIN. "A Formula for Measuring Syntactic Complexity: A Directional Effort." *Elementary English* 49 (1972): 513–516.

BURKE, CAROLYN L., and GOODMAN, KENNETH S. "When a Child Reads: A Psycholinguistic Analysis." *Elementary English* 47 (1970): 121–129.

CAREY, ROBERT F. "Cloze Encounters of a Different Kind." *Reading Horizons* 19 (1979): 228–231.

DAINES, DELVA, and MASON, LYNNE J. "A Comparison of Placement Tests and Readability Graphs." *Journal of Reading* 15 (1972): 597–603.

DALE, EDGAR, and CHALL, JEANNE. "A Formula for Predicting Readability: Instructions." *Educational Research Bulletin* 27 (1948): 11–20.

D'ANGELO, KAREN, and WILSON, ROBERT M. "How Helpful Is Insertion and Omission Miscue Analysis?" *The Reading Teacher* 32 (1979): 519–520.

DANKS, J. H. "Grammaticalness and Meaningfulness in the Comprehension of Sentences." *Journal of Verbal Learning and Verbal Behavior* 8 (1969): 687–696.

DAVIS, EVERETT E., and EKWALL, ELDON E. "Mode of Perception and Frustration in Reading." *Journal of Learning Disabilities* 9 (1976): 448–454.

EARLY, MARGARET. "Identifying Reading Needs." In *Speaking of Reading*, edited by John K. Sherek. Syracuse, New York: Annual Reading Conference Papers, 1964, 43–51.

FLESCH, RUDOLPH F. "A New Readability Yardstick." *Journal of Applied Psychology* 32 (1948): 221–233.

FRY, EDWARD. "A Readability Formula That Saves Time." *Journal of Reading* 11 (1968): 513–516, 534–538.

FRY, EDWARD. "The Readability Graph Validated at Primary Grades." *The Reading Teacher* 22 (1969): 534–538.

FRY, EDWARD. "Fry's Readability Graph: Clarifications, Validity, and Extension to Level 17." *Journal of Reading* 23 (1977): 242–252.

FRY, EDWARD, and DEPIERRO, JOSEPH. "A Partial Validation of the Kernal Distance Theory for Readability." In *Reading: Disciplined Inquiry in Process and Practice*, edited by P. David Pearson and Jane Hansen. Clemson, South Carolina: Twenty-seventh Yearbook of the National Reading Conference, 1978, 121-124.

GANIER, ANN. "The Post-Oral-Reading Cloze Test: Does It Really Work?" *Reading World* 16 (1976): 21–27.

GOODMAN, KENNETH S. "A Linguistic Study of Cues and Miscues in Reading." *Elementary English* 42 (1965): 639–643.

GOODMAN, KENNETH S. "Analysis of Oral Reading Miscues: Applied Psycholinguistics." *Reading Research Quarterly* 5 (1969): 9–30.

GOODMAN, KENNETH S. "Behind the Eye: What Happens in Reading." In *Theoretical Models and Processes of Reading*, edited by Harry Singer and Robert Ruddell. 2nd ed. Newark, Delaware: International Reading Association, 1976, 470–496.

GOODMAN, KENNETH S. "Reading: A Psycholinguistic Guessing Game." In *Theoretical Models and Processes of Reading*, edited by Harry Singer and Robert Ruddell. 2nd ed. Newark, Delaware: International Reading Association, 1976, 497–508.

GOODMAN, KENNETH S., and GOODMAN, YETTA J. "Learning about Psycholinguistic Processes by Analyzing Oral Reading." In *Inchworm, Inchworm: Persistent Problems in Reading Education*, edited by Constance M. McCullough. Newark, Delaware: International Reading Association, 1980, 179–201.

GOODMAN, YETTA M. "Reading Diagnosis—Qualitative or Quantitative?" *The Reading Teacher* 26 (1972): 32–37.

GOODMAN, YETTA M., and BURKE, CAROLYN L. *The Reading Miscue Inventory: Manual.* New York: Macmillan, 1972.

GUNNING, ROBERT. *The Technique of Clear Writing.* Revised edition. New York: McGraw-Hill, 1968.

GUTHRIE, JOHN T., SEIFERT, MARY, BURNHAM, NANCY, and CAPLAN, RONALD. "The Maze Technique to Assess, Monitor Reading Comprehension." *The Reading Teacher* 28 (1974): 161–168.

HARRIS, ALBERT J., and SIPAY, EDWARD R. *How to Increase Reading Ability.* 7th ed. New York: David McKay, 1980.

HITTLEMAN, DANIEL R. "Seeking a Psycholinguistic Definition of Readability." *The Reading Teacher* 26 (1973): 783–789.

HORTON, R. J. "The Construct Validity of Cloze Procedure: An Explanatory Factor Analysis of Cloze, Paragraph Reading, and Structure of Intellect Tests." *Reading Research Quarterly* 10 (1974–75): 248–251.

HUNT, ADRIANNE, and REUTER, JANET R. "Readability and Children's Picture Books." *The Reading Teacher* 32 (1978): 23–27.

IRWIN, JUDITH W., and DAVIS, CAROL A. "Assessing Readability: The Checklist Approach." *Journal of Reading* 24 (1980): 124–130.

JONES, MARGARET B., and PIKULSKI, EDNA C. "Cloze for the Classroom." *Journal of Reading* 17 (1974): 432–438.

KLARE, GEORGE R. *The Measurement of Reading.* Ames, Iowa: Iowa State University Press, 1963.

KLARE, GEORGE R. "The Role of Word Frequency in Readability." *Elementary English Journal* 65 (1968): 12–22.

KLARE, GEORGE R. "Assessing Readability." *Reading Research Quarterly* 10 (1974–1975): 62–102.

KOENKE, KARL. "Another Practical Note on Readability Formulas." *Journal of Reading* 15 (1971): 203–208.

LOWELL, ROBERT E. "Problems in Identifying Reading Levels with Informal Reading Inventories." In *Reading Difficulties: Diagnosis, Correction and Remediation*, edited by William K. Durr. Newark, Delaware: International Reading Association, 1970, 120–126.

McCRACKEN, ROBERT A. "Contrived Readability in the 5th and 6th Grades." *Journal of Educational Research* 52 (1959): 277–278.

McCRACKEN, ROBERT A. "Informal Reading Inventories: Diagnosis within the Teacher." *The Reading Teacher* 26 (1972): 273–277.

McLAUGHLIN, HARRY G. "SMOG Grading—A New Readability Formula." *Journal of Reading* 12 (1969): 639–646.

MUIR, SHARON. "Cleaning the Air of Fog and Smog." *Reading Horizons* 18 (1978): 285–288.

PAGE, WILLIAM D. "The Post Oral-Reading Cloze Test: New Link between Oral Reading and Comprehension." *Journal of Reading Behavior* 7(1975): 383–389.

PALMER, WILLIAM S. "Readability, Rhetoric, and Reduction of Uncertainty." *Journal of Reading* 17 (1974): 522–558.

PAUK, WALTER. "A Practical Note on Readability Formulas." *Journal of Reading* 13 (1969): 207–210.

PEARSON, P. DAVID. "The Effects of Grammatical Complexity on Children's Recall, and Conceptions on Certain Semantic Relations." *Reading Research Quarterly* 10 (1974–1975): 155–192.

PIKULSKI, JOHN, and PIKULSKI, EDNA C. "Cloze, Maze and Teacher Judgment." *The Reading Teacher* 30 (1977): 766–770.

POWELL, WILLIAM R. "Reappraising the Criteria for Interpreting Informal Inventories." In *Reading Diagnosis and Evaluation*, edited by Dorothy L. De Boer. Proceedings of the Thirteenth Annual Convention. Newark, Delaware: International Reading Association, 1970, 100–109.

RAKES, THOMAS A., and McWILLIAMS, LANA J. "A Cloze Placement Table." *Reading Improvement* 16 (1979): 317–319.

RANKIN, EARL F., and CULHANE, JOSEPH W. "Comparable Cloze and Multiple-Choice Comprehension Scores." *Journal of Reading* 13 (1969): 193–198.

RANKIN, EARL F., and THOMAS, SUSAN. "Contextual Constraints and the Construct Validity of the Cloze Procedure." In *Perspectives in Reading Research and Instruction*, edited by Michael L. Kamil and Alden J. Moe. Washington, D.C.: Twenty-ninth Yearbook of the National Reading Conference, 1980, 47–55.

RANSOM, PEGGY. "Determining Reading Levels of Elementary School Children by Cloze Testing." In *Forging Ahead in Reading*, edited by J. A. Figurel. Newark, Delaware: International Reading Association, 1968, 477–482.

RAYGOR, ALTON L. "The Raygor Readability Estimate: A Quick and Easy Way to Determine Difficulty." In *Reading: Theory, Research and Practice*, edited by P. David Pearson and Jane Hansen. Clemson, South Carolina: Twenty-sixth Yearbook of the National Reading Conference, 1977, 259–263.

SCHNEYER, J. W. "Use of the Cloze Procedure for Improving Reading Comprehension." *The Reading Teacher* 19 (1965): 174–179.

SHAFFER, GARY L. "An Investigation of the Relationship of Selected Components of Readability and Comprehension at the Secondary School Level." In *Reading: Theory, Research and Practice*, edited by P. David Pearson and Jane Hansen. Clemson, South Carolina: The National Reading Conference, 1977, 244–252.

SHEPHERD, DAVID L. *Comprehensive High School Methods*. 2nd ed. Columbus, Ohio: Charles E. Merrill Company, 1978.

SINGER, HARRY. "The SEER Technique: A Non-Computation Procedure for Quickly Estimating Readability Level." *Journal of Reading Behavior* 7 (1975): 255–267.

SMITH, WILLIAM L. "The Effect of Transformed Syntactic Structures on Reading." In *Language, Reading, and the Communication Process*, edited by Carl Braun. Newark, Delaware: International Reading Association, 1971, 52–62.

SPACHE, GEORGE. "A New Readability Formula for Primary Grade Reading Materials." *Elementary School Journal* 53 (1953): 410–413.

STOODT, BARBARA D. "The Relationships Between Understanding Grammatical Conjunctions and Reading

Comprehension." *Elementary English* 49 (1972): 502-504.

TAYLOR, WILSON L. "Cloze Procedure: A New Tool for Measuring Readability." *Journalism Quarterly* 30 (1953): 415–433.

TORTELLI, JAMES PETER. "Simplified Psycholinguistic Diagnosis." *The Reading Teacher* 29 (1976): 637–639.

VAUGHN, JR., JOSEPH L. "Interpreting Readability Assessments." *Journal of Reading* 19 (1976): 635–639.

VAUGHN, JR., JOSEPH L., and MEREDITH, KEITH. "Reliabil-

ity of the Cloze Procedure as Assessments of Various Language Elements." In *Reading: Disciplined Inquiry in Process and Practice*, edited by P. David Pearson and Jane Hansen. Clemson, South Carolina: Twenty-seventh Yearbook of the National Reading Conference, 1978, 175–180.

ZINTZ, MILES V. *The Reading Process: The Teacher and the Learner*. 2nd ed. Dubuque, Iowa: Wm. C. Brown Company Publishers, 1975.

Bibliography

BRADLEY, JOHN M., and MEREDITH, KEITH. "The Reliability of the Maze Procedure for Intermediate and Junior High School Students." In *Reading: Disciplined Inquiry in Process and Practice*, edited by P. David Pearson and Jane Hansen. Clemson, South Carolina: Twenty-seventh Yearbook of the National Reading Confernce, 1978, 186–189.

BURMEISTER, LOU E. "A Chart for the New Spache Formula." *The Reading Teacher* 29 (1976): 384–385.

FINN, PATRICK J. "Word Frequency, Information Theory, and Cloze Performance: A Transfer Feature Theory of Processing in Reading." *Reading Research Quarterly* 13 (1977–1978): 508–537.

FRY, EDWARD. "Comments on the Preceding Harris and Jacobson Comparison of the Fry, Spache, and Harris-Jacobson Readability Formulas." *The Reading Teacher* 33 (1980): 924–926.

GOODMAN, KENNETH S., and GOODMAN, YETTA M. "Learning about Psycholinguistic Processes by Analyzing Oral Reading." *Harvard Educational Review* 47 (1977): 317–333.

JOHNSON, MARGARET S., and KRESS, ROY A. *Informal Reading Inventories*. Newark, Delaware: International Reading Association, 1965.

LAYTON, JAMES R. "A Chart for Computing the Dale-Chall Readability Formula above Fourth Grade Level." *Journal of Reading* 24 (1980): 239–244.

MAGINNIS, GEORGE H. "The Readability Graph and Informal Reading Inventories." *The Reading Teacher* 22 (1969): 516–519, 559.

MANZO, ANTHONY V. "Readability: A Postscript." *Elementary English* 47 (1970): 962–965.

MARSHALL, NANCY. "Research: Readability and Comprehensibility." *Journal of Reading* 22 (1979): 542–544.

MEREDITH, KEITH, VAUGHN, JR., JOSEPH. "Stability of Cloze Scores across Varying Deletion Patterns." In *Reading: Disciplined Inquiry in Process and Practice*, edited by P. David Pearson and Jane Hansen. Clemson, South Carolina: Twenty-seventh Yearbook of the National Reading Conference, 1978, 181-184.

POPP, HELEN, and PORTER, DOUGLAS. *Measuring the Readability of Children's Trade Books*. Unpublished study, Harvard Graduate School of Education, July 1975. ERIC Ed 113684.

4 ASSESSING STUDY SKILLS

OVERVIEW

To help their students read and study better, teachers must be fully aware of their current abilities. They will then be able to provide the kinds of instruction and activities best suited to their students' needs. In this chapter, three types of reading and study skills tests are discussed in terms of what they measure and what they can tell teachers. Examples of various tests are given, as well as suggestions for making testing a successful part of one's curriculum.

TO BE EFFECTIVE, teachers concerned about their students' progress and ability as they read in the content areas must move from a teacher-oriented program to a learner-oriented program. A program focused on learners is based on the ideas that learning to read in the content areas is a continuing process and that all students in any given age group are not expected to reach the same level of achievement. Also inherent in such a program is the practice of providing instruction at the students' level of understanding and ability, while encouraging progression in their use of the necessary reading and study skills. All students need time and attention from the teacher. The more specific and direct the contact, the more learning is likely to take place. This result is achieved both through large and small group instruction and individual attention. It is far better to teach the reading and study skills considered necessary for efficient learning of subject matter content than to have to remediate misunderstandings and poor reading skills.

Why is assessment of reading skills important?

In the content areas, assessment is a preventive measure used to determine how students perform in a given reading situation, and subsequent instruction is adjusted to meet these needs. Instructional decisions are based on the assessment of what students can do and of what particular skills need strengthening. Inherent in this concept of teaching is the idea that evaluation is an ongoing activity that serves as a basis for instruction.

Informal measures are used to assess the strengths and weaknesses of a student's reading and study skills through planned observation and testing. This assessment is an inference made by a teacher about the student's performance in a specified skill. Classroom assessment should be continuous; it is productive only to the extent that follow-up procedures are formulated and implemented, and to the extent that the desired learning is achieved. Assessment of students' needs includes determining both good and poor performances, the influencing factors, and the resultant steps to be followed. The preventive aspect of evaluation is for all students, including the nonachievers, the achievers, and the gifted.

Informal measures of abilities are task oriented, and they are used to measure students' progress in specific skills of concern to the teacher. The results of such assessment serve as a basis for making curriculum decisions about classroom instruction as well as the materials and practices necessary to meet students' needs. Assessment is an integral part of teaching in the content areas.

Students' reading needs in the content areas can be assessed by standardized tests, criterion-referenced tests, and informal procedures. Each form of assessment yields information that helps in planning instruction and selecting materials. Standardized tests are usually norm-referenced and provide grade placement, percentiles, and measures of central tendencies. Generally, the scores of group achievement tests are used to indicate how well a student or class compares with another student or group of the same age and grade. Criterion-referenced tests measure a student's performance in relation to a specific behavioral objective. Informal measures devised by teachers are used to assess information that is not always available in other tests. This chapter emphasizes informal procedures that can be used to assess study skills in the content areas. In addition, the purposes of standardized achievement or survey tests and criterion-referenced tests are briefly reviewed.

STANDARDIZED READING TESTS

There are two general classifications of standardized reading tests—survey and diagnostic tests. These tests are designed to yield scores that compare a student's performance with that of a group or a norm established by group scores such as grade-placement, age-placement, or percentile scores. They are called norm-referenced tests. Survey tests provide gross measures of overall performance. Students may receive the same score obtained through different combinations of subtest scores. The diagnostic tests are planned to ascertain a student's strengths and weaknesses in specific skills such as word perception, understanding sentence and paragraph meanings, and identifying main ideas and details.

How can standardized reading tests be used to facilitate the teaching of reading?

Survey tests are administered either to a group or to an individual student. The group norms furnished with standardized tests enable a teacher or other school district personnel to make general comparisons between individuals, groups of students, schools, or general population. Standardized reading tests scores may also be used as a rough indication of growth in reading skills for both individuals and groups.

Survey tests often overestimate students' reading abilities. The grade equivalent scores indicate that students read better than their actual ability. Frequently, the grade scores on standardized tests are higher than students' instructional reading levels (McCracken 1962, Sipay 1964, Leibert 1965, Harmon 1975, Otto 1976, Karlin 1977, Estes and Vaughn, Jr. 1978, and Harris and Sipay 1979). This discrepancy is even greater for students who are having difficulty in reading. Furthermore, standardized tests do not always include the various skills required of students in the various content areas. Standardized tests have a definite place, however, in a comprehensive program. The results can be used to estimate the range of students' achievements, and plans can then be made to test more precisely students receiving low scores (Farr 1969 and Farr and Roser 1979, Karlin 1977, and Estes and Vaughn, Jr. 1978).

The Buros Mental Measurement Yearbook, the *Buros Reading Tests and Reviews*, and publications by the International Reading Association and the Educational Resources Information Center/Clearinghouse for the Retrieval of Information and Evaluation on Reading (ERIC/CRIER) are important sources for information about tests, including reading tests. The reviews give specific information about the tests, such as the groups for which a test is intended, if it is a group or individual test, if the test is machine scorable, the parts and levels of the test, reliability and validity of the test, cost of the test, time needed for administration of the test, author and publisher of the test.

CRITERION-REFERENCED TESTS

Criterion-referenced tests are useful for measuring students' mastery of specific objectives and standards of performance. The goal of criterion-referenced assessment is to describe reading behavior in relation to preestablished standards deemed essential by the teacher. Criterion-referenced measurement provides a way for teachers to adjust day-to-day instruction to the specific reading needs of students (Hill 1974).

What do criterion-referenced tests measure?

Glaser used the term "criterion-referenced test" to refer to the measurement of performance in relation to educational objectives. Setting standards of student performance is the key to using criterion-referenced tests in classroom instruction. Criterion-referenced tests are to be used to identify the reading behaviors that students can or cannot perform and to individualize reading instruction. Criterion-referenced tests are designed to describe a student's test performance without reference to the performance of other students. Since their achievement is shown in terms of the specific learning tasks that each student has or has not mastered, the results are helpful for planning instruction in the skills where further learning is needed. The completion of certain tasks is presumed to evidence the mastery of such skills (Glaser and Klaus 1962, Glaser 1963, Glaser and Nitko 1970, Hill 1974, Womer 1974, Davis 1974, Harris and Sipay 1979).

Criterion-referenced tests are limited in the measurement of mastery, the criteria to use, and the sequence and importance of the many skills (Popp 1975 and Meskauskas 1976). Although there is insufficient research to guide the process of designing criterion-referenced tests, Gronlund (1973, Ch. 1) suggests five steps to follow:

1. Delimit the achievement area to be tested.
2. State the objectives in specific and performance terms.
3. Establish standards for student performance.
4. Measure expected learning outcomes.
5. Provide for scoring and interpreting test results to determine mastery of learning.

INFORMAL MEASURES

How can informal measures be used to improve reading instruction?

Informal tests are defined as nonstandardized procedures for gathering information about students. Informal measures include teacher-developed instruments designed to assess readers' understanding and progress in specified reading and study skills. Assessment of daily assignments, checklists, worksheets, and observations are examples of other informal measures. Informal tests made and administered by the teacher give immediate information about each reader in reference to learning objectives selected by the teacher. Such measures can be used at a later date to recheck and verify students' maintenance of specific skills. Informal reading tests are usually easy to administer and check. The results of such measures should be recorded and shared with the students so they may plan with the teacher how to reach certain goals.

A major purpose for using informal reading tests for classroom diagnosis is to secure sufficient information about students' strengths and weaknesses in specific skills to guide a teacher in planning appropriate instruction and practice. The value of diagnosis based on informal tests is determined by:

1. The purpose of the test.
2. The preparation and arrangement of the test items.
3. The administration procedures of the test.
4. The interpretation of the test results.
5. The way the test results and interpretation are utilized.

Informal measures developed by teachers are classified into two categories: individual and group tests. Each type of test offers both strengths and weaknesses. Individual tests are administered on a one-to-one basis. Such tests usually enable the teacher to obtain more information about the reading behavior of a student and about the kinds and number of reading errors than can be recorded. Individual testing requires more teacher time.

Group testing makes it possible to gather data in a relatively short time since the tests are administered to several students at the same time. The size of the group may vary. Efficient scoring procedures minimize correcting time, making group tests both easy and economical to administer. These tests should contain enough items to ensure that each skill is adequately sampled, and the exercises should require the students to demonstrate their knowledge of the skill. In general, it is inadvisable to gather group data from verbal responses: students might be influenced by the responses of other students and distracted from the task, thus changing their original answer. In most instances, informal tests are administered to groups of students. However, any group tests can be administered individually when more specific observation of reading behavior is desired.

The purposes of informal group tests should be made clear to the students. More accurate information is usually obtained if students are committed to taking the test. This is especially true when students understand that test results will be used to assist them improve particular skills.

In addition to determining areas to which attention should be given, informal teacher-made tests aim to identify growth areas in reading and study skills where the students are progressing satisfactorily. Initial assessments should precede and influence instruction. Additional evaluations should be given to check the students' mastery of the skills related to reading in the content areas.

Students' responses in a test situation can be placed into two categories: recognition and production. Production-type responses usually require a higher level of thinking than a recognition response. At the recognition level, a reader is asked to identify a picture, a date, the meaning of a word, a main idea, or relevant details, and so on. At the production level, a reader is asked to put an idea into writing or to express it verbally and respond at the application or creative levels.

ADMINISTRATION OF INFORMAL TESTS

It is essential to follow the directions of informal tests. Inconsistency in giving directions for the same test to different students may change the intent and results of a test. Varying the scoring pattern also will cause the results to be diverse. The scoring patterns used by the teacher must be realistic about the mastery level of tasks expected of students. These patterns of giving directions and scoring influence tests and decisions about instruction, materials, and practices. Thus, advance planning and consistency in administering, scoring, and interpreting tests are essential.

RECORD KEEPING

Why is record keeping so important?

Keeping records will facilitate teacher guidance and instruction in reading. Patterns of students' achievement and progress in reading skills are discerned more readily when the results of tests, observations, checklists, informal tests, and so forth are organized in a record form. Record keeping is an indispensable facet of effective instruction. Retrieval or record keeping systems used by teachers should be simple and easy to maintain. The information placed on records helps a teacher decide what instruction is needed, which students have similar needs and might be grouped together for instruction, what materials to use, the kind and amount of practice needed, and the type of follow-up evaluation to utilize. It also is important that students learn to keep records of their progress in using different reading skills and of the books read.

An overview of a student's pattern of reading skills in a content area is readily obtained if the results of informal tests and other information have been organized on a record form. This information serves as a basis for teaching to meet an individual need or a group of students who have the same need.

Two examples of forms to record instructional needs are shown. They can easily be adapted to the specifications of any teacher.

TEACHER OBSERVATION

What role should teacher observation play in teaching reading?

Observation is not a passive process of merely watching the reading behavior of students. It is a purposeful act and involves a plan to observe for specific reading and study patterns displayed by students. Therefore, the teacher

Reading Skills Information

Names of Students	Sets Purpose	Adjusts Rate	Skimming	Scanning	Comments
	Date:	Date:	Date:	Date:	

Reading Record

Assessment Information			Individual Conferences			
Subject:			Date	Textbook Used	Skill Checked	Comments and Recommendations
Name:						
Date	Test	Results				

needs to know which reading skills are relevant and consequential for a particular subject.

Daily observation is an informal, ongoing activity of an effective teacher. It takes place during class instruction, class discussion, study periods, individual or group project development, and in the library. Observations should constantly be employed in making appraisals of students' needs and growth and attitudes toward reading content and related materials.

A teacher's experiential background provides information and attitudes for the identification, interpretation, and evaluation of that which is observed. Since conditions and situations may change from day to day, the teacher needs to have an adequate sampling of students' skills in reading and study situations. Inferences or deductions from classroom observations are a significant part of assessing student needs in reading content area materials.

There are many reading behaviors that a teacher might observe as students study subject matter materials and as they respond to questions on an informal test. This information can be used to plan instruction and practice activities for the students. Reading behaviors for which a teacher might observe include:

1. Does the student follow directions?
2. Does the student sustain effort on a task?
3. Does the student complete his assignments?
4. Does the student know how and where to locate information?
5. Does the student seek help?
6. How often and from whom does he seek assistance?
7. Does the student possess an experiential background for the task?
8. Does the student ask questions?
9. Does the student listen to the ideas of others?
10. Does the student volunteer to answer questions?
11. Does the student use the language of the subject?
12. Does the student contribute relevant ideas to a discussion?
13. Can the student identify the topic of a paragraph or longer selection?
14. Can the student select, interpret, and evaluate main ideas?
15. Can the student recognize relevant detail?
16. Does the student know how to organize information?
17. Does the student use context to understand word meanings?
18. Does the student use multi-meanings of words?
19. Does the student get an idea and carry it through to a logical conclusion?
20. Does the student know how to set reading purposes?
21. Does the student know how to use previewing, skimming, and scanning skills?
22. Does the student adjust the rate of reading to purposes, type of materials, etc.?
23. Does the student know how to use graphic aids?
24. Does the student know how to organize and express ideas in writing?
25. Does the student enjoy the activities of a challenging situation?

INFORMAL STUDY SKILLS TESTS

What specific informal study skills tests might you use to improve your students' reading ability?

It is important that teachers help students improve their reading comprehension of content materials. Informal assessment of needed study skills is one of the more effective ways to prevent problems before they arise. First, it is necessary to determine the skills students need to study a particular subject. After these decisions are made, they serve as a focus for assessment. Teacher-made tests can be used to measure the strengths and weaknesses of students in these specified skills.

To construct a teacher-made test, it is necessary to have clearly in mind what skills are to be assessed and how the results will be used. Samples of group informal tests, or parts of tests, used to assess study skills are presented below. Teachers have tried these tests in their classrooms. They have used them at the beginning of a new unit, as a preassessment before a new skill is introduced, or to test the proficiency of students in using a skill. Most of these examples can be adapted to different grade levels and subject matter.

Know Your Textbook

Directions: Your answers to the following questions will indicate how well you use your textbook. See how many questions you can answer correctly in five minutes.

1. On what page does Chapter 7 begin? Page _____ .
2. How many chapters does this textbook contain? _____ chapters.
3. How many units does this textbook contain? _____ units.
4. On what two pages is Herbert Hoover mentioned? Pages _____ and _____ .
5. On what page is the map showing the amounts of rainfall along the western coast of the United States? Page _____ .
6. Who invented the cotton gin? _____
7. What is the growth rate of the southwestern states? _____ _____
8. What is the definition of the phrase *trade deficit?* _____ _____ _____
9. In what state is the Grand Canyon located? The state of _____ .
10. On what page is the definition of the word "employment?" Page _____ .
11. On what pages are the Northern Rocky Mountain States mentioned? Pages _____ .
12. Examine the map on page 336 and list the states which contain oil shale deposits. _____ _____

Student responses to the above test will indicate if they know how to use textbook aids. Such information will help determine the success of follow-up instruction.

Book Utilization

Directions: This test is to determine your skill in using your textbook. Read each question and place the number matching your answer in the blank opposite the question.

1. Appendix   3. Foreword
2. Bibliography   4. Glossary

5. Graphs   9. Maps
6. Headings   10. Parts
7. Index   11. Preface
8. List of illustrations   12. Table of contents

_____ You have been told that your book contains a full color illustration of Gerald Ford. Where would you look in the textbook to verify what you have been told?

_____ You remember that you want to check on Andrew Jackson's monetary policy while he was President. Where would you look to see if the topic is covered in the textbook?

_____ What term is used when a chapter is divided into sections?

_____ Since the book was written, the author has died. To update the book a colleague of the author's has been called in to write an introduction to the book. What would you call such an introduction?

_____ Where would you find the correct spelling of a word, its meaning, or its pronunciation?

_____ Which source would you use to find the history of the stock market?

_____ What do we call an author's introduction to his work?

_____ How would the Mormon trek across the desert be shown?

_____ Where would you look to find what chapter 3 is about?

_____ Where would you locate a supplementary list of books on the subject of your text?

The responses of students to these questions will provide some information about instructional needs concerning their skills in using their textbook.

What Do You Know?

Directions: This inventory is to find out how much you know about Chapter 6 in your textbook before your read it. Read the directions for each of the four parts before you answer the question.

A. Match the vocabulary with the correct meaning.

_____ 1. labrum

_____ 2. abdomen

_____ 3. Malpighian tubules

_____ 4. spiracles

_____ 5. nymph

a. stages from molt to molt
b. the changes through which an insect passes in its life
c. a single tongue-like structure
d. numerous small tubes at the juncture of the small intestine and the stomach
e. the outside of each mandible
f. rough-edged jaws

_____ 6. metamorphosis

_____ 7. pupa

_____ 8. instars

_____ 9. mandible

_____ 10. maxilla

g. this is composed of eleven segments

h. the inactive stage of an insect

i. the young stage of a grasshopper

j. the upper lip of an insect

k. this is attached to the prothorax

l. these are small openings on each of the first eight segments of the abdomen.

B. Put a check in front of the following statements that are true.

_____ 1. The first appendages on an insect at its front end are a pair of antennae.

_____ 2. There are three kinds of muscle tissue in a grasshopper.

_____ 3. The digestive tract of an insect is large, with a crop preceding the stomach.

C. Put a check in front of the following generalizations which are true.

_____ 1. All insects have all of the characteristics of anthropoids.

_____ 2. All insects undergo a complete metamorphosis.

_____ 3. If we understand the metamorphosis of an insect, we can control it more effectively.

D. Write your answer to the next question in the space provided for you.

Why do you think it is important to study about insects and their behavior?

The responses of students to these questions will provide information about their familiarity with this topic that can guide planning for instruction and enrichment activities.

Locating Information

Directions: This test is to help determine your skill in locating information. Sources of information have been numbered from one to ten. Read each question. Then place the number of the correct source in the blank opposite the question.

1. Almanac
2. Atlas

3. Bartlett's Familiar Quotations

4. Card Catalogue	8. Guinness Book of Records
5. Dictionary	9. Reader's Guide to
6. Encyclopedia	Periodical Literature
7. ERIC	10. Specialized Periodicals

_____ Where would you look to confirm that *Tom Sawyer* was written by Mark Twain?

_____ Where would you find who was the heaviest person in recorded history?

_____ Your teacher has assigned you to write a paper about Menachem Begin. If you wanted to quickly become informed about his life, where would you look?

_____ You are writing a speech and you want to include a quotation about honesty. Where would you look to find the quotation?

_____ You are a camera bug and want to determine quickly what is new in the field. Where might you look?

_____ Your school library does not contain enough information on the topic you are studying. What library service might help you to secure the titles of additional books on the subject?

_____ If you wished to know the rainfall in Kentucky last year, in which source would you look?

_____ What source would give you a list of magazine articles relating to atomic energy?

_____ Where would you look to determine the origin and course of the Nile River?

_____ The quickest way of determining the population of Chicago, Illinois, would be to use what specific source?

Students should be grouped together according to the questions they missed to receive instruction and a demonstration on how to locate information. Relevant practice should follow.

Using a Dictionary

Directions: Use your dictionary to answer the following questions. Write your answer in the space after each question.

1. If you were looking for the word "neuron," would you open the dictionary to the front third, middle third, or last third? _____
2. If you were looking for the word "peaceful," would you look in the front third, middle third, or last third of the dictionary? _____
3. What do the following abbreviations stand for?

   a. Brit. _____ .   d. lb. _____ .

   b. bro. _____ .   e. Miss. _____ .

   c. dau. _____ .   c. mtn. _____ .

4. Who was George Gershwin? Where did you find this information in the dictionary? _____

_____

5. Look up the word "hear." Which definition fits the usage of the word "hear" in the following sentence? "The judge decided to *hear* the case." _____

_____

Questions should be added to this test so that it includes a greater variety of dictionary skills. The students' responses will provide some information about their instructional needs pertaining to dictionary usage.

Context Clues

Many teachers test the ability of students to use context clues by asking them to define the meaning of words in sentences. To prepare the test, select several paragraphs from a passage that the students have not read, depending upon the author's style of writing and the reading abilities of the students. Choose and underline words that can be defined by the way they are used in a sentence or paragraph. Students are to write a sentence defining each underlined word according to the way it is used by the author. The definitions written by the students will provide some information about their abilities to use context clues. This test may be given to students individually, and their responses may be verbal. Sentences showing the use of context clues follow.

Peggy likes to go with her friends to eat in a *restaurant*.

Please *cooperate* with your committee members and help them make the map.

Bill doesn't have brothers or sisters; he is a *singleton*.

The big car came to a sudden, *abrupt* halt.

He is *ambidextrous* and can use both hands equally well.

Jean is so *inquisitive*; she is always asking questions.

Discovering Main Ideas

Directions: On these pages are ten short paragraphs. You are to discover the main idea of each paragraph. Follow each step listed below.

1. Read the paragraphs one at a time.
2. After reading each paragraph, determine its main idea.
3. Write the main idea in a sentence, using your own words.
4. Write your answers on a separate sheet of paper.

Select ten short paragraphs to use for this test. It is more difficult for students to paraphrase the ideas of an author than to select an idea from a group of statements or to quote the author. Discussion of an idea will help students with this skill when more practice is needed.

Hidden Thoughts

Directions: This is a test of your skill in determining ideas that are not specifically mentioned in a story. Read the story "Stars Over Arizona." Follow the directions to record your answers to questions about the story.

1. Record on tape your name.
2. Record your answers to the questions listed below.
3. Place the tape back in the envelope when you have finished.
4. Place the envelope in the basket on the teacher's desk.

Questions to be answered after reading "Stars Over Arizona."

1. Captain Lang faced two problems. What were they?
2. What responsibility was given to Bill on the flight?
3. Why didn't Captain Lang wait to see what Bill wanted?
4. What idea was Bill beginning to formulate?
5. Why do you think Captain Lang didn't know about Bill's ideas?

This test is to determine whether students can infer major thoughts that are not stated directly by an author. This is a more difficult task than identifying a main idea that is included in a passage. Discussion about the clues found in a passage will help students develop the skill of inferring ideas from context.

Scanning Skills

Directions: Open your Utah History book to page 196. You have five minutes to scan Chapter 4 to answer the following questions.

1. When was Cache County settled? _____
2. Are the principal industries of Rich and Piute counties identical?
   _____
3. Which of the three following counties has the greatest area per square mile?

   Garfield _____
   Kane _____
   Salt Lake _____

4. Which county derived its name from the early discovery of iron ore?
   _____
5. Which county has had a percentage increase of 221 in population?
   _____

Pertinent questions should be added to this test to make it longer. Since the emphasis is on scanning, a rapid reading skill, it is a timed test. If students cannot complete the questions correctly in the allotted time, they should receive instruction in the reasons for scanning and how to scan for information. Practice should be included with the instruction.

Reading a Map

Directions: Examine your map of Utah and use it to help you answer the following questions. Write your answers in the blank spaces.

1. The city located at B5 is _____ .
2. Dinosaur National Monument is located at _____ .
3. The largest city in the northern part of the state is _____ .
4. The county where mining is the main occupation is _____ .
5. The county with the largest land area is _____ .
6. The transportation center of the state is _____ .
7. What are the two largest lakes in the state and where are they located?
   _____ .
8. Which county has the largest city? _____ .

Other questions might be added to make this a longer and more accurate test. Students should receive instruction in those areas of map reading in which they are having difficulty.

Notetaking skills in a listening situation might be tested by the use of a tape on which has been recorded a speech or lecture. Related skills of underlining, outlining, and mapping can be assessed through the use of a passage taken from a textbook. An informal test can be devised to determine the ability to read maps, interpret graphs, and follow directions.

SUMMARY

The use of informal measures to assess and verify study skills students can and cannot use in reading subject matter materials is an essential part of teaching. Assessing the growth of students is necessary for making decisions related to instruction.

Teachers can construct informal measures if they are aware of the reading skills to be measured. The reading skill or behavior needs to be clearly stated and understood if an appropriate test and materials are to be prepared. Teacher-made tests, because of their ease in construction, are readily adapted to checking daily or weekly progress of students' learning in the content areas.

Standardized tests and criterion-referenced tests are other measures for assessing the study skills of students. However, observation and informal assessment procedures should be used as a base for planning instruction in reading and study of content area material.

Reinforcement Activities

1. Examine a textbook used by your students, and determine the skills necessary to read the text. Put this information into list form, and write a performance objective for each skill selected. Choose one of the objectives and plan an informal test to assess your students' use of the study skill. Include the directions for the test and for the scoring pattern to correct and interpret the test.

2. Administer the test to some of your students. Afterwards, make any necessary adjustments to improve the tests. Also, prepare a form to record the results of this and other tests. Design the form to make the retrieval of the information convenient to facilitate the planning of instruction and student practice.

References

DAVIS, FREDERICK B. "Criterion-Referenced Tests: A Critique." In *Measuring Reading Performance*, edited by William E. Blanton, Roger Farr, and Jaap Tuinman. Newark, Delaware: International Reading Association, 1974, 44–50.

ESTES, THOMAS H., and VAUGHN, JR., JOSEPH L. *Reading and Learning in the Content Classroom*. Boston: Allyn and Bacon, Inc., 1978.

FARR, ROGER. *Reading: What Can Be Measured?* Newark, Delaware: International Reading Association, 1969.

FARR, ROGER, and ROSER, NANCY. *Teaching a Child to Read*. New York: Harcourt Brace Jovanovich, Inc., 1979.

GLASER, R., and KLAUS, D. J. "Proficiency Measurement: Assessing Human Performance." In *Psychological Principles in Systems Development*, edited by R. M. Gagné. New York: Holt, Rinehart and Winston, 1962, 419–474.

GLASER, R. "Instructional Technology and the Measurement of Learning Outcomes." *American Psychologist* 18 (1963): 519–521.

GLASER, R., and KLAUS, D. J. "Proficiency Measurement: Assessing Human Performance." In *Psychological Principles in Systems Development*, edited by R. M. Gagné. New York: Holt, Rinehart and Winston, 1962, 419–474.

GRONLUND, NORMAN E. *Preparing Criterion-Referenced Tests for Classroom Instruction*. New York: The Macmillan Company, 1973.

HARMON, D. "Reading Tests." *The National Elementary Principal* 54 (1975): 81–87.

HARRIS, ALBERT J., and SIPAY, EDWARD R. *How to Teach Reading: Competency-Based Program*. New York: Longman, 1979.

HILL, WALTER R. "Reading Testing for Reading Evaluation." In *Measuring Reading Performance*, edited by William E. Blanton, Roger Farr, and J. Jaap Tuinman. Newark, Delaware: International Reading Association, 1974, 1–14.

KARLIN, ROBERT. *Teaching Reading in High School: Improving Reading in Content Areas*. 3rd ed. Indianapolis: Bobbs-Merrill Educational Publishing, 1977.

LEIBERT, ROBERT E. "An Investigation of the Difference in Reading Performance on Two Tests of Reading." Unpublished doctoral dissertation. Syracuse, New York: Syracuse University, 1965.

McCRACKEN, ROBERT. "Standardized Reading Tests and Informal Reading Inventories." *Education* 82 (1962): 366-369.

MESKAUSKAS, JOHN A. "Evaluation Models for Criterion-Referenced Testing: Views Regarding Mastery and

Standard Setting." *Review of Education Research* 46 (1976): 133–158.

OTTO, WAYNE. "Evaluating Instruments for Assessing Needs and Growth in Reading." In *Assessment Problems in Reading*, edited by Walter H. MacGinitie. Newark, Delaware: International Reading Association, 1973, 14–20.

POPP, HELEN M. "Current Practices in the Teaching of Beginning Reading." In *Toward a Literate Society*, edited by John B. Carroll and Jeanne S. Chall. New York: McGraw-Hill Book Company, 1975, 101–146.

SIPAY, EDWARD. "A Comparison of Standardized Reading Scores and Functional Reading Levels." *The Reading Teacher* 17 (1964): 265–268.

WOMER, FRANK B. "What Is Criterion-Referenced Measurement?" In *Measuring Reading Performance*, edited by William E. Blanton, Roger Farr, and J. Jaap Tuinman. Newark, Delaware: International Reading Association, 1974, 34–43.

Bibliography

ALLINGTON, RICHARD, and STRANGE, MICHAEL. *Learning through Reading in the Content Areas*. Lexington, Mass.: D. C. Heath and Company, 1980.

AMMONS, MARGARET. "Evaluation: What Is It? Who Does It? When Should It Be Done?" In *The Evaluation of Children's Reading Achievement*, edited by Thomas C. Barrett. Newark, Delaware: International Reading Association, 1967, 1–12.

BLANTON, WILLIAM E., FARR, ROGER, and TUINMAN, J. JAAP, eds. *Measuring Reading Performance*. Newark, Delaware: International Reading Association, 1974.

BURNS, PAUL C., and ROE, BETTY D. *Teaching Reading in Today's Elementary Schools*. Chicago: Rand McNally College Publishing Company, 1980.

BUSH, CLIFFORD L., and HUEBNER, MILDRED H. *Strategies for Reading in the Elementary School*. New York: Macmillan Publishing Company, Inc., 1979.

DEBOER, DOROTHY L., ed. *Reading Diagnosis and Evaluation*. Newark, Delaware: International Reading Association, 1970.

DECHANT, EMERALD V. *Improving the Teaching of Reading*. 2nd ed. Englewood Cliffs, New Jersey: Prentice-Hall, Inc., 1970.

EARLE, RICHARD A. *Teaching Reading and Mathematics*. Newark, Delaware: International Reading Association, 1976.

ECKWALL, ELDON E. *Locating and Correcting Reading Difficulties*. Columbus, Ohio: Charles E. Merrill Publishing Company, 1975.

FRY, EDWARD. *Reading Instruction for Classroom and Clinic*. New York: McGraw-Hill Book Company, 1972.

HARRIS, LARRY A., and SMITH, CARL B. *Reading Instruction: Diagnostic Teaching in the Classroom*. 2nd ed. New York: Holt, Rinehart and Winston, 1976.

KARLIN, ROBERT. *Teaching Elementary Reading: Principles and Strategies*. 2nd ed. New York: Harcourt Brace Jovanovich, Inc., 1975.

KENNEDY, EDDIE C. *Classroom Approaches to Remedial Reading*. 2nd ed. Itasca, Illinois: F. E. Peacock, Publisher, Inc., 1977.

MACGINITIE, WALTER H., ed. *Assessment Problems in Reading*. Newark, Delaware: International Reading Association, 1973.

MAGER, ROBERT F. *Measuring Instructional Intent: Or Got a Match*. Belmont, California: Fearon Press, 1973.

PERRONE, VITO, coordinator. *Testing and Evaluation: New Views*. Washington, D.C.: Association for Childhood Education International, 1975.

SMITH, CARL B., SMITH, SHARON L., and MIKULECKY, LARRY. *Teaching Reading in Secondary School Content Subjects: A Book-Thinking Process*. New York: Holt, Rinehart and Winston, 1978.

The Reading Teacher 24, No. 4 (January 1971). (The whole issue is devoted to the subject of testing.)

THELEN, HELEN. *Improving Reading in Science*. Newark, Delaware: International Reading Association, 1976.

VIOX, RUTH G. *Evaluating Reading and Study Skills in the Secondary Classroom: A Guide for Content Teachers*. Newark, Delaware: International Reading Association, 1968.

WILSON, ROBERT M. *Diagnostic and Remedial Reading for Classroom and Clinic*. 3rd ed. Columbus, Ohio: Charles E. Merrill Publishing Company, 1977.

ZINTZ, MILES V. *Corrective Reading*. 2nd ed. Dubuque, Iowa: William C. Brown Company, Publishers, 1972.

5 TEACHING STUDY SKILLS

OVERVIEW
Students who approach learning and reading in a disorganized, haphazard manner learn little from their studies. Students should have an organized plan for deriving all the information they possibly can from written and oral materials. But students do not acquire such skills on their own, and teachers must be prepared to give formal instruction in study skills. Contained in this chapter are some of the basic skills teachers need to know to help their students transform the materials they encounter into meaningful knowledge.

EFFECTIVE TEACHING of any subject matter includes instruction in the use of those study skills that help students to understand and integrate the ideas and skills contained in lessons and related tasks. Study skills, the key to independent learning, enable readers to gain and use information effectively as they read. Students need study skills to contend with the vast array of materials used in different subjects, and the skills are best taught in relation to specific content areas. Focusing on the tasks to be achieved rather than on the skills to be mastered will also enhance the teaching of study skills. These study skills should be taught when the students need to use them but do not really know how to use them.

There is no general agreement about what comprises the complete set of study skills. In addition to word recognition, word study, and questioning strategies, there are many skills that enable students to engage in independent study (Daines 1972); they can be grouped into the general categories of:

1. Locating information
2. Using flexible reading techniques
3. Selecting and evaluating ideas
4. Organizing ideas
5. Following directions
6. Using graphic aids

Many of these study skills are dependent on each other, and so should be taught in logical sequence. For example, knowing the alphabetical order of letters would precede using an index, glossary, dictionary, or card catalog. And being able to identify main ideas and relevant details is a prerequisite to perceiving structure and outline when reading.

Information and ideas for teaching study skills in each of the six categories are presented in this chapter. These ideas can be adapted for use in different content areas and grade levels.

LOCATING INFORMATION

The ability to locate information in materials and in the library is of great importance. Reference sources that contain specialized information are used in all content areas. The great abundance of newspapers, magazines, encyclopedias, dictionaries, almanacs, books, textbooks, and other kinds of print and non-print materials have made the skill of finding information more important than ever.

The optimum grade for initial instruction in a locating skill has not been determined by research; however, experiences in classroom teaching have shown that regardless of the grade level, locational skills should be introduced when the students need to learn the skill to perform a task. Opportunities for practice and application are essential to maintaining such skills.

> What are study skills?

> Why is the ability to locate specific information an important study skill?

Why is knowing alphabetical order important?

Knowing the alphabet is an important skill for all students as they refer to dictionaries, encyclopedias, card catalogs, and other reference materials. If students need practice, they might (1) alphabetize words according to the first two, three, and four letters in each word, (2) find key words and information by using entry words and guide words in dictionaries and reference books, and (3) prepare lists of books to use in a bibliography. Students should be reminded that the articles *a, an,* and *the* at the beginning of a title are not used in alphabetizing; instead the next word is used.

Table of Contents and Lists of Graphics

What can a student learn from a table of contents or a list of graphics?

Readers should learn to use a table of contents and lists of graphics to determine if a book contains the information they seek. Sometimes a book provides a structured outline of its topics, or a list of major units or brief summaries. Illustrations, figures, and maps are listed separately. Students should learn that the table of contents and the lists of graphics indicate not only the contents of the book but also its plan of organization. They should also become familiar with the different formats in which tables of contents and lists of graphics are written.

Index

How can an index help a student study?

Topics in an index are listed in alphabetical order. Some indexes use the letters *p* or *m* along with the page numbers to denote pages with pictures or maps. Some indexes arrange subentries according to the page number on which a discussion of a topic begins; or the subentries of a topic may be arranged in alphabetical order. Students should become familiar with the styles of indexes, and know the topic to use in seeking specific information. Some sample index exercises follow.

1. What topics would you select to answer the questions "What was the purchase price for Alaska?" Alaska: acquisition, 211; exploration, 210–218; fossils, 222; hunting, 220; oil, 232; pipelines, 234; price, 212; Russia, 212; traders, 216. "Which war is known as the undeclared war of the United States?" Indian, 16; Spanish-American, 21; Civil, 22.
2. You are making candles for an art project. What page would tell you the kind of wax to purchase?
   Wax, bayberry, 19–20; bee's, 16–18; candelilla, 17; ceresin, 18; coloring, 59–61; formulas, 21–23; kettle, 31, 41, 47; montan, 19; candle paraffin, 16; spermaceti, 15–17; synthetic, 19–20.
3. Locate the map showing the California missions established during the Spanish exploration and colonization of the New World.
   Spanish exploration and colonization of the New World, 25–31, 196, 382; California missions, 17, 125, 257, 276; m. 266; Florida,

21–24; Louisiana, 194, 301–321; Southwest, 15, 17, 46–57; missions, 17, 125, 257-276, 301–321.

Glossary

A glossary defines and explains unusual and difficult words or expressions used by an author in a subject text. Sometimes a glossary includes a key to pronouncing words. The words included in a glossary are considered to be key words or expressions that readers must know to understand the ideas contained in the book. Part of a page from a glossary is shown below, and questions are listed for students to answer.

How can a glossary be used to improve study skills?

Abolitionist (ab′ə lish′ ən ist): A person who advocated and worked for the immediate end of slavery before the Civil War.

Alamo (al′ ə mo): A mission building in San Antonio, Texas; scene of the massacre of Texans by Mexican forces in 1863.

Alleghenies (al′ ə gā′ nēz): The mountain range extending from Pennsylvania to Virginia.

Armada (är mä′ də): A fleet of warships.

---

1. How are the words arranged on the page? _____
2. Use "armada" in a sentence. _____
   _____
3. Design a crossword puzzle using three words from the glossary.

Reference Materials

Searching reference material for needed information is an important skill, particularly for secondary school students, and knowing how to use an index is necessary when seeking specialized information. The *Reader's Guide to Periodical Literature* uses abbreviations and an unusual format. A key in front of the *Reader's Guide* explains how to use the book. Encyclopedias, "who's who" directories, *Roget's International Thesaurus*, the *World Almanac*, and other reference books require special skills to use. Teachers should present students with real problems to be solved through the aid of reference sources. Sample procedures to follow are presented below.

What is the value of reference material?

1. Prepare a transparency showing a page from the *Reader's Guide to Periodical Literature*. Draw attention to the page format and focus attention on the key that interprets the symbols used in the reference. Show a *Reader's Guide* entry and describe how it is to be used. Prepare several questions for the class to work on together. Afterwards, have several similar activities ready for students to use individually. Prepare a list of subjects related to a unit of study. Let the students select

a subject that they might research in the library. Before they start the search, ask the students to decide which topics they might look under to find the necessary information.

2. Ask students what kind of information they might find in an encyclopedia. Present a transparency that will show subject headings, an index, and an arrangement of entries. Let students research a topic of interest.

3. Present other reference books in a similar manner. Space these presentations over a period of several days or weeks, depending upon the grade level, reading skills, etc., of the students. Provide sufficient supervised practice.

Card Catalog

Why do students need to know how to use a card catalog?

In a school library the card catalog is an index to the entire collection of resources housed in the library, including books, filmstrips, films, picture files, records, tapes, and other print and non-print materials. The cards are filed alphabetically according to subject, title, and author. They provide information about these resources and about where the materials can be located in the library. Usually the Dewey Decimal classification system is recorded on the card to designate the location of the item. The media cards are often colorbanded, with a different color being used for each type of media. Sample exercises to acquaint students with the card catalog are shown.

1. Use an overhead projector to show the students facsimiles of title, subject, and author cards. Explain what information is placed on the cards, such as call numbers, author, title, publisher, place and date of publication, etc. Then obtain cards from the school librarian, and plan questions to accompany each card. Assign the students to work with these activities before they use the card catalog for research purposes.

2. Obtain a group of book and media cards from the librarian. Give the cards to individuals or teams, and ask them to locate the materials.

3. Identify information from this card by answering the following questions.

523.3	Johnson, Michael Louis, 1937–
J17	Life on the moon / Michael Louis Johnson.
1979	— 3rd ed. — Weiser, Idaho : Miken Press, Inc., 1979.
	152 p. : ill., maps : 24 cm.
	Bibliography: p. 98, 110, and 148.
	1. Moon—Photographs. I. Title.

a. Record the information you need to locate this book in the library.

_____

b. What information on the card tells you where to find other related references? _____

c. What does "152 p. illus." mean? _____

_____

d. What information is provided about the author? _____

_____

e. What is the copyright date of this book? _____

f. Is this a title, subject, or author card? _____

Book Classification Systems

School and community libraries have generally used the Dewey Decimal cataloging system. Some libraries are changing to the Library of Congress system. It is important that a student understand that the number on a card specifies the location of the book in the library and that needed books and media can be found easily. Teachers should prepare activities that will help students practice locating materials.

1. Take students to the library and discuss the location of the card catalog and its importance, the function of classification numbers, the arrangement of shelves, and other important information. Provide a list of the ten main headings used in the Dewey Decimal System, and assist the students in locating books.

   000–009 General Works
   100–199 Philosophy and Related Disciplines
   200–299 Religion
   300–399 Social Science
   400–499 Language
   500–599 Pure Science
   600–699 Technology (Applied Science)
   700–799 Arts and Recreation
   800–899 Literature and Rhetoric
   900–999 General Geography and History

   Return to the classroom and present a list of book titles, and instruct the students to match the titles with the proper headings. For example:

   Life in the Rain Forest (Social Science)
   Thorndike-Barnhart Dictionary (General Works)
   The Village Blacksmith (Literature)

After the students can classify books according to the Dewey Decimal System, provide a copy of the subtopics for one of the Dewey Decimal System headings, accompanied by book titles or subjects, and instruct students to match the titles or subjects with the appropriate number. For example:

Science
510—Mathematics
520—Astronomy and Allied Sciences
530—Physics
540—Chemistry and Allied Sciences
550—Earth Science
560—Paleontology
570—Anthropological and Biological Sciences
580—Botanical Sciences
590—Zoological Sciences

Examples: *Life on the Moon Planet* (520)
Physical Chemistry (540)

Bibliographic and Note Cards

How can the use of note cards improve a student's ability to study effectively?

Students are usually unaware of the many sources used by an author to compile and write content materials and that these same sources can be researched for more specific knowledge. When students research references for information to include in reports, they often overlook the importance of listing these sources. Even third grade students can learn to acknowledge a limited number of references used to write their reports. As secondary school students research a topic, they should be taught to use cross-reference cards and to record information on bibliographic and note cards.

Determining the key word is crucial in locating information about a topic. Since there is no assurance that a key word will always lead to the information students are seeking, they may need to research related topics or use information printed on a cross-reference card or "SEE" card.

```
Moon      Johnson, Michael L.

SEE

Astronomy
Man on Moon
Moonwalk
Solar System
Space Exploration
```

Practice, under the direction of the teacher, in using cross-reference cards and in writing bibliographic and note cards should precede independent student research. The following are procedures for writing and using bibliographic and note cards.

1. Make bibliographic references on 3 x 5 cards, using one card for each book.
2. All information should be recorded in the same order.
   a. Author (last name first)
   b. Title of book (underlined)
   c. Publisher and copyright date
   d. Call number
   e. Number of pages
   f. If desired, a word, phrase, or sentence to describe content of book.
3. All cards should be arranged alphabetically by the last name of the author for quick access to a particular card.
4. Place reading notes on 4 x 6 or 5 x 8 cards. At the top of each card, place the following information.

Topic	Author or reference Title of work	Page numbers

5. Cards can be sorted according to topics. The author's name provides a reference to the bibliographic card and information. The page number is to be used when acknowledging a quotation or use of an idea.
6. Record information on the remainder of the card. More cards should be used if necessary.

Fishes and Streams

Water Pollution   Callahan, Paul   29–36

Detergent pollution has caused massive
"Billows of for
to heights of

Water Pollution Miller, Ed 125–148

Environmental Problems

Some cities dumping sewage into
rivers. Waste products from large
industries are fed directly into
rivers. Results in fewer fish for
community.

7. Note cards can be sorted and used in making an outline before writing a report.

HAVING FLEXIBILITY IN READING PURPOSES

An efficient reader does not read all material at a single fixed speed. A flexible reader adjusts his speed to the kind of material being read, his knowledge of the topic, and the purpose for which he is reading. He must be able to identify words rapidly, retain ideas, and relate them to each other. A flexible reader has as his goal comprehension, and he adjusts his reading rate accordingly. He does not create a gap between his reading rate and his thinking rate. The greater the reader's capacity to grasp concepts and the meaning of words in context, the greater the possibility of increasing his speed and improving his comprehension.

Skimming and scanning are two forms of rapid reading. Skimming is the fast processing of material to obtain key ideas. Knowing the patterns of textbook organization is basic to skimming. If a reader merely wants to grasp the central thoughts of the passage he can read key sentences in paragraphs and the summary. By skimming the first sentences of a paragraph, a reader can usually determine if the material should be read more carefully. A rapid perusal of the material will reveal main ideas and some key details to the reader who wants to obtain more than just an overview of the material.

When scanning, a reader uses rapid reading to locate specific data on a page of print. His purpose—to find a date, a telephone number, an address, the temperature, and so forth—occupies his attention; he pays little heed to other information, and remembers little of the content as he scans the page for specific facts. It is a quick search that lasts only until the information is found, and it is a faster operation than skimming.

Most of the instructional material used in classrooms is read at slow rates, particularly in the areas of science and mathematics. Helping students determine the purposes for whch they are reading will allow them to develop flexibility by adjusting their reading rates accordingly. Providing opportunities to apply the skills of skimming and scanning in real situations will help students develop this ability to read with flexibility.

Skimming

How can skimming aid studying?

Skimming, a form of rapid reading, is used to obtain the general idea of the material, or what an author has to say. It can also be used to determine how a book is organized, some of the main ideas expressed in the chapters, the mood of a selection, and the sequence of ideas. This skill can be taught to children in the first grade. It becomes a more useful and important skill for older students and should be taught regularly. Many techniques can be used to teach skimming.

1. Demonstrate the following steps to teach students to skim a book.

    a. Examine the title and subtitle for an idea about the book's content.

    b. Read the publisher's description of the book on the jacket. It is loaded with information.

    c. Examine the preface and other introductory material. The purpose and scope of the book are stated in these parts.

    d. Read the table of contents. It lists the major topics, and the chapter titles, if read in order, will provide a concise summary of the content.

    e. Examine the first chapter. It sometimes reveals the overall content of the book.

    f. Examine the remaining chapters. The introductory and concluding paragraphs contain important ideas.

    g. Examine the concluding chapter. The author usually summarizes the main ideas or expounds the major ideas in greater detail.

2. Say, "How much can you learn in two minutes? Use your skimming skills to read this short article" (or an unread passage from the textbook). Time the students, and then let them share with a partner all the main ideas they were able to read in the allotted time. Instead of sharing information with a partner, they could answer questions prepared by the teacher. This activity can be varied by increasing the length of the material to be read and recording the reading time before questions are answered.

Scanning

Scanning is a more rapid reading skill than skimming, since it is used to locate a date, fact, name, time schedule, etc. The reader's eyes glance rapidly down a page to find the necessary detail. Initial instruction in scanning might be started with lists, timetables, directories, dictionaries, and similar materials. These kinds of materials are recommended at the beginning because the narrow column facilitates the straight-down-the-middle eye movements. It also teaches readers that reading is not always done with a left-to-right, line-by-line approach. The following ideas might be used to teach scanning skills.

What are the uses of scanning?

1. Make a transparency of a short newspaper article. Demonstrate how to scan for a target word or date by saying, "Find the date of the recent eruptions of the Mt. St. Helen's volcano." After explaining the procedure, ask the students to open their texts to a specified page. Pose questions that can be answered by scanning the page, such as:

    "What kinds of fossils are found in the State of Alaska?"

    "How are these fossils located?"

    "Look at the table of square roots. Tell me the square of 25, 100, etc."

    "When was Gerald Ford elected President?"

2. Organize students into small groups. Pose specific questions that can be answered by scanning a passage from a textbook. After a two minute period let students devise questions to ask their peers.

3. Prepare a list of questions for students to answer by scanning. Time their responses. Let them chart the time and observe the progress they make as they practice.

SELECTING AND EVALUATING IDEAS

The reading of textual materials involves identifying significant ideas and details in paragraphs and in larger units of information. All other interpretive reading skills are secondary to determining the essential meaning of the material. Students must learn to react to the author's ideas as they read, which requires an accurate comprehension of words, phrases, sentences, and longer passages. Students' reading is ineffectual if they cannot ascertain the theme of the material or if they cannot perceive implied meanings. Before students can interpret, analyze, synthesize, or evaluate ideas, they must be able to paraphrase the main thought; this is more difficult than recognizing or recalling it.

Looking for Main Ideas

Why is it important to be able to locate main ideas?

In teaching students to identify and evaluate ideas, the teacher must point out that narrative and expository treatment of information are quite different. In expository materials, the meaning of a paragraph is generally explicit; main ideas and topics are clearly stated. In contrast, meaning is usually implied in narrative materials. The purpose of expository passages is usually to explain a series of ideas. Narration is descriptive, and readers react to what they read, using their emotions and value systems. Therefore, the task of determining a main idea differs according to the type of material being read.

Main ideas can be found anywhere in a paragraph. Initial instruction should focus on helping students distinguish between the essential and non-essential ideas, regardless of their placement in the paragraph. This process necessitates the students' using a reasoning process of selecting and comparing ideas. When students master this task, they should proceed to finding main ideas in longer selections and books. Identifying implied main ideas is more difficult and will take practice.

How does one locate main ideas?

The first step in teaching students to select a main idea is to help them recognize what a passage is about. Students can usually find the major topic or subject by asking, "What is this paragraph (or chapter) about?" Ideas for identifying and evaluating main ideas are presented below:

1. Ask students to name the topic of the following sentences. This type of exercise should be extended to include paragraphs and longer selections.

The dog was Bruce's best friend. _____

Rice is a common food in the Middle East. _____

Water conservation is a way of life in the Southwestern states. _____

Coal is an important source of energy. _____

2. Ask students to read the following paragraph and to answer the questions.

The purpose of a taxonomy is to classify organisms. In classifying organisms they are first divided into large kingdoms on the basis of natural relationships. Linnaeus set up a system based on structural similarity. Other kingdoms are formed on the basis of cellular organization and biochemical and genetic similarity. These kingdoms are subdivided into smaller and smaller groups, such as phylum, class order, family, genus, and species. Species is the smallest group.

a. Select the topic of this paragraph.

_____ organisms

_____ species

_____ taxonomy

b. In this paragraph, a taxonomy is:

_____ a kingdom of organisms

_____ to classify organisms

_____ to show relationships

c. Select the main idea of this paragraph.

_____ Linnaeus set up a system based on structural similarity.

_____ The purpose of a taxonomy is to classify organisms.

_____ Kingdoms are divided into smaller and smaller groups.

3. Read this short paragraph and answer the questions.

Syllables in Spanish have two levels of intensity, stressed and unstressed. In English, accented syllables are held longer than those of secondary stress, whereas in Spanish all syllables, stressed or unstressed, are of approximately the same duration. The result is a "machine gun" effect of evenly spaced syllables. Spanish uses differences in stress to make differences in meaning.

What is the topic of the paragraph? _____

What is the main idea of the paragraph? _____

4. Read this paragraph and write your answers to the questions.

The measuring system that the United States currently uses has unrelated measures for dry and liquid volume. The metric system uses one set of units for both gases and liquids and dry measurement, such as ingredients in recipes. Volume is presented by the unit name *litre*, which is a unit of capacity. The desired measures of capacity follow the same pattern as the metre by successive multiplication or divisions by 10.

What is the main idea expressed in this paragraph? _____
_____

Write two details that provide information about the main idea. _____
_____
_____
_____

5. The following additional activities can be used to teach main ideas.
   a. Ask students to find the sentence that states the main idea of a paragraph.
   b. Ask students to paraphrase the main idea of a selection or book.
   c. Ask students to make a mural depicting the main events in a story.
   d. Ask students to write a telegram in ten words or less to convey the main idea of a paragraph or story.

Details

Why is the ability to recognize details and see their relation to main ideas important?

Proficiency in reading requires the assimilation of relevant details. The purpose is not to remember isolated bits of information, but to identify relevant details and to understand their relationship to each other and to the main idea in a paragraph, chapter, or story. The relevant details are likely to be more easily determined when the purpose for reading is definite and clear. It is unlikely that a reader will be able to formulate a main idea or a summary if he cannot identify the supporting facts and details and relate this information to the central thought.

After a reader learns to select main ideas and relevant details, the next steps are to perceive relationships among ideas, classify ideas, make comparisons, see cause and effect relationships, and make judgments. To recognize and evaluate ideas is to engage in critical reading. Two major components of critical reading are a reader's background of experience and knowledge of the subject: both influence a reader's understanding and evaluation of the information he reads. The following list represents some of the skills related to selecting and evaluating ideas:

1. Finding main ideas.
2. Determining implied ideas.
3. Recognizing relevant details.
4. Understanding the meanings of words and phrases.
5. Comprehending the meanings of sentences and paragraphs.
6. Understanding the meaning of longer selections.
7. Forming summaries and conclusions.
8. Making critical evaluations.

It is important that the teacher help students identify relevant details that support a main idea. Nonessential details are interesting, but unnecessary to understanding and evaluating central messages. Here are some suggestions for helping students select relevant details:

1. Tell students the main idea of a passage in a text. Then ask them to read the paragraph to find details to support the main thought.
2. Ask students to read a short selection in which you have inserted a few irrelevant words or sentences. Tell them to identify these words or sentences.
3. Ask students to answer questions you have written about the details of a paragraph or longer selection.
4. Ask students to match a series of details with a list of main ideas.
5. Ask students to list words describing a character whose actions have been discussed in a story.
6. Ask students to examine a painting and then describe it.
7. Ask students to draw a picture illustrating the details of a story.
8. Ask students to list the details that occur in a story as preparation for dramatizing it.
9. Ask students to prepare charts based on information that they have read, such as population growth in their state.
10. Ask students to make an outline showing the relationship between a main point and its supporting details.
11. Ask students to do editorial work on a class or school newspaper.
12. Let students make careful notes about a concept in their science or mathematics textbook. Ask them questions about facts related to the concept.

ORGANIZING IDEAS

Organizing ideas consists of placing thoughts in an orderly and systematic form. This skill consists of arranging, in an organized system and by levels of importance, concepts gleaned from reading one or several sources. Distinguishing relationships among ideas enables a student to outline main and subordinate ideas in a logical order.

Organizing what has been read can be accomplished by using different approaches, such as previewing, making structured overviews, taking notes, outlining, mapping, and summarizing. Efficient readers, with practice and teacher guidance, will learn to use all of these skills and to select the approach that best fits their purposes. Organizing what has been read, by one of these approaches, will help the students to better perceive and retain the relationships among ideas.

Previewing

An efficient reader previews what is to be read as an initial step in reading content materials. The purpose for previewing is to give a student some idea of what he is to read. Comprehension and retention are increased if a student possesses some basic information about the concepts to be read. Previewing skills should be taught as the first step to studying in all subject areas. A

How can previewing help one organize ideas?

student needs to be taught that previewing expository material is only a way of becoming acquainted with information to be read and that it is not a substitute for the careful study of materials. Following are several examples of previewing and study techniques.

How does one use advance organizers?

Advance Organizer   Ausubel (1960, p. 271 and 1968) introduced the idea that learning and retention of unfamiliar verbal materials can be "facilitated by the advance introduction of relevant subsuming concepts." The advance organizer is used to prepare a student for a reading task. The student reads a short passage that precedes a selection or chapter of a text; the passage is written at a higher level of generality and abstractness than the text that follows. This previewing technique directs the student's attention to the concepts that are to be read and prompts a recall of what is already known about the topic. If a student has some knowledge of the topic, an advance organizer included in a text is a helpful link with what is to be read, and leads to higher comprehension. Two sample advance organizers are shown.

1. There is a close agreement between the way a Spanish word is written and the way it sounds. This consistency between symbols and sounds facilitates learning to speak Spanish.

2. A composer of music uses melody, rhythm, and harmony in the same way an architect works with building materials. A composer designs a plan using musical materials to form music that can be recognized and enjoyed.

Structured Overview   The structured overview relates new concepts to those previously learned. Barron (1969) first proposed the idea of structured overviews as a way of arranging key vocabulary words into a diagrammatic form or visual map to let students see the relationships of concepts and to facilitate learning and retention of text in a new reading assignment. It aims to integrate a reader's prior knowledge with new information. According to Ausubel, (1960 and 1968) and Smith (1978) existing knowledge of a subject is a key factor in learning. If this information is well organized, new learning is expedited, whereas if it is unstructured the new learning is hindered.

A structured overview—a variation of the advance organizer—helps students to prepare for reading an assignment by presenting a diagram that shows the relationships between important concepts by the use of key vocabulary. The presentation of an overview may take five to ten minutes, depending upon the complexity of the overview and the students' background concepts and experience with the subject. Guidelines for the construction of an overview are:

1. Analyze the unit to be studied and identify the key vocabulary that represents the important concepts.
2. Arrange the words into a diagram or visual map that shows the relationships between the concepts. Use words that are known and unknown to the students.

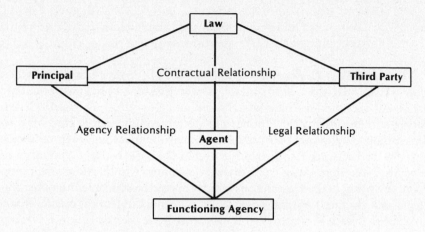

Structured Overview of a Unit in Business Law

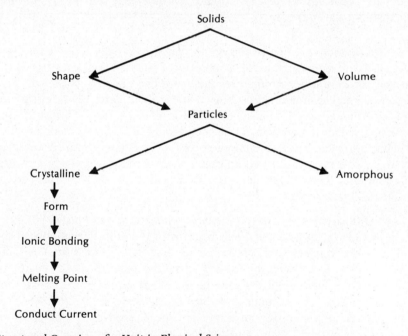

Structured Overview of a Unit in Physical Science

3. Present the diagram to the students by using the chalkboard or an overhead transparency as a preview to reading text. Explain why the words are arranged as shown. During the presentation preteach the structure and meaning of the key vocabulary words representing the important concepts.

4. Ask students to contribute information, and let them refer to the diagram as they read. After the students have studied the chapter,

they can restructure the overview to include new understandings. (Barron 1969, Earle 1969 and 1973, Vacca 1977, Estes and Vaughn, Jr. 1978, Singer and Donlan 1980, and Cunningham and Arthur 1981.) Two structured overviews are shown on page 103.

Graphic Post Organizer   Students received higher test scores when they constructed their own structured overview or graphic post organizer following a reading-learning task (Barron and Stone 1974, Barron 1979, and Moore and Readence 1980). Barron and Stone recommend that students construct their own graphic post organizer by arranging 3 x 5 cards on which they have written technical terms related to the basic concepts contained in a written selection. Using cards allows the students to rearrange the placement of words. Students can compare their post organizers with other students and use them when reviewing text information. (A post organizer is a structured overview constructed by students after they complete a reading assignment.) Students can be placed into small or large groups to defend their post organizer. A teacher should examine, but not grade, the post organizers of the students.

SQ3R Strategy   This strategy is designed to provide middle and secondary school readers with (1) a preview of information to be read, (2) questions to be answered while reading, and (3) a review of the concepts learned, to increase retention (Robinson 1961, 1970, Pauk 1974, Burmeister 1978, and Singer and Donlan 1980). The teacher should demonstrate the procedure with a chapter from a text; then groups of students should practice SQ3R until they can use the technique successfully without urging or prompting. To be effective, this procedure requires using materials that are written at the students' instructional or independent reading levels. There are several versions of this strategy.

How will SQ3R help a student organize reading materials?

1. SQ3R stands for "survey, question, read, recite and review."
   a. Survey the entire chapter. Begin with the title. Then glance at the introductory chapter outline to find what topics or ideas are included. If there isn't a chapter outline, read the section headings. Examine any illustrations, maps, charts, and graphs. Take time to read the captions and titles under the graphic aids. Read the author's summary of important ideas. Read questions posed by the author. Finally, look for a list and definition of technical terms used in the chapter. If the words are not defined, locate the meanings in a glossary or dictionary.
   b. Ask questions as the chapter is surveyed such as, "What does the title mean?" or "What is the significance of the photograph?" Another way is to pose a question about the different chapter headings. A heading entitled "Freedom from Domination" might become "What does freedom mean?" or "What does freedom from

domination mean?" Ask questions that go beyond the recall of fact. "What is the writer's purpose in attacking this policy?" "What does he want me to believe?"

    c. Read to answer the questions posed during the survey. Reading should be an active search for answers. Notes can be taken while reading the information.

    d. Stop to recite at the end of each section in the chapter. Answer the questions, verbally or in writing, without referring to the book. Paraphrase the author's words and use examples to substantiate answers. Pose questions, read, and recite for each subsequent section.

    e. Review the information when the chapter has been completely read, to check the recall of ideas, events, names, and so on contained in each section.

2. PQRST is a variation of SQ3R used with science materials (Spache 1963, p. 94). The acronym stands for "preview, question, read, summarize, and test."

3. SQRQCQ, another variation, is suggested for use in mathematics by Fay (1965, p. 93). The process consists of survey, question, read, question, compute, question, and check answer.

Outlining

Outlining is a way of organizing information. It is a complex skill. The main idea should be identified and the relation of the relevant details to the main thought should be indicated in a logical sequential pattern. Doing so requires that students be able to separate essential and nonessential ideas and to organize them into an outline form. For younger students, the outline can consist of only a few main points. Students at the secondary level should learn to make more formal outlines.

What are the essentials of effective outlining?

Since outlining is a study tool for organizing information, students should learn that information is to be placed into a hierarchical pattern that shows relationships. In order to show relationships, one must be able to select and evaluate ideas. Students should also learn that grouping ideas into an outline will increase their comprehension, retrieval, and retention of the information. The teacher should provide guided practice until the students can write a complete outline without assistance. Sample of an outline is shown.

    Energy

   I. Kinds of energy
      A.   Kinetic Energy
         1. Energy of motion
         2. Potential energy set free

       B.   Potential energy
            1. Energy of position or condition
            2. Stored up energy

II. Forms of energy
     A.   Main Categories of Energy
          1. Mechanical, heat, electrical, wave, chemical, and nuclear
          2. Mechanical energy seen most often
     B.   Transformation of Energy
          1. One form of energy can be changed to another form
          3. When energy is changed to another form, other forms of energy are also produced

III. Matter and Energy
     A.   Conservation of Matter and Energy
          1. Matter or energy can be changed to other forms of matter or energy
          2. Total amount of matter and energy in universe always remains the same
     B.   1.
           2.

Notetaking

Effective notetaking is a high-level organizing skill (Butcofsky 1971, Palmatier 1971, and Estes and Vaughn, Jr. 1978). Notetaking requires that a student differentiate between essential and nonessential ideas, see relationships between thoughts, and organize them into a pattern. Two sources of notetaking are lecture and reading.

What is the purpose of taking notes?

    Lecture notetaking requires a student to analyze what is said, to synthesize the ideas, and to make notes while listening. The difficulty of the task increases when the lecture is not well organized. Reading notetaking also requires a student to analyze and synthesize ideas and to record the information in his own words. This complex task becomes impossible if the text is too difficult and inappropriate for the student.

    The students' intention, when they take notes from a text, can affect the kind of notes they take and the amount of information they recall later. Notetaking is actually an initial phase of study, especially if the text information is to be recalled for test situations. After students complete their notetaking, they need to engage in recitation or other active study processes to ensure later retrieval of the information (Orlando 1980). Students should practice the complex skill of notetaking under the guidance of their teachers.

    Kollaritsch (1969) suggested a method of reading notetaking that requires little writing. The procedures give students practice in selecting and organizing main ideas and stating them in their own words. This form of notetaking can be used with remedial students, children in upper elementary grades, secondary students, and adults. The method consists of six steps.

3/3 Local Government pp. 284-289

I The Nature of Local Government

√√ A. Provides services (p. 284)
    1. Tax money used

√√ B. Roads (p. 285)
    1. Builds and maintains county roads and city streets

√√ C. Water supply (p. 285)
    1. Constructs and maintains reservoirs and pipelines

√ D. Public health (p. 285)
    1. Medical clinics
    2. Vaccinations, X-Rays, etc. for children
    3. Health and sanitation code for public buildings

√ E. Welfare services (p. 286)
    1. Care for aged, handicapped, and unemployed
    2. Institutional care provided

√√ F. Police and fire protection (p. 287)
    1. Maintains law and order
    2. Regulation of traffic
    3. Fire protection

√√ G. Education (p. 288)
    1. Public school system, buildings, etc.
    2. Teachers and other employees

√√ H. Public libraries (p. 289)
    1. Andrew Carnegie donation
    2. Operated at public expense

1. The student sets a goal of how many pages to read and make notes on. The pages are previewed. Then the name of the chapter, pages, and date are recorded.
2. The first section heading in the chapter is recorded with the page number on which it is found.
3. The first paragraph under the section heading is read, and then the main idea is written in one sentence or phrase. If applicable, the number or kinds of things to be remembered might be included. This process is repeated for each paragraph. All notes should be numbered to facilitate locating the paragraphs later.
4. The process in step three is repeated with each section heading in the chapter.
5. The information read is reviewed. The review is made with the textbook open to the page of the assignment. A check is placed beside the number of each paragraph that can be recalled without referring to the text.
6. The material is reviewed at a later date, and a second check mark is placed by the paragraph for which the content is recalled.

Mapping

How can mapping improve a student's study skills?

Mapping is a technique of recording main ideas and related details in graphic form. It can be used as a study technique with SQ3R, as a recall approach to

This final step completes the graphic outline.

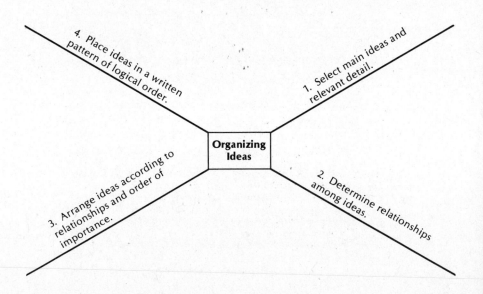

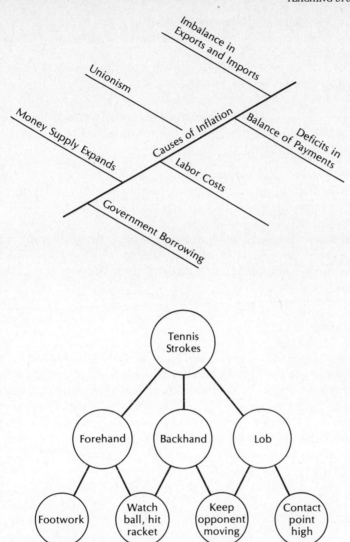

rapid reading, and as a substitute for notetaking and outlining (Hanf 1971). The technique involves the higher levels of thinking and the placing of ideas into a hierarchical order. This graphic form of organizing ideas is an aid to the retrieval and retention of ideas. Mapping consists of two steps:

1. Record the title or main idea of the passage or book anywhere on the page of a notebook. Sufficient room should be left to add additional information around it.
2. Organize the secondary ideas that support the main idea by placing them in a planned pattern around it. This detail is added after the

source material has been read. This step provides a graphic outline that can be used to review the information without referring to the text.

Underlining

How can outlining and
summarizing aid learning?

Another form of organizing information is underlining. Underlining requires that the reader complete, in sequence, the following steps:

1. Survey the chapter.
2. Read the chapter paragraph by paragraph (section by section).
3. After reading each paragraph, underline only key words or phrases that represent main ideas and supporting details.

Color coding can be used, with one color for main thoughts and a different color for details. Underlining enables a reader to review quickly what he has read. The purpose of underlining is defeated if too many words and phrases are marked.

Summarizing

Summaries include the main idea and essential facts in capsule form. Having students write a one sentence summary after each paragraph is a technique to help them remember the material they read. Summarizing ideas in the biological and physical sciences can involve lengthy listing of facts if caution is not exercised. To compose a summary, students must succinctly express the author's ideas in their own words. When students are reviewing information or preparing for a discussion or a test, the summarizing of ideas will reinforce what they have learned.

FOLLOWING DIRECTIONS

How can following directions
improve study skills?

Following directions requires that a student be skilled in determining key words and the sequence of instructions. Understanding oral directions given by a teacher or those read in a textbook are basic to success in completing school assignments. When a student fails in a task, not understanding the directions may be the cause, rather than the task itself. Before a student undertakes a task, all the requirements of the assignment should be understood. Checking the end product will usually reveal to both the student and teacher whether the directions were properly followed.

Students have the opportunity to learn how to follow directions when they perform tasks such as the following:

1. Demonstrating the use of objects.
2. Performing experiments.

3. Drawing charts and diagrams.
4. Classifying like and unlike items.
5. Developing a technique for interviews.
6. Preparing food to eat.
7. Filling out application forms.
8. Making maps and legends.
9. Maintaining records.
10. Illustrating ideas in sequence.
11. Computing math problems.
12. Writing research reports.
13. Exhibiting gymnastic feats.
14. Typing letters according to form.
15. Completing a test.

Directions for completing assignments become more prevalent and complex as students progress through the grades.

Learning to follow directions, both verbal and written, should begin with very simple procedures and then progress to the more complex. Start with one-step directions before proceeding to two-step directions, and then to three or more steps. Finally, students should be given directions for which the number of steps is not explicitly stated. Sample activities in following directions are given.

1. This assignment includes four directions to be followed by the students.

   Directions: In the sentences after these directions, complete the following:
   a. Underline each pronoun.
   b. Above each word, label it as subject, verb, direct object, object of preposition, indirect object, or possessive.
   c. Abbreviate the above labels as: subj., v., d.o., o.p., i.o., poss.
   d. Proofread your paper carefully before you submit it for correction.
      (1) Someone has given each of us a book.
      (2) As you know, our dog pulled that.
      (3) It was neither of us, Peggy nor me, whom Kay called.
      (4) Each of the children waved his hand at Geri and me.
      (5) The play begins at eight tonight, but Steve doesn't know it.

2. Give the directions needed to locate a specific place and have the students find it.

3. Read directions for a game of golf and follow them.

4. Obtain road maps for each student. Prepare a card with directions to reach different destinations. Let students do this in pairs.

5. Prepare a vocabulary game and let the students write the directions for the game. Afterwards, let them explain the steps to be followed before the game is played.

6. Prepare a group of one line directions that might be followed in a pantomime situation.
   a. A gardener cutting the grass.
   b. A police officer directing traffic.
   c. Someone doing the dishes.
   d. An attendant at a service station putting gas in a car.
   e. A farmer hoeing his garden.
7. Let a student direct classmates in making puppets or some other product.
8. Let students write recipes to be placed in a class book.
9. Prepare directions for students to follow in making a breadboard.
10. Clip ads from newspapers and magazines. Mount and laminate the ads. Prepare a set of directions that students might follow to test the claim of the manufacturer.

USING GRAPHIC AIDS

How can using graphic aids help a student study more effectively?

In the content areas, graphic aids such as maps, charts, graphs, tables, diagrams, pictures, and cartoons are used to facilitate the understanding and interpretation of textual materials. These aids can help students synthesize facts and detail into usable patterns of information. Reading and interpreting graphic and tabular aids requires the ability to understand what is stated directly and what is implied in the text.

The graphic aids in a textbook are used to help clarify difficult and abstract ideas, or to supplement them. Yet many students skip over this part of a text because they do not know how to use these aids and do not understand their importance for comprehending information. The teacher must

```
                    ┌─────────────────────┐
                    │   County Voters     │
                    └──────────┬──────────┘
                               │
                    ┌──────────┴──────────┐
                    │ Board of Commissioners │
                    └──────────┬──────────┘
                               │
                          ┌────┴────┐
                          │  Mayor  │
                          └────┬────┘
           ┌──────────┬────────┼────────┬──────────┐
      ┌────┴───┐ ┌────┴──────────┐ ┌────┴───────┐ ┌──┴────┐
      │ Finance│ │Public Transportation│ │Public Welfare│ │ Police│
      └────────┘ └───────────────┘ └────────────┘ └───────┘
```

City Mayor Plan of Government

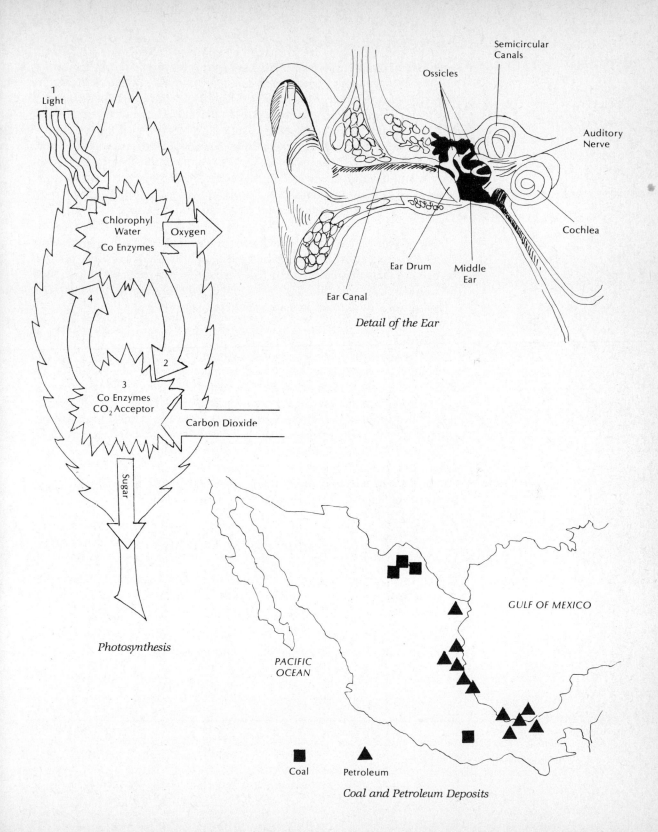

1
Light

Chlorophyl
Water
Co Enzymes

Oxygen

4

2

3
Co Enzymes
CO_2 Acceptor

Carbon Dioxide

Sugar

Photosynthesis

Ossicles

Semicircular
Canals

Auditory
Nerve

Cochlea

Ear Drum

Middle
Ear

Ear Canal

Detail of the Ear

PACIFIC
OCEAN

GULF OF MEXICO

Coal

Petroleum

Coal and Petroleum Deposits

begin with concrete experiences and then continue to more difficult concepts when teaching students to use graphic aids. Both literal and inferential information is gleaned from these support materials. Students must also learn how to use the symbols, signs, and codes in the legends included with tabular and graphic aids, particularly maps.

Students can be taught to read simple maps, charts, and graphs. Pictorial graphs are more easily interpreted. Circles, or pie graphs, two dimensional graphs, and line graphs are next in the order of difficulty. Vertical bars seem easier to read than horizontal bar graphs. However, the type of graph used should always be appropriate to the materials and the context in which it is used.

One of the very best ways to teach these specific study skills is to have the students construct tables, graphs, diagrams, and cartoons of their own on the basis of facts they have collected in their study of a particular topic. Used in this manner, graphic aids become a tool in teaching critical thinking skills. A few samples of graphic aids are shown on pages 112–113.

SUMMARY

Study skills are work skills used to perform particular learning tasks. The use of these skills helps students to better comprehend and apply the concepts explained in content area textbooks. Study skills should be taught when needed by students to perform specific tasks and to understand expository materials. Study skills are more efficiently learned within the context in which they are to be used. The many different study skills have been grouped into six classifications. They are (1) locating information, (2) using flexible reading techniques, (3) selecting and evaluating ideas, (4) organizing ideas, (5) following directions, and (6) using graphic aids.

Reinforcement Activities

1. For each of the six study skill categories, list one specific skill that is appropriate to the content area you teach. Explain the rationale for your selections.

2. Choose one specific skill and plan an activity to teach it to your students, using textual materials available in your classroom.

References

AUSUBEL, DAVID P. "The Use of Advance Organizers in the Learning and Retention of Meaningful Verbal Materials." *Journal of Educational Psychology* 51 (1960): 267–272.

AUSUBEL, DAVID P. *Educational Psychology: A Cognitive View*. New York: Holt, Rinehart and Winston, Inc., 1968.

BARRON, RICHARD F. "The Use of Vocabulary as an

Advance Organizer." In *Research in Reading in the Content Areas: First Year Report,* edited by Harold L. Herber and Peter L. Sanders. Syracuse, New York: Reading and Language Arts Center, Syracuse University, 1969, 29–39.

BARRON, RICHARD F. "Research for the Classroom Teacher: Recent Developments on the Structured Overview as an Advance Organizer." In *Research in Reading in the Content Areas: The Fourth Report,* edited by Harold Herber and James Riley. Syracuse, New York: Reading and Language Arts Center, Syracuse University, 1979, 171–176.

BARRON, R. F., and STONE, V. F. "The Effects of Student-Constructed Graphic Post Organizers Upon Learning Vocabulary Relationships." In *Interaction: Research and Practice and College-Adult Reading,* edited by Phil L. Nacke and Elizabeth Nelli. Clemson, South Carolina: Twenty-third Yearbook of the National Reading Conference, 1974, 172–174.

BURMEISTER, LOU E. *Reading Strategies for Middle and Secondary School Teachers.* 2nd ed. Reading, Mass.: Addison-Wesley Publishing Company, 1978.

BUTCOFSKY, DON. "Any Learning Skills Taught in High School?" *Journal of Reading* 15 (1971): 195–198.

CUNNINGHAM, J. W., CUNNINGHAM, P. M., and ARTHUR, S. V. *Middle and Secondary School Reading. New York: Longman, 1981.*

DAINES, DELVA. "Developing Reading Study Skills in the Content Areas." In *The Quest for Competency in Teaching Reading,* edited by Howard Klein. Newark, Delaware: International Reading Association, 1972, 214–221.

EARLE, RICHARD A. "Use of the Structured Overview in Mathematic Classes." In *Research in Reading in the Content Areas: First Year Report,* edited by Harold L. Herber and Peter L. Sanders. Syracuse, New York: Reading and Language Arts Center, Syracuse University, 1969, 49–58.

EARLE, RICHARD A. "The Use of Vocabulary as a Structured Overview in Seventh Grade Mathematics Classes." In *Research in Reading in the Content Areas: Second Year Report,* edited by Harold L. Herber and Richard F. Barron. Syracuse, New York:

Reading and Language Arts Center, Syracuse University, 1973, 36–39.

ESTES, THOMAS H., and VAUGHN, JR., JOSEPH L. *Reading and Learning in the Content Classroom.* Boston: Allyn and Bacon, Inc., 1978.

FAY, LEO. "Reading Study Skills: Math and Science." In *Reading and Inquiry,* edited by J. Allen Figurel. Newark, Delaware: International Reading Association, 1965, 92–94.

HANF, M. BUCKLEY. "Mapping, A Technique for Translating Reading Into Thinking." *Journal of Reading* 14 (1971): 225–230, 270.

KOLLARITSCH, JANE. "Organizing Reading for Detailed Learning in a Limited Time." *Journal of Reading* 13 (1969) 29–32.

MOORE, D. W., and READENCE, J. E. "A Meta-Analysis of the Effect of Graphic Organizers on Learning from Text." In *Perspectives in Reading Research and Instruction,* edited by Michael L. Kamil and Alden J. Moe. Washington, D.C.: Twenty-ninth Yearbook of the National Reading Conference, 1980, 213–218.

ORLANDO, VINCENT P. "A Comparison of Notetaking Strategies While Studying from Text." In *Perspectives in Reading Research and Instruction,* edited by Michael L. Kamil and Alden J. Moe. Washington, D.C.: Twenty-ninth Yearbook of the National Reading Association, 1980, 219–222.

PALMATIER, ROBERT A. "Comparison of Four Note Taking Procedures." *Journal of Reading* 14 (1971): 235–240.

PAUK, WALTER. *How to Study in College.* 2nd ed. Boston: Houghton Mifflin Company, 1974.

ROBINSON, FRANCIS P. *Effective Study.* New York: Harper and Row Publishing Company, 1961.

ROBINSON, FRANCIS P. *Effective Reading.* 4th ed. New York: Harper and Row, 1970.

SINGER, HARRY, and DONLAN, DAN. *Reading and Learning from Text.* Boston: Little, Brown and Company, 1980.

SPACHE, GEORGE. *Toward Better Reading.* Champaign, Illinois: Garrard Press, 1963.

VACCA, RICHARD T. "Readiness to Read Content Area Assignments." *Journal of Reading* 20 (1977): 387–392.

Bibliography

AARONSON, SHIRLEY. "Notetaking Improvement: A Combined Auditory, Functional and Psychological Approach." *Journal of Reading* 19 (1975): 8–12.

ALEXANDER, CLARA F. "Strategies for Finding the Main Idea." *Journal of Reading* 19 (1976): 299–301.

AUSUBEL, DAVID P., and ROBINSON, FLOYD G. *School*

Learning: An Introduction to Educational Psychology. New York: Holt, Rinehart and Winston, Inc., 1969.

AXELROD, JEROME. "Getting the Main Idea Is Still the Main Idea." *Journal of Reading* 18 (1975): 383–387.

CASTALLO, RICHARD. "Listening Guide—A First Step Toward Notetaking and Listening Skills." *Journal of Reading* 19 (1976): 289–290.

DeBOER, JOHN, and DALLMAN, MARTHA. *The Teaching of Reading.* 5th ed. New York: Holt, Rinehart and Winston, Inc., 1978.

DEMBO, MYRON H., and WILSON, DONALD A. "A Performance Contract in Speed Reading." *Journal of Reading* 16 (1973): 627-633.

DINNAN, JAMES A. "Library Skill—Whose Responsibility?" *Journal of Reading Behavior* 1 (1969): 31–37.

DONLAN, DAN. "Locating Main Ideas in History Textbooks." *Journal of Reading* 24 (1980): 135–140.

EARLE, RICHARD A., and SANDERS, PETER L. "Individualizing Reading Assignments." *Journal of Reading* 16 (1973): 550–555.

FIDLER, JERRY B. "Contemplative Reading: A Neglected Dimension of Flexibility." *Journal of Reading* 16 (1973): 622–626.

GRUBER, PAULETTE M. "Junior High Boasts Super Stars." *Journal of Reading* 16 (1973): 600–603.

HARRIS, ALBERT J. "Research on Some Aspects of Comprehension: Rate, Flexibility and Study Skills." *Journal of Reading* 12 (1968): 205–210; 258–260.

HAWKINS, J. A., JR. "How Should Reading and Study Skills Test Scores Correlate?" *Journal of Reading* 20 (1977): 570–572.

HERBER, HAROLD. *Developing Study Skills in the Secondary School.* Newark, Delaware: International Reading Association, 1969.

JENSEN, ROMA LYMAN. "An Evaluation of an Instructional Program Designed to Aid the Development of Critical Reading Skills and Study Skills among Intermediate Grade Pupils in Elementary School." Unpublished doctoral dissertation. Provo, Utah: Brigham Young University, 1974.

KARAHALIOS, SUE M., TONJES, MARION J., and TOWNER, JOHN C. "Using Advance Organizers to Improve Comprehension of a Content Text." *Journal of Reading* 22 (1979): 706–708.

KARLIN, ROBERT, *Teaching Reading in High School: Improving Reading in the Content Areas.* 3rd ed. Indianapolis: Bobbs-Merrill Educational Publishing, 1977.

LAMBERG, WALTER J., and LAMB, CHARLES. *Reading Instruction in the Content Areas.* Chicago: Rand McNally College Publishing Company, 1980.

PAGE, LINDA TURPIN. "Reading and Study Skills in Junior High History." *Reading Improvement* 6 (1969): 41–42.

PAUK, WALTER. "Super-Glue of Study Skills." *Reading World* 19 (1980): 303–304.

PIERCEY, DOROTHY. *Reading Activities in Content Areas: An Idea Book for Middle and Secondary Schools.* Boston: Allyn and Bacon, Inc., 1976.

POLICASTRO, MICHAEL. "Notetaking: The Key to College Success." *Journal of Reading* 18 (1975): 372–375.

RANKIN, EARL F. *The Measurement of Reading Flexibility: Problems and Perspectives.* Newark, Delaware: International Reading Association, 1974.

ROBINSON, ALAN. *Teaching Reading and the Study Strategies in the Content Areas.* Boston: Allyn and Bacon, Inc., 1978.

SARGENT, EILEEN E., HUUS, HELEN, and ANDRESEN, OLIVER. *How to Read a Book.* Newark, Delaware: International Reading Association, 1970.

SHERER, PETER A. "Skimming and Scanning: De-mything the Process with a College Student." *Journal of Reading* 19 (1975): 24–27.

SMITH, BRENDA G. "Speed Reading Scores in Perspective." *Journal of Reading* 19 (1975): 128–130.

THOMAS, ELLEN L., and ROBINSON, H. ALAN, *Improving Reading in Every Class: A Sourcebook for Teachers.* 2nd ed. Boston: Allyn and Bacon, Inc., 1977.

VOIX, RUTH G. *Evaluating Reading and Study Skills in the Secondary Classroom.* Newark, Delaware: International Reading Association, 1968.

6 WORDS, SENTENCES, AND PARAGRAPHS

OVERVIEW

Reading involves words, and the better one understands words the better one will read. To read well, a student must first understand words themselves—must develop vocabulary. The student must also understand how words are used in relation to one another—their syntax. Related to syntax is semantics, the variety of meanings of words. Syntax and semantics combine to create sentences, and sentences then find their way into paragraphs. Indeed, meaning can be manifested and manipulated in many ways, and knowing those ways will greatly increase one's reading ability.

What is the function of language?

READING IS A LANGUAGE based process. Words have meanings in relation to other words and also in relation to experiences. Thinking, itself, necessitates the use of words. The ability to express ideas and communicate clearly depends upon having a stock of words and experiences and upon the ability to choose the *right* words. Language, then, is at the heart of learning, and the study of words is an indispensable part of teaching reading in the content areas.

A word is a verbal representation of a concept; Vygotsky (1962, p. 132) suggests that "thought is born through words." Vocabulary reflects experience. As a person's vocabulary grows, so does the ability to form and express concepts, for language not only supplies labels for concepts but also helps to generate ideas by the way it is written and used. When students know the language of a subject they can participate in the communication of its concepts. Obviously, if students do not know the language used to convey knowledge about a subject, the language itself can interfere with their comprehension of that information. Therefore, vocabulary plays a central role in learning subject matter content.

What role does language play in the content areas?

Language development is a complex and sensitive social process. Intelligence influences the potentialities for language growth, but the extent and richness of the experiential backgrounds of students—their environments—also determine the development of their communication skills. A positive relationship exists between a student's concept of self and his language fluency. Socioeconomic criteria can influence language patterns. Students learn to speak the dialect of the language and culture in which they live, and they learn to think and organize their ideas according to the view of the world shared by those with whom they live and associate. Teachers should consider these various factors as they plan for vocabulary development and related activities in the content areas.

VOCABULARY AND CONCEPT DEVELOPMENT

How does a student acquire understanding?

Reading is a thinking process, and language is its vehicle for transmitting ideas and meanings. But while meaning is conveyed by words, meaning is not *in* words themselves. Meaning exists in the thinking of the reader, as a result of his previous experiences. Background knowledge interacts with and often even overrides syntactic factors (Pearson 1974–1975 and Anderson 1977). And a reader extends his understanding of a subject by using his past experience as a base for interaction with the ideas conveyed by an author's words and sentences. A student who already knows a great deal about a subject will gain more information from reading about it than the students who know little about the subject. One reads to gain experience; yet more is gleaned from the reading if one has had more experiences, since previous knowledge affects comprehension (Chall 1947, Rumelhart and Ortony 1977), and Friedman and Rowls 1980, p. 27).

A significant aspect of concept development is the growth that takes place when a word is recognized as the verbal expression of a concept. Concept acquisition and vocabulary development, the products of meaningful experiences, occur simultaneously. The cultivation and extension of word meanings involve the development of concepts. The general meaning a word connotes to the reader represents a concept. Concepts are altered and refined, little by little, through many meaningful experiences with objects, ideas, and people. It is important that teachers help students build background experience about a topic before a reading assignment is given.

The behavioral and thought structures of intelligence are continually changing through interaction with the environment. Students will encounter conflicts and inconsistencies as they learn concepts; but they must be led on to discover relationships of ideas at increasingly higher levels of analysis and synthesis. What one already knows in any subject strongly influence the learning and retention of new material. A student gains confidence and satisfaction when he is successful in processing new information.

It is obvious that in order to acquire an extensive vocabulary and ideas about which to think, talk, write, and read, a student needs many rich, meaningful experiences involving language. Dale and O'Rourke (1971, Ch. 1) stress three key points in their book about teaching vocabulary:

How does a student acquire vocabulary?

1. Vocabulary development is concept development. Vocabulary and concept growth occur together. Every word is a concept, but a concept usually consists of more than the meaning of a single word.
2. Vocabulary development is the result of a planned program. A systematic program provides opportunities for students to build new concepts and word meanings.
3. Vocabulary development evolves within the context of a communication triad comprising speaking and listening, visualizing and observing, and reading and writing.

Building concepts and understanding the words used with them can be achieved by employing an instructional program that includes the following three approaches (Tinker and McCullough 1975, Ch. 7):

1. The provision of a wide variety of first-hand and vicarious experiences.
2. A continuous opportunity for extensive reading of both fiction and non-fiction materials.
3. Continuous guidance in word study.

These three approaches should be implemented in every classroom and not left to a chance inclusion in the lives of students. Providing students with regular opportunities for wide and extensive reading is one of the most profitable ways to develop vocabulary. This approach needs to receive considerably more attention at all grade levels.

LANGUAGE OF A SUBJECT

How does vocabulary development relate to learning about the content areas?

Vocabulary development is vital in the acquisition of subject matter concepts. To a large extent, each discipline has its own special language. Basic concepts are expressed in terminology peculiar to each subject; students often find that the technical words of a subject have special meanings, and words with which they are familiar sometimes have new meanings. If a learner is to understand and communicate ideas concerning subject related concepts, he must have facility with the technical language in which the various concepts are expressed.

Vocabulary and concept development in a content area are functional. When the basic concepts in each subject are understood, long term memory improves (Gipe 1978–1979). The technical terms representing those concepts should serve as a basic list of words to be taught to students prior to the reading and study of a chapter, a unit, or their textbooks. Dale and O'Rourke (1971, Ch. 1), Karlin (1977, Ch. 5), Herber (1978, Ch. 6), Lamberg and Lamb (1980, Ch. 6), Singer and Donlan (1980, Ch. 16), Cunningham, Cunningham, and Arthur (1981, Ch. 5), and Pressley, Levin, and Miller (1981) all suggest that the key concept words, the importance of the units, and the competence and needs of students are the criteria to use when selecting the vocabulary to preteach before students read assignments. Knowing the meaning and pronunciation of one, two, or three key concept words will help students to understand better the new concepts they encounter in content materials.

There isn't sufficient time (nor is it even necessary) to teach every important word in each unit. After the key concept words are taught, utilizing context, structure, or phonics, the remaining words should be pronounced for the students. The meaning may be given for some of the words, depending on how the author has used the word. Or the teacher may have the students help in defining these words. Word analysis, word recognition, and word meaning are important in teaching technical words in the content areas. Exercises can be used with students to help them develop greater vocabulary.

New vocabulary comes rapidly in the content areas. The most important instructional strategies are those that help students understand word meanings *before* they read their textbooks. The four classifications of words to include in these plans are:

1. Basic words for communicating ideas, feelings, and actions (commonly used verbs and nouns).
2. Technical words that deal mainly with a specific field of knowledge (uncommon verbs and nouns).
3. Proper nouns used throughout printed matter.
4. Connective words used to join and express complex relationships among sentences.

A significant aspect of concept development is the growth that takes place when a word is recognized as the verbal expression of a concept. Attentively listening to the speech of others and studying the proper use of words is necessary for the development of a good vocabulary. There should be ample opportunities in all school activities, in addition to the content areas, for students to study word meanings and to talk and write about the concepts they encounter in various kinds of experiences.

SYNTAX

Syntax is derived from the Greek word *syntassein,* meaning to join together or arrange. Syntax refers to the way words are ordered or arranged to convey meanings in phrases and sentences. Word order forms the basis of meaning in English sentences. "The cat ate the mouse" has a different meaning from "The mouse ate the cat." These two sentences contain the same words, but each sentence expresses an entirely different meaning. Syntax also includes the ways in which the same word may function in different sentence patterns, either as verb, noun, or adjective. For example:

> Kick the ball.
> That kick sent the ball flying.
> It is a kick ball.

It is probable that a bilingual or bidialectical student is more aware of syntactic structures because of the contrasting systems he uses.

A reader deciphers meaning by identifying ideas represented by words and by recognizing the patterns used to express those ideas. The meaning desired by the encoder, speaker, or writer determines the grammatical structure of the words combined to make a sentence. Written language is understood by having "meaning brought to it" (Smith 1978, p. 76). Smith further explains that a reader uses his knowledge of how letters and words go together to make a meaningful sequence, and that predictions of meaning depend on prior knowledge of language and subject matter.

Syntax, the sum of processes that operate on vocabulary to generate an infinite number of sentences, is an important aspect of word meaning and thus of reading for understanding. Since the comprehension of printed matter also involves making predictions and confirming or rejecting them as one reads, clear writing gives the reader clues for predicting correctly. Dawkins (1975, p. 1–44) explains how the rules of language produce complex syntax and how syntax influences the reading ease or difficulty of materials. Some of the aspects of syntax that generate variety are:

What is the relationship between syntax and meaning?

1. *Arrangement* of a simple sentence includes subject and verb: The man spoke.
2. *Rearrangement* changes a simple sentence from one form to another: The strike has begun. Has the strike begun? The wind turned the windmill. The windmill was turned by the wind.

3. *Addition* produces longer or more complicated sentences: Mike survived the walk, but he never went again. Running to the field, Jim didn't see the ball. The reporter who saw you wrote your story.

4. *Deletion* omits certain words or parts of sentences: The dress that I bought is blue. The dress I bought is blue. The dog ran down the street and barked at the cat. The barking dog ran down the street.

5. *Substitution* replaces one item by another: The boy ran fast. He was afraid. The boy who was afraid ran fast.

6. *Agreement* is the process of adjusting one word to conform to another when rules of grammar require it: The boy runs. The boys run. Each of the boys is a good athlete.

Perhaps most important is the rearrangement of sentences that changes the sentence from one form to another. Rearranging the conventional sentence order adds a degree of difficulty. Here are a few examples of the rearrangement of simple sentences.

The small girl found the books. The books were found by a small girl.

The man drove the tractor. The tractor was driven by a man.

The boy found the books when he went home. The boy, when he went home, found the books.

SEMANTIC AND CONTEXT CLUES

An important goal in vocabulary development is word power, the power to deal with unfamiliar words and make them part of an active vocabulary. Since the teaching of words in isolation is usually ineffective, word meanings should be taught as an integral part of a balanced program for concept development. Students should realize that the exact meaning of a word usually depends upon the context in which it is placed.

As a sentence becomes more complex, comprehension of it may become more difficult. Context clues—the method of comprehending new words by examining the surrounding context—become an element in reducing the complexity of sentence structure. Using context as a key to comprehension involves the use of syntax and semantics to interpret a word, or words, and its meaning (Farr and Roser 1979, p. 169). The examination of known words in context, in a sentence or paragraph, is one of the most important aids to identifying the meanings of new words. Most words have more than one meaning, and context determines the meaning of a word. Semantic clues draw on a reader's general knowledge and his knowledge of language. An author's language and a reader's concepts are the building blocks to contextual meaning (Page and Pinnell 1979, Ch. 2).

What context may reveal to a reader will depend upon his previous experiences with words and concepts. The key words in the context may indicate to the experienced reader that a definition, example, or a restatement is being given, whereas the inexperienced reader may completely miss this

How can understanding syntax and semantics aid a student in reading?

information. Thus, the inexperienced reader will derive less help from context clues than the experienced reader. Poor readers also fail to extract contextual clues essential for word identification and meaning, according to Steiner, Weiner, and Cromer (1971).

There are two patterns of writing that curtail definition by context. First, if the context that explains an unfamiliar word precedes it, even by a paragraph, the effectiveness of the clue is limited. Second, if there is not some definite connection between the unfamiliar word and the context that clarifies it, the clue is again limited. This latter problem may be resolved by repeating the phrase, substituting a synonym, or by using phrases such as *like, for example, such as this.*

Explaining syntax clues to the reader automatically includes teaching semantics: syntactic and semantic clues are interrelated. Other words in a sentence and surrounding sentences may give semantic clues to the way a word is used in context. A reader uses prior knowledge and experience along with the semantic clues to predict a word's meaning. A reader also uses syntactic expectations of the redundancy of grammar, such as synonyms, to analyze unknown words in context, since an unknown word can become known in association with a known word of a similar meaning. A syntactic clue, such as knowing the function of a modifier of a noun, assists a reader to find the semantic clues within that particular grammatical structure.

Ames (1966) conducted a study concerning contextual aids that served as clues to word meanings. Readers often inferred unknown words from what they knew and anticipated concerning word patterns in sentences. He arranged the contextual aids into fourteen categories and suggested that in using semantic clues a reader depends on one or more of them:

1. familiar expressions
2. modified phrases or clauses
3. definition and description
4. words connected in a series
5. comparison and contrast
6. synonyms
7. tone, setting, and mood
8. referents and antecedents
9. association
10. main ideas and supporting details
11. question-answer pattern of paragraph
12. prepositions
13. nonrestrictive clauses and appositive phrases
14. cause and effect patterns

Synonyms, Antonyms, and Homonyms

The study of synonyms, antonym, and homonyms contributes to learning about the relationship of words and concepts. The words *synonym, antonym,* and *homonym* are formed from the Greek root *onym,* meaning *name.*

What can synonyms, antonyms, and homonyms teach students about meaning?

Synonym, from *syn* meaning *together* or *like*, and *onym* meaning *name*, refers to words with like or similar meanings. Synonyms usually do not have exactly the same meaning; instead, very fine distinctions in meanings exist. For example, "I loathe him" represents a typical linguistic pattern. Other ways of constructing the same sentence are:

I detest him.
I hate him.
I abhor him.

Each communicates a slightly different shade of meaning.

The study of synonyms provides an opportunity to introduce the concepts of denotative and connotative meanings. The denotation of a word is the exact, literal meaning. Connotation refers to the implied meaning. Students learn to make fine distinctions between one synonym and another with practice and experience; thus, they need to have ample opportunities to make these discriminations by discussing concepts encountered in their reading and in practice exercises that relate to their study of subject content.

Synonyms operate as semantic clues to help students make distinctions between similar, yet different, words and concepts. For example:

Gaye and Geri are sisters. They are siblings.
They were asked to pacify the rulers. To appease them, costly gifts were sent to their cities.

Note that, while similar, the synonyms represent subtle differences of concept.

Antonyms are words opposite in meaning. Using antonyms as semantic clues helps the students think in terms of contrasting statements and concepts. Studying antonyms can be made a part of word analysis by illustrating how the addition of certain prefixes and suffixes to root words can create words with opposite meanings. For example:

prepaid— postpaid
prewar— postwar
underfed— overfed

When students learn a new word they might also learn its opposite. Examples are:

The cake was sweet, but the sauce was very bitter.
The robin is classified as a diurnal animal, and the bat is a nocturnal animal.

Homonyms are words that are identical in pronunciation, but different in meaning and spelling. Context generally indicates the meanings of these words. Homonyms frequently present recognition and spelling problems for some students. To illustrate their differences, the teacher must use them in various contexts. For example:

The justice of the peace had the right to conduct the marriage rite.

The bear was climbing the large bare elm tree.

As with synonyms and antonyms, students need practice in discriminating between one homonym and another. Following is a sample of a few common homonyms.

beach — beech

birth — berth

coarse — course

ewe — yew

fair — fare

feet — feat

fir — fur

idle — idol

sew — sow

slay — sleigh

some — sum

steal — steel

whole — hole

write — right

wrote — rote

Prefixes, Suffixes, and Roots

Base or root words and affixes are morphemes, the smallest meaningful elements in a word. Root words can stand alone as a word, whereas affixes are always attached to a base word. Prefixes are always affixed to the front of the root word, and suffixes are appended to the end of the base or root word. Most two and three syllable words are composed of a root and a prefix and/or a suffix. When a student knows root words and affixes, the meaning of many new words can be determined, especially if context clues are used to confirm the word meaning. Being able to break a word into its root, prefix, and suffix is a valuable skill for increasing word power.

How can understanding prefixes, suffixes, and roots enhance understanding?

Students should not be expected to memorize long lists of unfamiliar prefixes, suffixes, and roots. Instead, prefixes, suffixes, and roots should be learned by starting with known words and moving to the unknown words. Inductive or discovery methods are effective ways for students to learn derivative words. For example, most students know the words *telephone*, *telecast*, and *television*. From them, they can deduce that the root word *tele* means *far away* or *distant*. Then they might list other words they know that begin with the root *tele*.

Although prefixes cannot stand alone, they play important roles, for they modify the meanings of the root words to which they are attached. A small

Prefix	Meaning	Example	Prefix	Meaning	Example
ab	from	abdicate	in	not	inhospitable
ad	to	adhere	macro	large	macrosopic
ante	before	antebellum	meta	between, after	metaphysics
anti	against	antipathy	micro	small	microscope
auto	self	automatic	neo	new	neolithic
be	by	bedecked	para	beside, beyond	paradoxical
bi	two, twice	biannual	peri	around	perimeter
circu(m)	around	circumscribe	poly	many	polychrome
com	with	commingle	post	after	postscript
counter	against	counterblow	pre	before	precede
de	from	dehydrate	pro	in front of	proceed
dis	apart	discount	re	back	recite
en	in	enamored	sub	under	submerged
ex	out	exhale	super	above	supercilious
fore	in front	forecast	trans	across	transmit
hyper	over	hypersensitive	ultra	beyond	ultralight
hypo	under, beneath	hypodermic	un	not	uncontrolled
in	into	inject			

number of prefixes account for most of the common English words containing prefixes (Stauffer 1975, p. 284, Stotsky 1977, and Graves and Hammond 1980). They are listed above.

A suffix comes at the end of a word and is usually part of a two or three syllable word. It is attached to a root word, and modifies its meaning. The suffix often indicates which part of speech the word is. The suffix -*ion* indicates the word is a noun, such as *foundation*. The -*ly* at the end of a root indicates the word is an adverb, as *fondly*. The suffix -*able* means "capable of (being)," as in *washable*. The inflectional suffix -*s* added to a noun denotes plural meaning, such as *thoughts*.

The root is the main part of a word. Root or base words, which form the core of vocabulary, cannot be broken into smaller elements. Knowing the roots of words is the key to determining the meanings of many words. Adding a prefix or suffix to a root word changes its meaning. Some roots are unique, and some are members of "families." Classifying words—prefixes and suffixes as well as roots—according to families is a common way to learn many words. For example, the Greek root *graph*, meaning to write or record, can help a student determine and remember words like autograph, lithograph, monograph, photograph, polygraph, and telegraph.

The English language contains innumerable prefixes, suffixes, and roots. Many of them have been borrowed from other languages. Analyzing Greek and Latin prefixes, suffixes, and roots can help derive the meaning of unfamiliar words.

Signal Words

Writers use signal words to direct the reading of their ideas. These words qualify or modify the meaning of a sentence. For example:

> He goes to the park to swim.
>
> He always goes to the park to swim.

How can signal words affect meaning?

The word *always* changes the meaning of the sentence. Other signal words are placed into categories and sentences to serve as examples.

Time Markers   Words that relate to the expression of time:

after, after that	next
before, before that	now
earlier	since, since then
formerly	soon
last	then
later	to begin with

Before Al entered the room, he paused and listened to their merriment. Then, he slowly opened the door and sauntered into the room.

To begin with, they were not prepared for the snow storm. They had only one blanket, a limited supply of food, and three matches. Soon the food was gone and later the dry wood became scarce to find.

More to Say   Words that indicate one or more additional ideas are to be expressed.

also	furthermore
beside	in addition
for example	moreover

Peggy is a friend of Kay. Peggy is always willing to help her in the garden. Besides, she never expects a favor in return.

The old school house has been empty for three years. Cobwebs are everywhere. Also, several windows and steps are broken.

Consider Both Sides   Words that indicate another, or a different, viewpoint is to be expressed:

however	on the other hand
in spite of	to the contrary
nevertheless	whereas

His headache was relieved by taking the medication. However, his fever is still high.

Make a Summary or Conclusion   Words that are used to indicate a summary or concluding statement:

as you can tell	hence
finally	in conclusion
for this reason	therefore

The postman could not get to our house this morning to deliver the mail. The snow on the steep path to our house melts a little at midday. Therefore, we need to place salt on the ice.

Signals of Order   Words that indicate sequence:

first	fourth
second	fifth
third	sixth

First, set the oven at 450 degrees. Second, place the unthawed casserole in the oven. Third, bake the casserole for one hour and forty five minutes. Fourth, remove the casserole from the oven and serve immediately.

Punctuation

What role does punctuation play in conveying meaning?

In addition to marking syntactical units, punctuation represents the intonation of speech, and so helps to convey meaning to the reader. The intonation patterns of pauses, pitch, and stress are replaced in writing by the use of punctuation. Punctuation indicates to the reader whether the written expression is a command, question, or statement, conveying satire, anger, surprise, and so on. The comma and semicolon indicate a pause. The comma is used to set off nonrestrictive clauses, to note a series, and to set off an appositive. A period is used to end a statement. A question mark indicates there would be a sharp rise in the voice. The exclamation point is used to end a command, show surprise, etc., and indicates a change in pitch and stress on words.

Read the following sentences without punctuation. Then, notice the ease of reading and of grasping the meaning when punctuation is added to the sentences.

"The clouds formed the rain came and rivers ran in the streets"
"The clouds formed, the rains came, and rivers ran in the streets."

"Those plants are found in wooded areas grassy plains and mountainous regions"

"Those plants are found in wooded areas, grassy plains, and mountainous regions."

"John the star of the basketball team broke his leg"
"John, the star of the basketball team, broke his leg."

"Get a look at this"
"Get a look at this!"

"Help I am over here!"
"Help! I am over here."

"What's this detergent"
"What's this, detergent?"

"They took over the cooking chores Chris and Nancy built the fires"
"They took over the cooking chores; Chris and Nancy built the fires."

Greater efficiency in reading is achieved if the importance of punctuation is taught in written expression, oral reading, rapid reading, and in reading subject content.

Figures of Speech

Figures of speech provide different ways of expressing ideas and extending sensory images. They add to the beauty and appeal of language. Figurative language refers to several ideas at the same time, like the synchronization of movement. Readers must use their imagination and semantic clues to recognize this less familiar form of language.

How does one derive meaning from figures of speech?

Figures of speech require that teachers pay special attention to helping students, particularly young children, understand their meanings. Students often interpret these expressions literally, even though they use figures of speech themselves, especially in slang language. Written forms of figurative language are difficult for them. Figures of speech place a strain on students' understanding of familiar words, and require that a student perceive an extension of meanings. It is the statement of one thing in terms of another that underlies figurative language and creates puzzlement for listeners and readers. Perhaps the easiest approach to understanding figures of speech is to call attention to their prevalence in everyday speech, to discuss them during class, and to share the "discovery" of new figures of speech.

Figures of speech are often used by speakers and writers to persuade or affect the listener or reader. Figurative speech is picturesque, and it is used to heighten the effect of a comparison or to identify an idea with a more familiar idea. There are many classifications of this special kind of speech, such as:

An *allegory* is a story in which objects or ideas are symbolized. Allegories often deal with the moral and spiritual nature of man, usually in long complicated stories.
Aesop's Fables, Gulliver's Travels and Pilgrim's Progress are examples of allegories.

A *euphemism* is used to express a disagreeable or unpleasant fact indirectly.

"TICKLING A FANCY"

> He gave up the ghost.
> God has released her. (Southey)

Hyperbole is an exaggeration in which truth is stretched for effect.

> He hit the ball a mile.
> He was so angry he was boiling.

Metonymy is the use of the name of one thing for another it suggests; thus one thing is said but another is meant.

> The pen is mightier than the sword.
> A watched pot never boils.

Metaphor makes an implied comparison between two things by transferring a term from the object it normally denotes to another.

> He raced like lightning down the street
> Language is the dress of thought. (Johnson)

Personification gives personal or human qualities to inanimate things or ideas.

> City of the Big Shoulders. (Sandberg)
> The green trees whispered low and mild. (Longfellow)

Simile makes a direct comparison between things, using the words *as* or *like*.

> She walks in beauty like the night. (Byron)

Similes in everyday speech include:

> As busy as a bee   Neat as a pin

As clumsy as an ox	Pretty as a picture
As easy as pie	Proud as a peacock
As free as a breeze	Quick as a wink

Synecdoche is speech in which a part is used for the whole, and something has to be supplied to what is said.

> The retiring golfer hung up her clubs.
> She gave her hand in marriage.

PARAGRAPH STRUCTURES

Comprehension, the cognitive processing of language, is a multidimensional operation. It consists of understanding sentences in paragraphs and paragraphs in longer discourse. The comprehension of a paragraph requires the comprehension of its sentences and their relationships in the paragraph. The paragraph is the basic unit for presenting a central thought and a group of closely related ideas.

How can understanding the nature of paragraphs help a reader?

Karlin (1975 and 1977, p. 186) contends that "paragraph reading is more complex than sentence reading." Paragraph structure implies the relations between sentences. Thus, the makeup of a paragraph depends on the kind of discourse in which it occurs, and the intent and content of the communication. When readers are aware of paragraph structure their reading patterns are more flexible, and they comprehend the information better. Karlin (1977, Ch. 7), Hittleman (1978, Ch. 8), Robinson (1978, Ch. 7), and Singer and Donlan (1980, Ch. 7) identify specific paragraph structures used in content area textbooks. Robinson describes seven paragraph structures:

Definitional Paragraphs

A definitional paragraph explains the meaning of one or several technical words, phrases, or clauses. The paragraphs are explanatory. Sometimes a paragraph will explain and define ideas. Typographical aids help readers to identify definitions. Italics or bold print is used, or the words are framed by heavy lines. Readers should be guided to locate key words, phrases, or clauses, and to determine their meanings. Two samples of definitional paragraphs are:

> An addition to our satellites was the Transit Series. These are navigational satellites, or satellites that help ships and airplanes tell where they are. The Transit Satellites send information to earth every two hours about storms, winds, tides, and other navigational aids.

> The ratio of the measure of a side opposite a given angle of a right triangle to the measure of the hypotenuse depends on the measure of the angle and not on the measure of the sides. The ratio is called *sine* of the measure of the angle and is abbreviated *sin.*

Descriptive Paragraphs

Descriptive paragraphs are used throughout literature and, occasionally, in other content areas as well. When readers skim or skip descriptive paragraphs they miss information as well as the expression of feeling about an idea. Some social studies and science paragraphs are descriptive because writers want to provide an overall impression of description, and at the same time use the paragraph to present facts and ideas. If the description is complex, students should be asked to verbalize or draw a picture using labels to describe the ideas. Here is a paragraph where facts are used to describe and provide information.

> Modern ferns range in size from very small to as large as trees. Large ferns reach a height of ten to fifteen meters. They are usually found in tropical regions. In temperate areas, ferns often grow as low shrubs on the forest floor. Some ferns float in water or are rooted in mud. Several species live in very dry areas such as on cliffs. Species living in these dry regions are dormant when moisture is not available. When water is present they quickly resume life activities.

Explanatory Paragraphs

Explanatory paragraphs explain, inform, or tell about something factual. They are the most common paragraph structure used in the content areas, with the exception of literary writing. Readers should be instructed to (1) not skip unknown words, (2) look for definitions, (3) determine the main idea of paragraphs, and (4) relate graphs to information explained in paragraphs. The following paragraph illustrates an explanatory paragraph.

> Plants of Phylum Tracheophyta have vascular tissue and (in most forms) true roots, stems, and leaves. The sporophyte generation is predominant. These plants lead a more complete land life than bryophytes. Included in this phylum are early forms found mostly in warm, tropical climates. The most widespread tracheophytes are those which reproduce by seeds.

Introductory Paragraphs

Introductory paragraphs usually establish the purpose for reading a selection. This type of paragraph is not as densely packed with ideas. An introductory paragraph should be read before proceeding to study a chapter to observe words or expressions that signal what to expect in the remainder of the selection. Locating questions or statements that help set the purpose for reading the selection is important. The following is an introductory paragraph.

> This chapter describes how feudalism faded in western Europe. It tells how the kings, aided by the rising middle class, began to replace the local

governments of feudalism with strong central authority. Thus a few nations, united and protected by new centralized governments, and by the loyalty and support of the people, took the place of hundreds of separate fiefs. Finally, the chapter shows how the development of nations varied from country to country, moving rapidly in some and slowly in others.

Narrative Paragraphs

Narration is most often used in literature, particularly fiction. However, in expository writing narrative paragraphs often introduce a chapter or section. The purpose is to focus a reader's attention on the information to be explained, or to create and sustain interest. Narrative paragraphs are also used to introduce important ideas or to connect information that is to be explained in ensuing explanatory paragraphs. A narrative paragraph used in expository material is shown below.

> Sarajevo is a remote little village in the Balkans. There, one Sunday in June, 1914, two pistol shots were fired that were to send up in smoke the dreams of millions of peace lovers around the world. For these pistol shots were the immediate cause of World War I.

Summarizing and Concluding Paragraphs

These paragraphs serve the reader as a previewing aid, as a comprehension check, and as a review. Sometimes summarizing and concluding paragraphs occur throughout a chapter or unit as deemed necessary by the writers. The summarizing paragraphs restate the most important ideas presented in the section, chapter, or unit. Students should be guided to read these paragraphs and to check their understanding of the ideas presented in capsule form. A summarizing paragraph follows.

> In this chapter, you have been introduced to the forms of local government. You have learned how these governments are formed at the desire of the people, and by the authority of the state. You studied the general forms of county governments into which our states are divided. You then examined the smallest political units, towns, townships, and villages. You learned about special districts, units of government which serve only one specified purpose, and other services performed for you and your fellow citizens by local governments.

Transitional Paragraphs

Transitional paragraphs summarize an idea and also introduce another idea. Questions may be used for this purpose. At times, a combination of interrogatories and declaratories are used. This type of paragraph serves to alert readers to review what they have read and to be prepared to read information that is new. Students should be taught to use the questions to review important ideas, and to give attention to what will be treated in the following paragraphs. Two samples of transitional paragraphs follow.

> Although law making is the main business of a Congressman, he does have other tasks to fill his days, and sometimes his nights. Just what does he do? How does he spend his time outside of sessions of Congress? What are the various ways he represents us?

> Name the hottest thing you can think of on earth. What would you guess the temperature to be? Can you name something even hotter? What we want to do now is find out what happens to a solid when we heat it. We also want to find out if the particle model of matter can account for all the things we see happening. Let's begin by doing an investigation.

DICTIONARY USAGE

How is a dictionary used to teach word meanings?

Samuel Johnson published his dictionary in 1755 after nine years of work. He had learned that he could only "register the language," not "form it." In other words, he could neither keep the language from changing nor report all that people knew about their language.

From the very beginning, students should learn to consult dictionaries as guides to a broad range of information about words. Students in elementary school first use dictionaries to find the meanings and spellings of words (but unless one already knows the first two or three letters of an English word, it is difficult to locate it in a dictionary to check on its correct spelling). As students gain experience in using a dictionary, they can use it to acquire semantic, grammatical, and etymological information. By comparing dictionaries, students can learn that they sometimes differ about the spellings of words or their uses.

Nor do all the dictionaries contain the same kinds of information. The parts-of-speech labels explain the words' grammatical usages; the labels, such as Latin, Greek, French, or German, document the historical derivation of words. Word meanings are explained by illustrative phrases and sentences. In addition, the pronunciation, synonyms, and antonyms of words are usually included. Some classroom dictionaries contain special tables and indexes, giving biographical, metrical, historical, or geographical information.

Using a dictionary is an important aspect of word study for students of all ages. Young readers can learn the purpose and organization of dictionaries by starting with picture dictionaries. Middle grade and secondary school students can expand their dictionary skills to increase their vocabulary and understanding of word origin. Effective instruction should help readers to use a dictionary when:

1. They encounter a word that is not a part of their vocabulary.
2. The meaning of a word is not made known in context.
3. A precise meaning or multiple meanings of word are needed.
4. The correct pronunciation of a word is unknown.

In order to use a dictionary efficiently, students need to learn the following skills:

1. Locating words. This skill includes knowing the alphabet, guide words and their use, inflected and derived forms of words, and the special sections such as foreign words and phrases.
2. Deriving word pronunciation. This skill involves using the pronunciation key to identify vowel sounds, recognizing syllables, including unstressed syllables, using phonetic respellings and diacritical marks, and using primary and secondary accent marks.
3. Determining word meanings. This skill consists of using illustrative sentences to ascertain the apposite meanings, selecting a specific meaning for a word in a given context, and explaining meanings of root words.

As students learn to use a dictionary they should also learn to use a thesaurus. A thesaurus is a book of synonyms, antonyms, and related words. To find a related word such as a synonym, students must know how to use the index, select the word suitable for their purpose, identify the appropriate page number, and look up cross references. Thesauri are written for different levels of cognitive and linguistic development of students.

WORD ORIGINS AND CHANGE

The original basis of English is Anglo-Saxon, of the Germanic branch of Indo-European. However, a count from a dictionary reveals that only about 40 percent of English words are of Anglo-Saxon origin. Although the rest of our words are borrowed from almost every language, the Anglo-Saxon element comprises a large number of high frequency words such as the definite and indefinite articles, and common prepositions, conjunctions, adjectives, nouns, and verbs (Pei 1965, p. 151).

How does understanding word origins and changes relate to vocabulary development?

Lingustic change is continuous in sentence structure, word forms, pronunciation, and vocabulary. A knowledge of etymology, or word origins, and semantic changes increases a reader's interest in words.

When printing was invented in the fifteenth century, the spelling of English words became relatively fixed. However, spelling is complicated because of the many borrowed words from other languages (Bloomfield 1965 and Pei 1965). Many of these borrowed words are in constant use.

Dutch:	cole slaw, cookie, spree, bass, scow, spa, daffodil, Catskill, Harlem, bowery
French:	state, reign, judge, jury, soldier, soup, roast, chef, chauffeur, culdesac
German:	sauerkraut, dachshund, liverwurst, frankfurter, wiener, pretzel, waltz, kindergarten, blitzkrieg, delicatessen
Italian:	spaghetti, ravioli, sonata, virtuoso, piccolo, soprano, contralto, ballot, brigade, cavalry

Latin:	affidavit, deficit, exit, memorandum, minimum, recipe, stimulus, vacuum, veto, via
American Indian:	Massachusetts, Wisconsin, Michigan, Chicago, Illinois, Milwaukee, moccasin, papoose, totem, wigwam
Scandinavian:	cake, sky, ugly, geyser, saga, ski, slalom, oar, egg, bait

The meaning of words is linked with the psychology of both the individual and the masses. The relativity of meaning becomes paramount in the transfer from one language to another. The essential part of semantics is the acceptance of a given meaning. Few words retain the original meanings of centuries ago. For example, the original meaning of *foyer* is "fireplace"; *meat* was once food of any kind; *naughty* was "poor"; *perfume* was used to disinfect a room; *confetti* was once candy; *measles* had the meaning of "leper"; and *constable* was originally a stable companion, then an officer of high rank and finally a police officer.

When new words are created, or coined, their makers, such as scientists and authors, use known prefixes, roots, and suffixes. The language of aerospace scientists is an example. They have introduced many new words and phrases to the English language. A few of these words are: *booster rocket, downrange, G-force, interstellar flight, launch pad, lunar probe, retrorocket,* and *subsatellite.* Lewis Carroll, in *Alice in Wonderland,* created words such as *jabberwocky, frabjous,* and *chortle.* Jonathan Swift used the word *Lilliputian.* Rhyming words, such as *chin-chin, hurdy-gurdy,* and *tom-tom,* are used by children in games and by writers. The world of advertising has coined words such as *elasto, finast, simonize,* and *glamorize.* Some coined words in common use are:

amtrac	iron curtain
bamboo curtain	junkie
emcee	prefab
grassroots	spelunker
intercom	supermarket

The story of personal and family names is till another part of word origins and meanings. For example, *Smith* is the most common family name in both Britain and America. The name Smith has a counterpart in German (*Schmidt*), Dutch (*Smit*), Spanish (*Herrero*), and French (*Ferrier*). Several centuries ago family names represented trades, such as *Baker, Taylor, Butler,* and *Cook* (Dale and O'Rourke 1971 and Pei 1965). The origin of a few first names:

Annette:	French "little Ann"
Dorothy:	Greek "gift of God"
Clara:	Latin "bright"
Michael:	Hebrew "one who is like God"
Ivan:	Russian version of John
Charles:	Teutonic "strong"

SUMMARY

Each subject includes basic concepts that must be understood. The technical terms representing key concepts should be taught to students before they read textbook assignments. Concept development proceeds through enlargement of vocabulary, since a word is a verbal expression of a concept.

Students must understand syntactical structures (the way words are arranged in phrases and sentences) in order to extract meaning from their reading. Syntactic and semantic clues function together, and context serves as a key to interpreting the meanings of words and how they are related.

Learning about the relationship of words and concepts involves the study of synonyms, antonyms, homonyms, signal words, figurative language, base words, prefixes, suffixes, and word origins. This kind of information and knowing how to use a dictionary and thesaurus greatly enhance reading and writing skills.

At the sentence level, a knowledge of punctuation aids comprehension. The comprehension of a paragraph, in turn, requires the comprehension of its component sentences and their relationships in the paragraph. Several types of paragraph organization have been identified. When students understand paragraph structures and purposes, they can assimilate the information better.

Reinforcement Activities

1. Review a chapter or unit in a content area textbook. Select one, two, or three key concept words, and plan how you will preteach their pronunciation and meaning.

2. Choose two different facets of word or sentence study your students need to develop their linguistic skills. Outline the techniques you will use to teach the word skills you selected.

3 Determine the paragraph structures in a chapter of a content area textbook. Plan how you will teach the students to recognize and use the information about the different kinds of paragraphs.

References

AMES, WILBUR A. "The Development of a Classification Scheme of Contextual Aids." *Reading Research Quarterly* 2 (1966):57–82.

ANDERSON, RICHARD C. "Schema-Directed Processes in Language Comprehension." Urbana, Illinois: Center for the Study of Reading. Number 50, July 1977.

BARNITZ, JOHN G. "Syntactic Effects on the Reading Comprehension of Pronoun-Referent Structures by Children in Grades Two, Four, and Six." *Reading Research Quarterly* 15 (1980): 268–289.

BLOOMFIELD, LEONARD. *Language History From Language*, edited by Harry Hoijer. New York: Holt, Rinehart and Winston, 1965.

CHALL, JEANNE. "The Influence of Previous Knowledge

on Reading Ability." *Educational Research Bulletin.* Ohio State University 26 (1947): 225–230.

CUNNINGHAM, JAMES W., CUNNINGHAM, PATRICIA M., and ARTHUR, SHARON V. *Middle and Secondary School Reading.* New York: Longman, 1981.

DALE, EDGAR, and O'ROURKE, JOSEPH. *Techniques of Teaching Vocabulary.* Palo Alto, California: Field Educational Publication, Inc., 1971.

DAWKINS, JOHN. *Syntax and Readability.* Newark, Delaware: International Reading Association, 1975.

FARR, ROGERS, and ROSER, NANCY. *Teaching a Child to Read.* New York: Harcourt Brace Jovanovich, Inc., 1979.

FRIEDMAN, MYLES I., and ROWLS, MICHAEL D. *Teaching Reading and Thinking Skills.* New York: Longman, 1980.

GIPE, JOAN. "Investigating Techniques for Teaching Word Meanings." *Reading Research Quarterly* 14 (1978–1979): 624–643.

GRAVES, MICHAEL F., and HAMMOND, HEIDI K. "A Validated Procedure for Teaching Prefixes and Its Effects on Students' Ability to Assign Meaning to Novel Words." In *Perspectives in Reading Research and Instruction,* edited by Michael L. Kamil and Alden J. Moe. Washington D.C.: Twenty-ninth Yearbook of The National Reading Conference, 1980, 184–188.

HERBER, HAROLD. *Teaching Reading in Content Areas.* Englewood Cliffs, New Jersey: Prentice-Hall, Inc., 178.

HITTLEMAN, DANIEL R. *Developmental Reading: A Psycholinguistic Perspective.* Chicago: Rand McNally Publishing Company, 1978.

KARLIN, ROBERT. *Teaching Elementary Reading.* 2nd ed. New York: Harcourt Brace Jovanovich, Inc., 1975.

KARLIN, ROBERT. *Teaching Reading in High School: Improving Reading in the Content Areas.* 3rd ed. Indianapolis, Indiana: Bobbs-Merrill Company, Inc., 1977.

LAMBERG, WALTER J., and LAMB, CHARLES E. *Reading Instruction in the Content Areas.* Chicago: Rand McNally College Publishing Company, 1980.

PAGE, WILLIAM D., and PINNELL, GAY S. *Teaching Reading Comprehension.* Urbana, Illinois: National Council of Teachers of English, 1979.

PEARSON, P.D. "The Effects of Grammatical Complexity on Children's Comprehension, Recall, and Conception of Certain Grammatical Relations." *Reading Research Quarterly* 10 (1974–1975): 155–192.

PEI, MARIO. *The Story of Language.* 3rd ed. Philadelphia: J. B. Lippincott Company, 1965.

PRESSLEY, MICHAEL, LEVIN, JOEL R., and MILLER, GLORIA E. "How Does the Keyword Method Affect Vocabulary Comprehension and Usage?" *Reading Research Quarterly.* 16 (1981): 213–226.

ROBINSON, H. ALAN. *Teaching Reading and Study Strategy.* 2nd ed. Boston: Allyn and Bacon, Inc., 1978.

RUMELHART, DAVID, and ORTONY, ANDREW. "The Representation of Knowledge in Memory." In *Schooling and the Acquisition of Knowledge,* edited by Richard C. Anderson, Rand J. Spiro, and William E. Montague. Hillsdale, New Jersey: Eribaum 1977, 99–135.

SINGER, HARRY, and DONLAN, DAN. *Reading and Learning from Text.* Boston: Little, Brown and Company, 1980.

SMITH, FRANK. *Understanding Reading: A Psycholinguistic Analysis of Reading and Learning to Read.* New York: Holt, Rinehart and Winston, 1978.

STAUFFER, RUSSELL G. *Directing the Reading-Thinking Process.* New York: Harper and Row Publishers, 1975.

STOTSKY, SANDRA L. "Teaching Prefixes: Facts and Fallacies." *Language Arts.* 54 (1977): 887-890.

STEINER, ROLLIN, WEINER, MARTIN, and CROMER, WARD. "Comprehension Training and Identification for Poor and Good Readers." *Journal of Educational Psychology.* 62 (1971): 506-513.

TINKER, MILES, and McCULLOUGH, CONSTANCE. *Teaching Elementary Reading.* 4th ed. Englewood Cliffs, New Jersey: Prentice-Hall, Inc., 1975.

VYGOTSKY, LEV SEMENOVICH. *Thought and Language.* Edited and translated by Eugenia Hanfmann and Gertrude Vakar. Cambridge: Massachusetts Institute of Technology Press, 1962.

Bibliography

Ammon, Richard. "Generating Expectancies to Enhance Comprehension." *The Reading Teacher* 29 (1975): 245–249.

Asimov, Isaac. *Words of Science and the History Behind Them.* Boston: Houghton-Mifflin, 1959.

Asimov, Isaac. *Words From the Myths.* Boston: Houghton-Mifflin, 1961.

Asimov, Isaac. *Word From History.* Boston: Houghton-Mifflin, 1968.

Braam, Leonard S. and Walker, James E. "Subject Teacher's Awareness of Reading Skills." *Journal of Reading* 16 (1973): 608-611.

Chomsky, Noam. *Aspects of a Theory of Syntax.* Cambridge: Massachusetts Institute of Technology Press, 1965.

Dechant, Emerald V. *Diagnosis and Remediation of Reading Disabilities.* Englewood Cliffs, N.J.: Prentice-Hall, Inc., 1981. Chapter 5.

Flavell, J. H. *The Developmental Psychology of Jean Piaget.* New York: Van Nostrand, 1964.

Forester, Leona M. "Idiomagic!" *Elementary English* 51 (1974): 125–127.

Funk, Charles Earle, Jr. *Heavens to Betsy.* New York: Warner Paperback Library, 1972.

Funk, Charles Earle, Jr. *Thereby Hangs A Tale.* New York: Warner Paperback Library, 1972.

Funk, Charles Earle, Jr. *Horse Feathers.* New York: Warner Paperback Library, 1972.

Funk, Charles Earle, Jr., *A Hog on Ice.* New York: Warner Paperback Library, 1973.

Funk, Wilfred J. *Word Origins and Their Romantic Stories.* New York: Grosset and Dunlap, 1950.

Goldfield, Ben. "Semantics: An Aid to Comprehension." *Journal of Reading* 16 (1973): 310–313.

Goodman, Kenneth, and Buck, Catherine. "Dialect Barriers to Reading Comprehension: Revisited." *The Reading Teacher* 27 (1973): 6–12.

Griese, Arnold A. *Do You Read Me? Practical Approaches to Teaching Reading Comprehension.* Santa Monica, California: Goodyear Publishing Company, Inc., 1977.

Kaiser, Robert A., Neil, Cheryl F., and Flosiani, Bernard P. "Syntactic Complexity of Primary Grade Reading Materials: A Preliminary Look." *The Reading Teacher* 29 (1975): 262–265.

Kaplan, Elaine M., and Tuchman, Anita. "Vocabulary Strategies Belong in the Hands of Learners." *Journal of Reading* 24 (1980): 32–34.

Kennedy, Larry D. "Textbook Usage in the Intermediate-Upper Grades." *The Reading Teacher* 24 (1971): 723–729.

Langen, John J. "Vocabulary and Concept Development." *Journal of Reading* 10 (1967): 448–456.

Lapp, Diane, and Flood, James. *Teaching Reading to Every Child.* New York: Macmillan Publishing Company, Inc., 1978.

Mickleson, Norma. "Meaningfulness, A Critical Variable in Children's Verbal Learning." *The Reading Teacher* 23 (1969): 11–14.

Miller, John W., and Charles A. Hintzman. "Syntactic Complexity of Newberry Award Winning Books." *The Reading Teacher* 28 (1975): 750–756.

Morris, William, and Morris, Mary. *Dictionary of Word and Phrase Origins.* New York: Harper and Row, Volume 1, 1962; Volume 2, 1967; and Volume 3, 1971.

O'Neill, Mary. *Words, Words, Words.* New York: Doubleday and Company, Inc., 1966.

Pei, Mario. *What's in a Word? Language: Yesterday, Today and Tomorrow.* New York: Hawthorne Books, 1968.

Rodgers, Denis. "Which Connectives?" Signals to Enhance Comprehension." *Journal of Reading* 17 (1974): 462–466.

Rystrom, Richard. "Language Patterns and the Primary Child." *The Reading Teacher* 26 (1972): 149–152.

Smith, Carl B. *Teaching Reading in Secondary School Content Subjects: A Bookthinking Process.* New York: Holt, Rinehart and Winston, 1978.

Smith, Frank. *Psycholinguistics and Reading.* New York: Holt, Rinehart and Winston, 1972.

Thomas, Ellen L., and Robinson, Alan H. *Improving Reading in Every Class.* Boston: Allyn and Bacon, Inc., 1977.

Tovey, Duane R. "Inseparable 'Language and Content' Instruction." *Journal of Reading* 22 (1979): 720–725.

Turner, Thomas N. "Figurative Language: Deceitful Mirage or Sparkling Oasis for Reading?" *Language Arts* 53 (1976): 758–761, 775.

Waterhouse, Lynn H., Fischer, Karen M., and Ryan, Ellen B. *Language Awareness and Reading.* Newark, Delaware: International Reading Association, 1980.

Zeman, Samuel S. "Reading Comprehension and Writing of Second and Third Grades." *The Reading Teacher* 23 (1969): 144–150.

7 READING FLEXIBILITY AND RAPID READING

OVERVIEW

Just as people find it desirable, even necessary, to drive at varying speeds, so should students learn to read different materials at different speeds, according to their purpose for reading. When reading highly technical material, one needs to understand all that is said and will naturally read at a much slower rate than when reading the evening newspaper. And not only will the speed differ: the entire approach to reading will too. This chapter contains information on increasing reading speed and comprehension and also on varying reading strategies according to the material being read.

"READING FLEXIBILITY" refers to the ability to adjust one's reading rate according to his purpose for reading, previous knowledge of the topic or subject matter, and the complexity of the material. An efficient reader adjusts his rate and approach to reading within a given selection and for various kinds of materials. The rate may vary from under fifty to several thousand words per minute. Striving for maximum comprehension is a necessary factor in achieving this flexibility, since a student cannot read faster than ideas can be comprehended.

Why should students learn to be flexible readers?

If one cannot be an effective reader without being a flexible reader, then students should receive direct instruction in adjusting their reading rates according to their reading purposes. According to Harris (1976), flexibility in reading is a fundamental part of basic reading instruction. He emphasized that reading programs that have not given attention to variability in reading purposes and rates may contribute to reading failures.

ADJUSTMENT OF READING RATE

The findings of several studies indicate that reading flexibility consists of many factors rather than one (Smith 1965, McDonald 1965, Stone 1965, Carver 1977-1978, and Harris and Sipay 1979). The flexible reader selects his reading rate according to (1) the purpose for which the material is being read, (2) his ability to read and comprehend the materials, (3) the complexity, content, and style of the text, and (4) his background experiences and interests in the subject (Rankin 1974 and Miller 1978). Development of this kind of flexibility should begin in the primary grades and focus on frequent instruction in these reading variables (Carrillo and Sheldon 1952, Berg 1967, Harris 1976, and Stauffer 1962).

The flexible reader varies his technique to match the kind of idea assimilation the reading task demands, whereas the rigid reader relies on a single approach to reading all printed materials. It is doubtful that the rigid reader even considers in advance how he is going to read a selection. He may not be aware of the appropriateness of a change in rate, or he may feel the risk of change is too great to undertake. To attain efficiency in comprehension requires a flexible approach to rate adjustment, rather than speed alone (Harris 1968). An investigation by Morasky (1972), for example, was concerned with the eye movements made by readers as they read to answer questions. The results showed that more visual fixations occur and the reading time is longer when the questions are placed after paragraphs than when they are placed before them. The researchers concluded that reading is more efficient when readers view questions before reading paragraphs. Thus, the change or adjustment in rate was the consequence rather than a cause of flexibility.

How should students select their reading rates?

An efficient reader reduces or increases the speed of reading according to his purpose. A slower rate may be selected to avoid creating a gap between reading and comprehension rates. An effective rate is achieved when the reader can employ a maximum unforced speed and obtain the desired meaning from the content (Hafner and Jolly 1972, p. 176). In contrast, the ineffective reader mechanically plods from word to word, and the comprehension attained is seldom related to a purpose for reading the selection.

Flexibility or rate of reading is influenced not only by the reader's purpose, but also by many other factors that pertain to the reader or to the materials. The reader's background experiences and his understanding of and interest in the topic are crucial components, because they influence his selection of and reaction to ideas. The reader's flexibility is also influenced by his mental ability, his personality, and his reading skills such as word decoding. The writing style of the author, the vocabulary and concept load, and the frequency of new, different, and abstract ideas affect one's reading rate, as do the typography of the book and the environment in which the reading takes place.

Since different materials are read for different purposes, teachers must provide systematic guidance. From what is known about the processes of reading, it appears that a teacher can stress the adjustment of reading as early as the fundamental reading skills are taught. This is necessary if students are to become self-reliant in determining their own reading purposes and appropriate rates. An even greater emphasis on rate adjustment, including rapid reading, should extend into the middle school, and into secondary and adult programs.

Henderson (1965) reported a significant relationship between the ability of readers to set a purpose for reading and general reading achievement. He found that fifth grade students can be taught to identify their purposes for reading and to vary their reading rates accordingly. Samuels and Dahl (1975) showed that fourth grade children read significantly faster when reading to obtain a general overview than when they are told to read for details. There is evidence from one research study that flexibility in reading rate can be taught to nine-year-old students. With only two weeks of training sessions, the young students learned to vary the rate of reading according to their purposes. The greatest improvements were in two areas: reading for the main idea and reading for specific facts (Harris 1976).

Troxel (1962) conducted a study in which two different groups of eighth grade students read the same expository mathematics materials. One group read the passages to determine the main idea; the other group read to respond to specific questions. The students' purposes for reading influenced the rate at which they read the materials. Direct instruction and practice improved the students' reading speed and accuracy. According to Labmeier and Vockell (1973), the reading rate and comprehension of the ninth grade girls who were in a reading development course were improved through systematic instruction and practice.

EYE MOVEMENTS

Reading begins as a sensory process involving the eyes, and depends upon the efficiency of one's oculo-motor habits. The term *vision* refers to this efficiency of the eyes. The perceptual processes are very dependent upon the information received through the eyes, since this visual perception makes possible the interpretation of what is seen.

The visual field includes both the foveal and peripheral vision. The functional center of the retina of the eyes reaches its highest degree of specialization for sharp vision in the two or three millimeter section known as the fovea or macula. Cone cells predominate in this small area, and the acuteness of form perception and completeness of color vision are greatest in the fovea and lowest in the extreme retinal periphery. Outside the fovea, away from the main focus of the eye, objects can be seen, but they are unclear and fuzzy; this is known as the area of peripheral vision (Kronfeld 1943, Jobe 1976, and Daines 1979).

The eyes are never still; they constantly make fine rotary movements unless there is an abnormality. In conventional reading, after each advance the eyes make short stops or fixations on a line of print. The fixation is the pause needed for perceiving and reacting to visual stimuli. These movements take place equally in each eye for both near and distant vision and whether one or both eyes are employed in fixation. Since a number of letters or words are seen in a single fixation, or visual span, the eyes do not proceed along the entire line, but indentations occur at either end. The rate of reading is influenced by the length and duration of the fixation pauses and by the reader's ability to assimilate ideas (Jobe 1976, and Daines 1979).

The perceptual span is the number of words that are recognized and understood at a single fixation by the reader. When the eyes move back or refocus on the line of print, it is known as regression. When a reader completes a line of print and the eyes return to the beginning of another line, it is called the return sweep. Readers, regardless of reading ability, use regression. When a reader encounters an unfamiliar word or more difficult and complex ideas, the number of regressions increases; and the fixation pauses are spaced closer together.

Approximately 90 percent of reading time is consumed by the fixation pause, and the remaining 10 percent of the time is spent on movement of the eyes between pauses. The duration and frequency of the fixation pause is influenced by the reader's word recognition skills, familiarity with the content and purposes, the amount of information acquired by the reader during the pause, and the difficulty level of the material as perceived by the reader. As a student develops reading efficiency, the number and length of fixations and regressions decrease. When the reading material becomes more difficult, and the reading purposes become more analytical, there are more and longer fixations.

How do eye fixation and peripheral vision relate to reading?

The integration of the information from one fixation to the next seems to be at a deeper level of encoding, such as letter and sound patterns, rather than just the shapes of letters and words. During a fixation, a reader acquires information primarily to the right of the center of vision. Words that are to the left of the center of vision have probably been identified during a prior fixation and are ignored by the reader. The amount of visual information a reader acquires and uses in reading varies from fixation to fixation (Tinker 1965, McConkie and Rayner 1976, *a* and *b*, Smith and Dechant 1977, and McConkie 1978).

Although there is a loss of detail and clarity in peripheral vision, there seems to be sufficient visual stimulus to direct a reader's eye movements. The detail may be ample enough in the periphery for a skilled reader to identify some words. This information perhaps reduces the processing of the visual stimulus and directs the eyes to new fixations. If the text contains extensive redundancy, the information in the peripheral vision becomes a basis for word identification. The language patterns and words that conform to expected shapes and syntactic and semantic context influence a reader's peripheral vision. A regressive movement on a later fixation occurs if the words do not fit an expected pattern of thought or context. The rapid movement of the eyes from one fixation pause to the next—the saccadic movement—positions the eyes to a specific location in text. Some evidence indicates that during the saccade and just before and after the eye locates on a new fixation, the visual sensitivity is lowered. The saccade is influenced by the information processed in the text (McConkie and Rayner 1976 *a* and *b* and McConkie 1978).

The eye-voice span refers to the number of words the eyes are ahead of the voice. A poor reader has a very narrow eye-voice span, and he does not move his eyes from a word until he has voiced it, whereas an able reader's eyes tend to be seven or eight words ahead of what he has spoken aloud. A span of several words is necessary for the proper interpretation of a passage, and phrase reading is just as important in silent reading as oral reading.

How do eye movements reflect thought processes?

Unless there is some visual anomaly, eye movements are reflections of a reader's thought process. Inefficient eye movements are symptomatic of other problems. The habitual use of round-robin reading in the early grades and the use of frustrational level materials are two common causes of inefficient eye movements. In round-robin reading, students have an unusual number of regressions and long fixation pauses; they start to subvocalize in an attempt to keep the same pace and rhythm in silent reading as the oral reader they are expected to follow. When students are given materials at their frustration levels, they encounter many difficult and unknown words and ideas. Thus, they use many regressions as they attempt to identify words, and their fixation pauses lengthen as they stumble in their attempt to complete a task. Poor decoding skills also cause inefficient eye movements and hinder flexibility and comprehension. Edfelt (1960) and Smith (1978) suggest that subvocalization is often caused when a student reduces his rate of reading for a difficult passage and thus articulates individual words.

RATE IMPROVEMENT STUDIES

Eye movement photography has shown that the eye movements of poor readers, when compared with those of good readers, are more erratic; the eye fixations are of longer duration, and eye regressions occur more often. Mechanical devices have been developed to help poor readers overcome these problems and increase efficient eye movements; many studies have been conducted to determine the role of machines in improving the reading skills and the speed of poor and able readers.

Gates (1953) evaluated the effectiveness of reading machines in increasing the rate of reading. He felt that if the device forced a student to read at an even speed, flexible reading would be destroyed. Berger (1968) reported a study in which the use of machines was less effective than the paperback scanning method for increasing the reading rate, comprehension, and flexibility of students. According to Weintraub (1968), children in the primary grades will not benefit from formal rate training because they have not matured sufficiently in visual perception or verbal development. Tinker (1967) expressed concern about the use of machines that force a reader's eyes to focus in three fixations per line at an equal speed line by line. He states that mechanical pacing devices, not tachistoscopes (an apparatus used for testing perception by exposing visual stimuli such as pictures, letters, or words for an extremely brief period), have motivational value if used properly as one aspect of reading improvement training. He further states that nonreading specialists too often overemphasize the mechanics of reading, which may result in a decrease in flexibility and adaptability of reading habits, and that such attempts to improve reading by training eye movements are useless or even harmful. Thus, he asserts that school monies might be better spent on books than on machines. Witty (1969) reviewed studies that pertained to increasing reading speed and comprehension. He found that early studies indicated that reading rates of readers of all ages could be improved within a few weeks or months. These gains were usually measured by the scores on standardized tests. Witty found that programs that did not employ mechanical pacing devices had equally satisfactory results as those programs where machines were used.

After reviewing research studies, Karlin (1958) stated that mechanical devices can be used to achieve gains in the rate of reading. But he also stated that instruction without the use of machines can surpass these gains. Later (1977), Karlin wrote that the use of mechanical devices motivates some students to increase their rate of reading and that the devices have acceptance

Why are reading machines considered less effective than other measures to improve reading rates?

among some high school teachers who conduct reading improvement programs.

Mechanical devices can be an asset, but they are not a necessity for a successful reading improvement program, according to Moore (1970). When the rate of reading is increased by the use of machines, there is little assurance that students will be able to transfer their training to textbooks (Olson and Ames 1972, p. 97). Morrison and Oakes (1970) demonstrated the effect that spending fifteen minutes each day on guided skimming had on the achievement of children in the second, third, and fourth grades; they concluded that skimming seemed to result in increased reading efficiency, especially for older children. A study by Swalm and Kling (1973) compared the effects of two methods for increasing the reading rates of students in the fifth and sixth grades. The methods used were timed reading drills and free reading with directions to read faster. The results showed that for these older children an abundance of independent reading coupled with timed exercises improved the reading rate better than free reading alone. These investigators felt that comprehension needs to be emphasized in a rate-training program with students in the upper elementary grades. Miller (1973) stated that a developmental reading program should include instruction in achieving flexible reading rates and should take into consideration the purposes and background experiences of the readers. Burmeister (1978, p. 310) stated that mechanical devices should be supplemental and purchased only if a wide variety of paperback books, textbooks, and other materials are available to students.

SPEED READING

What are the purposes and benefits of speed reading?

Two decades ago, reports written by Stauffer (1960) and Wood (1960) about speed reading excited reading specialists. The desirability of rapid reading was vigorously debated. Many researchers reject the claims of rapid readers. They believe that the maximum rapid reading rate is limited by the physiological structure of the eye, or that comprehension decreases as speed of reading increases (Spache 1962, Erlich 1963, Carver 1971, and Graf 1973). Other writers assert that reading at 2,000, 10,000, and 20,000 and more words per minute is possible with a high level of comprehension for mature readers who have adequate word recognition skills (Stauffer 1962, Himelstein and Greenberg 1974, Brown 1976, Hansen 1976, and Singer and Donlan 1980, pp. 204–205).

Although speed reading becomes more significant as students progress through the grades, it should never be considered separately from comprehension. Sailor and Ball (1975) examined the effects of reading rate training and peripheral vision training on speed of reading and reading comprehension. They found that reading speed was improved by rate training, and the subjects who received peripheral vision training improved in rate over subjects who received rate training only. Marcel (1974) examined the amount of material that children, age eleven, and adults gained from each fixation. Results showed that increases in reading speed are reflected by dealing with greater amounts of text at individual fixations. Both the words and typespaces perceived were increased.

Hansen (1976) designed a study to determine qualitative differences between the comprehension of university freshman students who were taught to use the Wood rapid reading technique and "normal" readers. Comprehension was measured by comparing pre- and post-test written recalls on a chapter from a psychology textbook. She reported that the rapid readers were not just skimming for main ideas. The students seemed to obtain better comprehension from reading a passage twice at high rates than reading once at slow rates. Given the same amount of time to master a passage, the rapid readers significantly outperformed normal readers. These rapid readers recalled more information units governed by reason and in gestalt relationships to other units of thought. The rapid readers responded more quickly to visual clues, as evidenced by recall of information not mentioned by the slower readers.

Rapid readers use less visual information to identify letters in words and words in meaningful sentences than isolated letters and unrelated sequences of words (Smith 1978, p. 78.) Smith also suggests that rapid and fluent readers are capable of making immediate word and meaning identification because of their abilities to use orthographic, syntactic, and semantic redundancy. It seems that these readers use syntax as a tool to predict the other words and confirm their predictions by using a minimum of visual clues.

Neisser (1967) and Gaardner (1970) have presented models that explain perception as an active process of construction during the reading process. Given a stimulus, the perceiver begins to organize data into significant and related units. In the process of organizing the stimuli, the reader refers to past experiences, organizes the information into significant clusters or chunks, and begins to construct hypotheses about the nature of the stimulus. According to this analysis-by-synthesis model, rapid readers search only for enough clues to make hypotheses about the probable meanings of words, phrases, and sentences. Once a reader has enough clues to suggest the meanings of a phrase or sentence, there is no reason for him to read and verify each individual word within the phrase or sentence.

McLaughlin (1969) suggests that speed readers appear to use their peripheral vision not only to examine words on each side of the fixation point but also to inspect the lines above and below. Techniques for increasing the reading rate of university students are described by Brown (1976); they include vocabulary development, teaching aids, student feedback, identifying and helping students overcome negative attitudes, visual expeditors and progress sheets, and the use of pacing for secondary school students and adults. Barrus and Brown (1977) reported a study in which seventeen graduate and university honors students participated. The rapid readers read faster, with fewer context errors. It appeared that they did not use a skimming or scanning technique; their rate of reading excelled over that of the control group, at rates of up to 3,000 words per minute. Johnson (1973) has described methods of instruction in rapid reading techniques and comprehension improvement, and there are many commercial programs available for developing rapid reading skills.

Speed readers do not read words in order. That is, their fixations do not follow the conventional pattern of seeing word by word. Speed readers usually pace their eye movements by moving a hand across the page in a rapid zigzag pattern, going from left to right to left or in a straight movement down the center of the page. Sometimes this same pattern is used from the bottom of the page to the top. Words are seen along several lines, in clusters or in phrases, the exact pattern depending on the background of the reader and his familiarity with the concepts and language patterns used by the authors. Perhaps more important, speed readers use overviewing techniques and checking procedures to increase and verify their comprehension of the material. The same rapid reading procedures are used with fiction and nonfiction materials.

Rapid Reading Skills

Why should students learn to read rapidly?

All students should learn the basics of rapid reading. Students who can read more material in less time with adequate comprehension have an advantage. They can read about many things and build up a tremendous background. Developing speed in reading requires direct training.

Rapid reading is very dependent upon a reader's purpose, reading abilities, and background, as well as the materials. High rates of speed in reading are to be taught only to mature readers. However, forms of rapid reading such as skimming and scanning should be taught to children in basic programs. Older chldren should be encouraged to increase their rate of silent reading. They need to learn that all materials are not read for the same purpose or at the same rate.

Skimming and scanning are forms of rapid reading to acquire information. Both are particularly important for reading in the content areas at all grade levels. *Skimming* is reading relevant parts of a selection for a purpose. It is an active process of placing ideas into a pattern to get a general impression or overview of the contents of a selection by reading main ideas and examining summaries. *Scanning* is used to locate specific information. It involves a quick search and is used whenever some particular information, such as a date, telephone number, or a relevant fact, needs to be found. When the information is located, the rate of scanning is usually reduced in order to assimilate the details. Scanning is the ability to read at a fast rate from point to point, searching out information.

Readers should be taught to read for different purposes and to adjust their rate of reading according to their purposes. For instance, when students read a selection to determine the reasons for the westward movement in the United

States, they should learn they are reading for main ideas, and that it isn't necessary to read the full paragraph at the same rate. Readers at the upper elementary, secondary, and postsecondary school levels should receive instruction in adjusting their rate to their reading purposes. They should also receive instruction in "out-of-word order" or "speed" reading from qualified teachers.

Some rapid reading techniques can be taught to children who are learning to read. Children in kindergarten and first grade might use pictures such as comic strips and rebus stories to learn to obtain information more rapidly. As soon as children have learned to read, they should learn to determine their purposes for reading. First grade children should skim for main ideas and scan pages for specific information. These same procedures started in the first grade should be continued at all grade levels.

In the higher grades these same skills of setting purposes, skimming, and scanning should be practiced daily. In addition, the previewing skills are to be taught and used as a part of all reading, including speed reading. Previewing what is going to be read is an active rather than a passive act: it becomes a process of anticipating and questioning. The reader's rate of reading and comprehension level are increased when preview techniques are used. Reading, including speed reading, should be followed by postviewing the material. Postviewing simply means reviewing after the selection has been read. The purpose is to note for a second time the important points which were read. This rapid review or postview of the materials will reinforce the main thoughts and aid in retention of the material.

Techniques for Increasing Reading Rates

A student's reading rate may be measured by either informal or standardized tests. However, standardized reading tests designed for use with primary grade children are not usually concerned with speed, because instruction during this period deals primarily with helping children acquire the basic reading abilities, upon which rapid reading depends. The speed of reading scores in standardized tests are calculated by noting the number of items the student attempts to answer within a set time limit. These scores are usually based on rather easy material with one set purpose. Furthermore, such scores do not relate to speeds in reading other kinds of materials.

What are some ways to improve students' reading rates?

A teacher can devise informal speed practice exercises that can be used at least once a day by students above the fourth grade. It is important that students maintain daily records of these exercises to show their progress in reading rates. Sample exercises and variations are shown below.

1. This test exercise can be used with middle grade and secondary school students.
   a. Select a few consecutive paragraphs or pages of prose from a content area textbook. The length of each selection might vary accord-

ing to the kind and difficulty of the materials and according to the reading levels and skills of the students. Initial passages should be no more than 400 to 1,000 words in length. Longer selections are used with more able readers; and as students improve the reading rate, longer passages can be used.

b. A set of questions should be prepared for each reading selection to help determine students' comprehesion of the materials. The length and purpose of the reading should determine the number of questions used. The number of questions might vary from five to fifteen. As an alternative to asking students to answer questions, they might be directed to write all they can remember about the selection.

c. Students are to record the time it takes to read each selection. The teacher can write the number of seconds at every ten second interval on the chalkboard, or hold up cards showing the time every ten seconds. This procedure should be started before any reader can complete the test. The number of words read per minute can be computed by the following formula:

$$\frac{\text{words read}}{\text{seconds}} \times 60 = \text{words per minute}$$

The scores of correctly answered questions and the time it takes to read the selection reveal both the speed and accuracy of the comprehension of the specific material read. If students write all the information they can recall, the teacher must have formulated a key to recognize the main ideas, contrasts, comparisons, relationships of cause and effect, and elaborations that are included in the discourse.

d. Students are not to reread the selection or to refer to it when answering the questions or when writing all they can recall about the passage. It is suggested that 85 percent accuracy or better on the questions indicates good recall and understanding. Seventy to 84 percent represents fair recall, and scores below 70 percent are considered to indicate poor comprehension. If the accuracy is 50 percent or less, the comprehension is very low. If a student's comprehension is high and the speed of reading is average or low, he will benefit from a program to increase his speed of reading. If both comprehension and speed are low or if comprehension is low and speed high, it will be more profitable to increase comprehension before the student is given training to increase speed.

e. Students are to record on a chart or graph the results of each test exercise. Keeping informed about progress is an important aspect of motivating students to realize their goals of increasing rate of reading and comprehension.

2. Select a passage and have students read the selection for one purpose, and then have them reread it for another purpose. Record the rate of reading and the comprehension level. If students were to use the same rate of reading for different purposes, whether it be fast or slow, it would be evident that they need to learn how to adjust their rate of reading. It is best to use materials other than the text for these exercises. Check students' comprehension with each exercise.

3. Use timed exercises. Select a passage of three hundred words to be read in one minute or less. Gradually use longer passages and expect greater speed. This can be expanded to include longer selections and books to be read in a designated time, such as five, fifteen, thirty or more minutes.

4. An adaptation of general rate training involving the scanning of paperbacks, as suggested by Berger (1972–1973), is another procedure that is profitable for use in a classroom.

   a. Students are to select a paperback that is easy to read or a paperback book they have read and would like to reread.

   b. Students are to read at their own pace for five minutes and record on a chart the average number of words per minute.

   c. Students are to read under time pressure at a skimming rate for each of the designated time intervals.

      (1) Skim eight seconds per page for two minutes.

      (2) Skim seven seconds per page for two minutes.

      (3) Skim the successive pages, each time reducing the reading interval by one second, until a page can be skimmed in two seconds.

      (4) Then spend two minutes skimming a page every ten seconds. At the end of each ten second interval, the student must turn the page and move on.

   d. Students are to continue reading for five more minutes at their own rate. The number of words per minute read during this five minute period is to be recorded on a chart.

   e. Students should then be allowed to read at their own rate for fifteen to twenty minutes.

5. Another version of practice reading under time pressure for skilled readers is as follows:

   a. Students select an easy-to-read story or novel.

   b. Students read eight pages using a finger pacing pattern.

   c. The students read the same eight pages using a finger pacing pattern at the rate of 12 seconds per page, three different times. Students record recall of the passage.

   d. The students read at the rate of six seconds per page for the fourth reading. Students record recall of the passage.

   e. The students read at the rate of four seconds per page for the fifth reading. Students record recall of the passage.

     f. A comparison is made of the three recorded recalls.

     g. This exercise can be expanded to include previewing and mapping techniques.

6. Still another exercise for general rate training that students can do without a teacher is the following:

     a. Students are to select a story from materials that are new to them.

     b. Students are to read the same selection for three or five, one-minute timed sequences. The stopping point for each reading is to be marked with a pencil. At the end of the exercise, the pencil marks are to be erased. A stop watch or a minute timer should be available for student use.

     c. Students are to select their fastest reading, count the total number of words read, and record the information on their charts.

     d. This exercise is to be repeated one to four tmes daily for several days or a few weeks. At regular intervals students should examine their reading habits to see if this exercise is helping them to improve their rate of reading.

Variations of these exercises for increasing reading rate should be prepared for student use at learning centers. Learning centers at both the elementary and secondary levels allow teachers the time to teach necessary skills, while the students themselves work independently on these rapid reading skills.

SUMMARY

A review of studies pertaining to flexibility and rapid reading shows that instruction in the adjustment of rates for different reading purposes should be included in basic programs at all levels. More emphasis on teaching these skills should be given at the middle school, high school, and adult levels.

The rapid reading techniques of skimming and scanning and the procedures of previewing and postviewing are necessary skills that should be taught in the content areas. Students who receive rate improvement training increase their reading speed and rate of comprehension. Teachers can develop exercises that can be used to help students increase their rate of reading. Able students can learn to read at extraordinary speeds with high levels of comprehension. However, trained personnel should teach speed reading to students.

Reinforcement Activity

Open this book to the next chapter. Time your reading for five minutes. How many words a minute did you read? How many ideas and relationships of these thoughts did you recall? If you decide your comprehension and rate of reading need to be improved, what procedures will you follow? How will doing this help you teach your students to increase their reading speed?

References

BARRUS, KIM B., and BROWN, BRUCE L. "Rapid Reading and the Transparency of Language." Study reported at the Third Annual Brigham Young University Reading Conference, 1977.

BERG, PAUL C. "Flexibility in Reading." In *Vistas in Reading*, edited by J. Allen Figurel, 1966 Convention Proceedings. Newark, Delaware: International Reading Association, 1967, 45–49.

BERGER, ALLEN. "Effectiveness of Four Methods of Increasing Reading Rate, Comprehension and Flexibility." In *Forging Ahead in Reading*, edited by J. Allen Figurel. 1967 Convention Proceedings. Newark, Delaware: International Reading Association, 1968, 588–596.

BERGER, ALLEN. "Increasing Reading Rate with Paperbacks," *Reading Improvement* 9 (1972–1973): 78–84.

BROWN, JAMES I. "Techniques for Increasing Reading Rate." In *New Horizons in Reading*, edited by John E. Merritt. Proceedings of the Fifth International Reading Association World Congress on Reading. Newark, Delaware: International Reading Association, 1976, 158–164.

BURMEISTER, LOU E. *Reading Strategies for Middle and Secondary School Teachers*. 2nd ed. Reading, Massachusetts: Addison-Wesley Publishing Company, 1978.

CARRILLO, LAWRENCE W., and SHELDON, WILLIAM. "Flexibility of Reading Rate." *Journal of Educational Psychology* 49 (1952): 299–305.

CARVER, RONALD P. *Sense and Nonsense in Speed Reading*. Silver Springs, Maryland: Revrec Publishing Company, 1971.

CARVER, RONALD P. "Toward a Theory of Reading Comprehension and Rauding." *Reading Research Quarterly* 13 (1977–1978): 8–63.

DAINES, HAZEN B., M.D. "Demonstration and Explanation of Eye Movements Used in the Reading Process." Salt Lake City, Utah, May 15, 1979.

EDFELT, AKE W. *Silent Speech and Silent Reading*. Chicago, Illinois: University of Chicago Press, 1960.

ERLICH, E. "Opinions Differ on Speed Reading." *National Education Association Journal* 52 (1963): 43–44.

GAARDNER, K. R. "Eye Movements and Perception." In *Early Experience and Visual Information Processing in Perceptual and Reading Disorders*, edited by F. Young and D. B. Lindsley. Washington, D.C.: National Academy of Sciences, 1970, 79–94.

GATES, ARTHUR I. *Teaching Reading: What Research Says to the Teacher*. Washington, D.C.: Department of Classroom Teachers and American Educational Research Association, for the National Education Association, 1953.

GRAF, R. J. "Speed Reading: Remember the Tortoise." *Psychology Today* 7 (1973): 112–113.

HAFNER, LAWRENCE E., and JOLLY, HAYDEN B. *Patterns of Teaching Reading in the Elementary School*. New York: The Macmillan Company, 1972.

HANSEN, DOROTHY. *A Discourse Structure Analysis of the Comprehension of Rapid Readers*. Doctoral Dissertation. Provo, Utah: Brigham Young University, 1975. Dissertation Abstracts International, 1976, 36(11)7293–A (University Microfilm No. 76–9839).

HARRIS, ALBERT J. "Research on Some Aspects of Comprehension: Rate, Flexibility and Study Skills." *Journal of Reading* 12 (1968): 205–210, 258–260.

HARRIS, ALBERT J., and SIPAY, EDWARD R. *How to Teach Reading*. New York: Longman, 1979.

HARRIS, THEODORE L. "Reading Flexibility: A Neglected Aspect of Reading Instruction." In *New Horizons in Reading*, edited by John E. Merritt. Proceedings of the Fifth International Reading Association World Congress on Reading. Newark, Delaware: International Reading Association, 1976, 27–35.

HENDERSON, EDMUND H. "A Study of Individually Formulated Purposes for Reading." *Journal of Educational Research* 58 (1965): 438–441.

HIMELSTEIN, H., and GREENBERG, G. "The Effect of Increasing Reading Rate on Comprehension." *Journal of Psychology* 86 (1974): 251–259.

JOBE, FRED W. *Screening Vision in Schools.* Newark, Delaware: International Reading Association, 1976.

JOHNSON, BEN E. *Learn to Rapid-Read.* Indianapolis: Howard W. Sams and Company, Inc., 1973.

KARLIN, ROBERT. "Machines and Reading: A Review of Research." *Clearing House* 32 (1958): 349–352.

KARLIN, ROBERT. *Teaching Reading in High School: Improving Reading in Content Areas.* 3rd ed. Indianapolis, Indiana: Bobbs-Merrill Educational Publishing, 1977.

KRONFELD, PETER C. *The Human Eye in Anatomical Transparencies.* Rochester, New York: Bausch and Lomb Press, 1943.

LABMEIER, ANGELA M., and VOCKELL, EDWARD L. "A Reading Development Course." *Reading Horizons* 13 (1973): 64–71.

MARCEL, TONY. "The Effective Visual Field and the Use of Context in Fast and Slow Readers of Two Ages." *British Journal of Psychology* 64 (1974): 479–492.

MCCONKIE, GEORGE W., and RAYNER, KEITH. "Identifying the Span of the Effective Stimulus in Reading: Literature Review and Theories of Reading." In *Theoretical Models and Processes of Reading*, edited by Harry Singer and Robert B. Ruddell. Newark, Delaware: International Reading Association, 1976a, 137–162.

MCCONKIE, GEORGE W., and RAYNER, KEITH. "An On-Line Computer Technique for Studying Reading: Identifying the Perceptual Span." In *Theoretical Models and Processes of Reading*, edited by Harry Singer and Robert B. Ruddell. Newark, Delaware: International Reading Association, 1976b, 163–175.

MCCONKIE, GEORGE W. "Stimulus Control in the Study of Reading." In *Reading: Disciplined Inquiry in Process and Practice*, edited by P. David Pearson and Jane Hansen. Clemson, South Carolina: Twenty-seventh Yearbook of the National Reading Conference, 1978, 206–211.

MCDONALD, ARTHUR S. "Research for the Classroom: Rate and Reading Flexibility." *Journal of Reading* 8 (1965): 187–191.

MCLAUGHLIN, HARRY G. "Reading at Impossible Speeds." *Journal of Reading* 12 (1969): 449–454; 502–510.

MILLER, LYLE L. "Speed Reading in the Seventies." *Educational Leadership* 30 (1973): 623–627.

MILLER, PHYLLIS A. "Considering Flexibility of Reading Rate for Assessment and Development of Efficient Reading Behavior." In *What Research Has to Say about Reading Instruction*, edited by S. Jay Samuels.

Newark, Delaware: International Reading Association, 1978, 72–83.

MOORE, GLADYS B. "To Buy or Not to Buy." *Journal of Reading* 13 (1970): 437–440.

MORASKY, ROBERT L. "Eye Movement as a Function of Adjunct Question Placement." *American Educational Research Journal* 9 (1972): 251–261.

MORRISON, IDA E., and OAKES, MARY LUCILLE. "The Effect of Skimming on Reading Achievement." *Abstracts, Fifteenth Annual Convention*, Newark, Delaware: International Reading Association, (1970), 59.

NEISSER, ULRIC. *Cognitive Psychology.* New York: Appleton-Century-Crofts, 1967.

OLSON, ARTHUR V., and AMES, WILBUR S. *Teaching Reading Skills in Secondary Schools.* Scranton, Pennsylvania: Intext Educational Publishers, 1972.

RANKIN, EARL F. *The Measurements of Reading Flexibility: Problems and Perspectives*, Newark, Delaware: International Reading Association, 1974.

SAILOR, A. LOUISE, and BALL, STEVE E. "Peripheral Vision Training in Reading and Speed and Comprehension." *Perceptual and Motor Skills* 41 (1975): 761–762.

SAMUELS, S. JAY, and DAHL, PATRICIA R. "Establishing Appropriate Purpose for Reading and Its Effect on Flexibility of Reading Rate." *Journal of Educational Psychology* 67 (1975): 34–43.

SINGER, HARRY, and DONLAN, DAN. *Reading and Learning from Text.* Boston: Little, Brown and Company, 1980.

SMITH, HELEN K. "The Development of Evaluation Instruments for Purposeful Reading." *Journal of Reading* 8 (1965): 17–23.

SMITH, FRANK. *Understanding Reading: A Psycholinguistic Analysis of Reading and Learning to Read.* New York: Holt, Rinehart and Winston, 1978.

SMITH, HENRY P., and DECHANT, EMERALD V. *Psychology in Teaching Reading.* 2nd ed. Englewood Cliffs, New Jersey: Prentice-Hall, Inc., 1977.

SPACHE, GEORGE D. "Is This a Breakthrough in Reading?" *The Reading Teacher* 15 (1962): 258–262.

STAUFFER, RUSSELL G. "A Magnificent Ambition." *The Reading Teacher* 14 (1960): 74, 92.

STAUFFER, RUSSELL G. "Speed Reading and Versatility." In *Challenge and Experiment in Reading*, edited by J. Allen Figurel. Proceedings of the International Reading Association, New York: Scholastic Magazines 7 (1962): 206–210.

STONE, DAVID R. "Reading Flexibility as Related to Levels

of Reading Complexity." In *Proceedings of the College Reading Association*, edited by Clay A. Ketcham. 6th ed. Easton, Pennsylvania: College Reading Association, 1965, 63–67.

SWALM, JAMES, and KLING, MARTIN. "Speed Reading in the Elementary School." *The Elementary School Journal* 74 (1973): 158–163.

TINKER, MILES A. *Bases for Effective Reading*. Minneapolis, Minnesota: University of Minnesota Press, 1965.

TINKER, MILES A. "Devices to Improve Speed of Reading." *The Reading Teacher* 20 (1967): 605–609.

TINKER, MILES A. "Devices to Improve Speed of Reading." *The Reading Teacher* 20 (1967): 605–609.

TROXEL, V. "The Effects of Purpose on the Reading of Expository Mathematical Materials in Grade Eight." *Journal of Educational Research* 55 (1962): 221–227.

WEINTRAUB, SAMUEL. "Factors Related to Reading Rates." *The Reading Teacher* 21 (1968): 663–669.

WITTY, PAUL. "Rate of Reading—A Crucial Issue." *Journal of Reading* 13 (1969): 102–106; 154–163.

WOOD, EVELYN N. "A Breakthrough in Reading." *The Reading Teacher* 14 (1960): 115–117.

Bibliography

BALDRIDGE, KENNETH P. *Seven Reading Strategies*. Greenwich, Connecticut: Baldridge Reading Instruction Materials, Inc., 1977.

BERGER, ALLEN, and PEBBLES, JAMES D., compilers. *Rates of Comprehension: An Annotated Bibliography*. Newark, Delaware: International Reading Association, 1976.

BRAAM, LEONARD. "Developing and Measuring Flexibility in Reading." *The Reading Teacher* 16 (1963): 247–251.

FLYNN, PEGGY. "Speed Is the Carrot." *Journal of Reading* 20 (1977): 683–687.

FRIEDMAN, MYLES I., and ROWLS, MICHAEL D. *Teaching Reading and Thinking Skills*. New York: Longman, 1980.

HANSEN, DOROTHY. "Correlations between Reading Out of Word Order and Current Linguistic Theory." Unpublished Master's Thesis. Provo, Utah: Brigham Young University, 1970.

HOFFMAN, JAMES V. "Developing Flexibility through Reflex Action." *The Reading Teacher* 33 (1979): 323–329.

JENSEN, POUL ERIK. "Theories of Speed Reading and Comprehension." *Journal of Reading* 21 (1978): 593–599.

MITCHELL, ADDIE S. "The Effects of Rate Training on the Academic Performance of Good Readers at the College Level." Unpublished doctoral dissertation, University of Chicago, 1965.

MOORE, WALTER J. "The Skimming Process in Silent Reading." In *Challenge and Experiment in Reading*, edited by J. Allen Figurel. Proceedings of the International Reading Association, New York: Scholastic Magazines 7 (1962): 203–206.

PIERCY, DOROTHY. *Reading Activities in the Content Areas: An Idea Book for Middle and Secondary Schools*. Boston: Allyn and Bacon, Inc., 1976.

SMITH, BRENDA G. "Speed Reading Scores in Perspective." *Journal of Reading* 19 (1975): 128–130.

SPACHE, GEORGE D. "Reading Rate Improvement—Fad, Fantasy, or Fact?" In *Improvement of Reading through Classroom Practice*, edited by J. Allen Figurel. Conference Proceedings. Newark, Delaware: International Reading Association, 1964.

STAUFFER, RUSSELL G. *Directing the Reading–Thinking Process*. New York: Harper and Row, Publishers, 1975.

THOMAS, ELLEN L., and ROBINSON, H. ALAN. *Improving Reading in Every Class: A Sourcebook for Teachers*. 2nd ed. Boston: Allyn and Bacon, Inc., 1976.

TINKER, MILES A. "Eye Movement in Reading." *Journal of Educational Research* 30 (1936): 241–277.

TINKER, MILES A. "Recent Studies of Eye Movements in Reading." *Psychological Bulletin* 54 (1958): 215–231.

TINKER, MILES A., and McCULLOUGH, CONSTANCE. *Teaching Elementary Reading*. 4th ed. Englewood Cliffs, New Jersey: Prentice-Hall, Inc., 1975.

WOOD, EVELYN N., and BARROWS, MARJORIE W. *Reading Skills*. New York: Henry Holt and Company, 1958.

8 QUESTIONING STRATEGIES

OVERVIEW

A great deal of learning takes place as teachers and students engage in discussions, with teachers asking those questions that will most effectively stimulate thought. Unfortunately, most of the questions asked in schools are not the kind that result in the higher levels of learning. Teachers must learn to ask the right questions if students are to learn all they are capable of, and it is to this purpose that this chapter is devoted.

QUESTIONING STRATEGIES play an important role in molding the quality of students' thinking. Questions can be used to help students process information; to examine their feelings, values, and attitudes; and to increase their depth of thinking. By the questions they ask and by guiding students in developing their questions, teachers can help students become critical processors and consumers of the ideas presented in subject matter materials. Classroom and study questions, like other learning activities, should lead students to develop autonomy of thought.

A teacher asks many questions during the school day as a way of directing the thinking and discussion of students. Nearly seventy years ago, Stevens (1912) found that a sample of high school teachers asked nearly 400 questions per day; a high percentage of those questions were of the recall type. In an analysis of the oral questioning activity of ten primary grade teachers, Floyd (1960) reported that they asked an average of 348 questions each during the school day. Fourteen fifth grade teachers each asked an average of sixty-four questions in a thirty-minute social studies lesson, according to Schreiber (1967). Guszak (1967) stated that students learn to adapt their way of reading to the types of questions they anticipate receiving from teachers. Guszak developed a Reading Comprehenson Question Response Inventory to describe the thinking modes required by teachers' questions. He determined that literal comprehension questions accounted for 70.4 percent of the questions teachers asked during reading lessons; many of these questions were classified as recall about minute facts. Hoetker (1968) found that junior high school English teachers ask a question every 11.8 seconds. In a low ability class the rate of questions rose to one every 5.6 seconds. At the high school level, Gallagher (1965) and Davis and Tinsley (1967) classified questions teachers asked gifted students and the questions of student teachers. More than half of the questions asked by both groups of teachers tested students' recall of facts. Gall (1970) suggested that teachers' questions emphasize the recall of factual information about three-fourths of the time, while students are required to think at higher levels about one-fourth of the time.

Several studies indicate that most teacher questions are posed at the literal level of comprehension. Fact or memory questions were preponderant in textbooks, according to Davis and Hunkins (1966). Sloan and Pate (1966) compared the questions asked by teachers of mathematics. They found that teachers of "new math" asked fewer recall questions and more higher level questions. Sloan and Pate suggested that the type of questions posed by teachers is greatly dependent on the type of curriculum materials available to them. Lanier and Davis (1972) stated that the largest proportion of questions included in teacher manuals are of the recall type. In a study conducted by Pfeiffer and Davis (1965) it was found that teachers use more fact questions than other kinds of questions in ninth grade social studies examinations. In a study reported by Hogg (1973), 87 percent of the questions asked by student teachers were factual. Too many teachers pose questions that ask for the mere recall of text based information, according to Allington and Strange

What purposes do questioning strategies serve?

What kinds of questions are most frequently asked?

(1980, pp. 196–197), who maintain that this type of question does not require an understanding of the content.

THE IMPORTANCE OF HIGHER LEVEL QUESTIONS

What is the value of higher level questions?

Teachers communicate their expectations of students through the questions they ask. Yet the findings of research indicate that the greater number of teachers' questions are at the fact or memory level. The findings also show that a slight increase in higher thinking questions posed by teachers yields higher thinking responses by students.

Gallagher and Aschner (1963) reported compatability between the level of teachers' questions and students' responses. Even a slight increase in the percentage of higher thinking questions yields a definite increase in higher thinking by students and encourages responses from several students to the same question. Taba (1964 and 1965) cited a high relationship between the levels of comprehension that students exhibit in their answers and the types of questions teachers ask. She too found that a slight increase in higher thinking questions posed by teachers yielded more divergent and evaluative responses by a greater number of students. The research of Parson and Shaftel (1967) found that the types of questions teachers ask are established early in their teaching career. They also stated that teachers find it difficult to formulate higher level questions. Ladd and Anderson (1970) investigated the level of questions in discussions and the effect these questions have on students' achievements, and concluded that the teachers' questioning behavior strongly influences students' achievements. A group of sixth grade students who were consistently asked high level questions produced significantly greater scores in social studies achievement than students who were asked only low level questions, according to Hunkins (1968 and 1974). Schafer (1975) found that the most frequent type of question asked by teachers sought the recognition or recall of factual information. Lucking (1976) found that adolescent students make more responses of interpretation to their reading of short stories when teachers are trained to ask hierarchically arranged questions that stimulate higher cognitive processes. In another study, Smith (1978) found that both second and fourth grade children formulate substantially longer average communication units in responding to interpretive questions than they do with factul questions. Smith also found that students from both the elementary and secondary grades average a higher number of words when answering higher cognitive level questions, compared to the number of words in responses to lower cognitive questions.

Teacher expectations of students should differ and be evident in the composition, sequencing, and pacing of questions, since the variable of differences among learners affects questioning strategies. This variable includes such differences as high and low abilities, different cultural backgrounds, different ways of perceiving and organizing information, different backgrounds of experiences and understanding, and different ages and stages of maturation and intellectual development. Questions can be devised to individualize instruction and meet the various needs of all these students (Singer and Donlan 1980). Comparative questions help students with different cultural backgrounds contrast their own experience with ideas presented in selections and books (Turner 1979). Limited research indicates that more literal level questions might be used to guide the thinking of students with limited reasoning abilities (Medley 1977). The unique differences among gifted students should also be accommodated: questions and other learning activities should be geared toward the higher levels of thought processes (Kaplan 1979).

The simplest way to learn something is to ask a question about it. Yet it was not until 1956 that Bloom and his associates introduced a hierarchical taxonomy for the cognitive domain. Later a taxonomy for the affective domain was presented by Krathwohl and his associates (1964). Since Bloom's and Krathwohl's works, many cognitive and affective systems for asking questions to improve students' reading comprehension have been devised (Sanders 1966, Taba 1967, Cunningham 1971, Hunkins 1972, Ruddell 1974, Carin and Sund 1978, and Aulls 1978). These taxonomies are based on the cognitive processes assumed necessary to ask and answer questions. The categories of each taxonomy proceed in order from the lowest levels of thinking to the highest levels. There are both simple and complex questions within each classification. The taxonomies are constructed as hierarchies, with each category subsuming and building upon each preceding category. It is thought that a certain kind of question will then elicit or lead to the same kind of thinking. However, all learners do not necessarily use the same processes to answer a question, nor does a question always lead to a single kind of thinking.

Effective questioning often includes questions from both the cognitive and affective domains. The purpose for reading, the concepts and values presented in content materials, and the background of students influence the combination and number of cognitive and affective questions asked in any learning situation. Fundamental to improving questioning techniques is learning how to classify them.

COGNITIVE DOMAIN QUESTIONS

The systematic use of questions assists students in reaching a higher level of understanding. Two taxonomies that serve this purpose are the Four-Step Question System and the Six-Step Question System. The question system of four sequential steps is based on the work of Taba (1967). Bloom's research (1956) serves as a foundation for the six-step question classification system.

Thought matures through a progressive and active organization and

How can questions be presented to students to help them achieve higher levels of thinking?

reorganization of the conceptual structures. When students receive information, they fit it into the conceptual schema they currently possess. Each instructional step ought to require a little more learning than did the preceding one, whether it be a centering or expanding function. Each increase in learning needs to be a challenge beyond what students can do at a given time, yet not so far beyond their current skills as to hinder their progress. Learning experiences that challenge students to apply what they have learned in one context to a new context are the most effective. Furthermore, each new learning experience should serve as a basis for the performance required in the subsequent one. This continuity implies that differences among groups as well as among individuals can be accommodated by providing challenging learning experiences within the reach of all students. These experiences should proceed from the concrete to the more abstract, with reinforcement being provided at certain points.

Although the sequence moves from the known to the unknown, from the concrete to more abstract reasoning in information processing, the same amount of time need not be spent on each level of a classification system. The initial questions depend on students' readiness and background in regard to the topic being studied. Possibly the most important difference among students is the varying amount of concrete thinking experience each needs before higher cognitive thinking can emerge.

Basic concepts are interwoven throughout subject matter content, and specific facts serve to develop these main ideas. Such facts are not significant in themselves; the function of such facts is to explain, illustrate, and develop main ideas. Thus, a specific knowledge of facts should serve as a foundation for the higher cognitive level questions. The major tasks a teacher faces in using any questioning strategy are to determine the students' level of knowledge about a topic, anticipate potential difficulties, and recognize when to proceed from examining specific facts to higher levels of thinking.

Continuous diagnosis of pupil performance is essential for effective teaching, and questions at a lower level can serve this function. The teacher can discover the content background of students and decide whether anything needs to be done to increase their base level of information. Throughout the study of the text, the teacher needs to assess the students' understanding and use of thought processes and products before deciding the adjustments to make, the procedures to follow, and when to progress to higher levels of thinking and activities.

Determining in advance the main ideas to be developed in a chapter or unit and the facts that will facilitate the development of these concepts are important teaching strategies. The inclusion of plans as to the skills and understanding to be developed at the other thinking levels will help facilitate the success of the learning experiences. Even though such questioning strategies have been planned, adjustments should be made to accommodate the needs of students.

Four-Step Question System

The plan of categorizing questions into a four-step sequence uses an inductive process of interpreting data. Regardless of the source of the content, whether it be a story, a film, an article, or a chapter in textual material, the procedure is to lead the students through a sequence of questions, from the facts through an analysis of relationships to the verbalization of abstractions that can be logically supported by data. When teachers use the questioning strategy of proceeding from one level to succeeding higher levels of thought, students clarify and extend their comprehension of ideas. This hierarchical process of using questions helps to focus the students' thinking from the simpler and more concrete information to the more complex structures.

What steps does the four-step question system involve?

Taba (1967) relied heavily on the teaching of Piaget for her research in questioning strategies. She stated that cognitive growth is related to the developmental level of the learner. Cognitive development follows a sequence in which simpler and more concrete information precedes and prepares the learner for more complex and abstract knowledge. Piaget views intelligence as the building of experiences on each other, forming ever more complex structures. Concrete operational thought, for example, must be mastered before formal symbolic thinking is possible. These sequences operate not only in cumulative maturing of thought through the years, but also in mastering a specific aspect of thinking. It seems that the knowledge of facts, trends, and terminologies is a prerequisite for functioning at higher cognitive levels of thinking (Piaget 1954, Taba 1967, Honstead 1968, Elkind 1974, Wadsworth 1978, and Duckworth 1979).

In this system, the questions are classified into four hierarchial categories identified by Taba and placed into a sequential pattern. The categories are (1) open questions, (2) focusing questions, (3) interpretive questions, and (4) capstone questions. This model of asking questions can be used many times a day, in every subject, and at any grade level.

Open Questions   Asking open questions is the first step in this model. The objective is to elicit specific relevant facts that will serve as a base for responding to higher cognitive level questions. Sufficient time should be taken to achieve this objective without dragging responses out of students. Facts should be pursued on the same level when more information is needed before proceeding to the next level of questions and discussion. Clarification should be requested when necessary.

"What did you see take place in this experiment?"

"What happened after that?"

"How did the people secure their food?"

"What evidence is there of trade?"

Focusing Questions   In the second step, questions should center students' attention on the specific facts or ideas considered to be significant. The question should specify both the process and the topic. For example, "Let's list all the fruit that grows in this valley," establishes the topic as that of fruit grown in a local valley and the process of enumeration from recall. The teacher or students might seek or give additional information and provide elaboration on or clarification of information already provided.

> "What two things did Josh do when Ben reached the cliff overhanging the river?"
>
> "Describe how Ben managed to join his father and the other riders."
>
> "List the ingredients that were added to the compound."
>
> "Tell what happened when heat was applied to the liquid."

After this task is accomplished, the teacher is to paraphrase the relevant information elicited from the students. The teacher also should check to determine if they are satisfied with the paraphrased statements.

Interpretive Questions   Interpretive questions are asked as the third step. Students are to explain the relationships the teacher considers important for them to understand about facts, issues, and events. In interpreting data, the procedure is to explain and elaborate on the information sought in the first and second steps.

> "How do you account for the differences between Ben and Josh?"
>
> "In what way did Ben emulate his father?"
>
> "In what ways are the two compounds similar?"
>
> "Compare the market value of the two compounds."
>
> "Explain why the one substance is of greater use in the colder regions than in the hot, tropical countries."

When students have wandered from the subject or deviated from the focus, a teacher is to restate or refocus on the original relationship question. Young students need frequent refocusing. A question should be rephrased if it isn't understood. The questions should broaden students' patterns of thinking.

Capstone Questions   The objective of the fourth and concluding step is to move the class discussion to the verbalization of an abstraction. Such a question is to complete the discussion by asking for a conclusion, prediction, evaluation, or generalization. Known facts about the topic being discussed serve as a basis for a response to a capstone question.

> "What would you predict happened to Josh as a result of these incidents?"
>
> "Evaluate the story by using this set of criteria."
>
> "What conclusion might you draw from these findings?"

The figure below depicts how the higher level categories build on the preceding classifications.

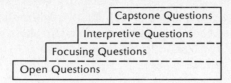

Four-Step System for Formulating Questions

Six-Step Question System

Bloom and associates (1956) presented a taxonomy in the cognitive domain as a basis for classifying educational objectives; it is one of the best known examples of logical analysis of the cognitive areas. They defined a number of intellectual processes and placed them into six major categories and subcategories. The Six-Step Question System is based on Bloom's taxonomy.

What steps does the six-step question system include?

The six sequential steps of this system consist of (1) knowledge, (2) comprehension, (3) application, (4) analysis, (5) synthesis, and (6) evaluation. The taxonomy is constructed as a hierarchy, with each category encompassing and building upon each preceding classification. That is, the category of comprehension includes knowledge, application comprises comprehension and knowledge, and so on. Evaluation, the highest cognitive level in the system, embodies all preceding categories or levels. The lower levels of thinking serve as a base for the higher and more complex levels. This taxonomy can be used in all content areas and at any grade level.

Knowledge   Answering knowledge level questions places emphasis on recall or memory processes. Thinking and responding at this level necessitates that readers be aware of and understand basic information. Responses are usually predictable because they are restricted to the information stated in expository materials. The knowledge level of questions includes the recall of: specific facts, terminology, trends and methods, specific ideas, principles, theories, and generalizations. For example:

"What is the second step to follow in performing this experiment?"

"What has been the growth of inflation during the past ten years?"

"List the criteria to follow when assessing programs presented during prime time television."

"What are the reasons for adjusting and fitting commercial patterns?"

"List the ways the community workers help us."

"At what temperature does water freeze?"

"Which of the following statements on the relationships between our diet and health is true?"

"In which classifications did you place these leaves?"

Comprehension   Questions in the comprehension category focus on the students' knowing what is being expressed in the literal message contained in a communication. This is a common level of thinking emphasized in our schools. Responses to such questions include (1) the translation of a message into another form of communication, (2) an interpretation of interrelationships among major ideas, and (3) the extension of ideas to make an inference or prediction.

"In your own words, tell what is depicted in the graph."

"Make a flow chart that describes the movements of fresh produce to the market."

"Contrast the American newspaper policies with that of Russia."

"Explain how the plot of this play is similar to what exists in our family relationships today."

"Examine this picture and tell what you think the story will be about."

"Examine these statistics of the migration of people in the United States and this map showing the location of proposed water projects. Tell where the greatest concentration of people will be living within the next twenty years."

Application   At the application level, students are expected to use previously acquired knowledge and comprehension of ideas to solve problems in new or unique situations. Comprehending an idea does not indicate that an individual will apply it correctly. Apparently there needs to be the opportunity for practice to develop this level of thinking or skill. Providing for achieving the level of application is an important aspect of curriculum planning and evaluation. Responses to questions at the application level require students to use their information and understanding to solve problems.

"Study the map of Magic Valley. Illustrate where you would locate a dam on the Snake River and indicate the reasons for the site you choose."

"Examine the barley plants in this experimental plot and demonstrate what you need to do to improve the growth conditions of the plants."

"Illustrate a light spectrum."

"Determine the drainage capacity of this soil. Indicate whether deciduous or evergreen trees would thrive better in the soil."

"John knows how much money he earned in four weeks. Demonstrate how he would find his average weekly earnings."

"Read this passage and identify all words classified as adjectives."

Analysis   Analysis emphasizes the breaking of given information or materials into parts. Analysis serves to develop greater comprehension as a prelude to independent thinking and evaluation of the material. Responses to questions at the analysis level require (1) an analysis of elements or parts, (2) the analysis of relationships, (3) an analysis of arrangements or organization, and (4) the determination of cause and effect.

"Analyze what caused the dam to break and tell how the disaster changed the lives of people living in the lower valley."

"From our discussion about human rights, relate the three basic assumptions that might be accepted."

"Analyze the idea of instant voter registration and discuss the major problems that might be encountered."

"Explain how these data support your hypothesis."

"Listen to this musical selection and distinguish where and how the melody is repeated."

"Examine Mike's painting. How did he relate the colors to express feelings of happiness?"

"Read these advertisements and determine how the words are used to influence the consumer."

Synthesis   Synthesis is the opposite of analysis—it is the placing of parts together to form a whole, a combining of parts in such a way as to form a pattern not clearly evident before. This is the category that provides for divergent or creative thinking. The students are expected to work within the limits set by the particular problems or materials. There is greater emphasis at the synthesis level on drawing upon elements from many sources and putting them together into a pattern or product that is more than they started to work with. Freedom from constraints and time to create are important elements in this category of thinking. Responses at the synthesis level are expected to include (1) the production of a unique communication, (2) the production of a plan or proposed set of operations, and (3) the derivation of a set of abstract relations.

"Write an essay telling why 'America is Great.' "

"Compose a musical selection to accompany this narration."

"Write a story to tell what happened to you during the expedition down the Salmon River."

"Use these specifications to design a house that would conserve energy."

"Hypothesize what you consider to be the reasons for the differences in the growth patterns of the animals."

"Analyze these factors and then formulate a hypothesis to test the use of this medication in treating acne."

"Plan a way you might divide these shapes into groups that are alike."

Evaluation   Evaluation is considered to be the most complex part of the taxonomy. It is regarded as requiring, to some extent, all the other categories. Evaluation is not necessarily the last step in problem solving. The evaluative process may in some situations be a prelude to seeking new knowledge, comprehension, application, a new analysis or synthesis. Evaluation involves the making of judgments about ideas, solutions, methods, and values. When judgments are made it is expected that the responses will be based either on internal or external standards (or criteria).

"Review the appeal the commissioner made for the need of enlarging the library. Judge the effectiveness of his case."

"Defend the urban renewal project."

"Evaluate the effectiveness of this lunch program by using the school district criteria."

"We devised standards as a guide for an effective class discussion. Evaluate today's discussion using these standards."

"Justify the banishment of James Reed from the Donner Party according to the available facts."

The figure below shows the sequence of the six categories of the cognitive domain question system. Each category subsumes the preceding levels and extends beyond the performance of each foregoing category.

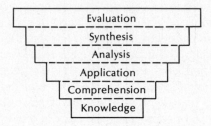

Sequence of the Six-Step System

AFFECTIVE DOMAIN QUESTIONS

What are affective domain questions, and what role should they play in teaching?

The affective domain deals with interests, attitudes, values, and appreciations that relate to intellectual knowledge and understanding. Students' feelings affect their learning, and their understanding affects their feeling and behavior. Questions in the affective domain are used in all subject areas, although they receive more emphasis in music, literature, writing, speech, drama, and social studies. Although less is known about affective education than cognitive learning, classroom discussion allows students and teachers to react to what they experience in the content areas.

It is anticipated that a teacher will employ questions during a discussion to help students clarify their values. Instructional procedures that promote the internalization of values include:

1. Using real issues and situations for students to consider.
2. Alternating concept and value questions with students.
3. Providing alternative choices when students are to make a selection.
4. Allowing enough time for students to consider alternatives and responses to higher affective domain questions.
5. Helping students develop criteria to evaluate their reactions to a situation.

6. Providing sufficient worthwhile experiences to help students form a cluster and pattern of attitudes.
7. Helping students to be pleased with and to support their choices.

Students, too, must have opportunities to pose affective questions. Therefore, their involvement in a discussion is crucial. Students need to learn how to examine their own questions and the questions of others, to examine their own values and the beliefs of others, and to accept the universalities and diversities they encounter. To achieve these ends requires attentive listening, sharing of thoughts, and making choices. It also means that students need to learn to support their reactions to affective questions with articulated rationales.

Teachers should be significant adults in the life of students if affective education is to be an active force in their learning. This means that a teacher must listen with understanding to the feelings of students, respect their ideas and concerns, give them encouragement and assistance when needed, and demonstrate confidence in them. Also needed are an environment in which high interest materials are provided to stimulate thought and sufficient time to experiment with information. To achieve these ends requires considerable planning and preparation on the part of teachers.

Both affective and cognitive classification schemes consist of arbitrary categories established for the convenience of researchers. The separation of these domains is not intended to suggest that they actually exist separately. Affective behaviors, particularly those elicited by motivation, influence achievement in the cognitive area: students who have clear values enjoy a more purposeful and favorable attitude toward learning in the content areas. This relationship between affective and cognitive learning is an important element in planning and using questions in the curriculum areas. In practice, questions based on these two classification systems are interwoven and often build on each other.

Affective Domain Question System

In the affective domain researched by Krathwohl and associates (1964), all levels of the system have a cognitive component, and the cognitive categories contain affective components.

Their affective domain taxonomy is a classification system that can be used to deal with questions about interests, attitudes, values, and appreciations. They placed the affective behaviors into five broad hierarchical categories and subcategories. The Affective Domain System for asking questions is based on these categories; it consists of (1) receiving, (2) responding, (3) valuing, (4) organizing, and (5) characterizing by values. Each category builds on the preceding classification. This continuum of levels to describe the range of affective behavior is ordered from the simple to the complex.

What is the affective domain question system?

Receiving At this, the lowest level, the students are to be willing to receive or attend to a fact, occurrence, event, or incident. This behavior can vary from merely being conscious of a phenomenon to a controlled awareness of a stimulus. Awareness, which appears to be cognitive behavior, is necessary for learning at this and the other levels. Background experience may either facilitate or hinder the learning. Responses to questions at the level of receiving require students (1) to be aware of a phenomenon, and (2) to notice and attend to a task.

"These are pictures of key leaders in the community. Tell me their names."

"If you had a free day, which of the following activities might you do? Consider each activity carefully and indicate your choices by placing a check in the appropriate column."

	Yes	Uncertain	No
1. Read a book.			
6. Visit a friend.			
10. Play tennis.			
14. Watch television.			
18. Take a nap.			
21. Go for a walk.			
27. Go surfing.			

"We are interested in your opinions regarding the following thirty statements about music. Please indicate your interests by placing a check mark (√) in the appropriate column to indicate your response."

	Like	Indifferent	Dislike
1. To sing Irish folk songs.			
8. To compose counterpoint songs.			
16. To use tones of syncopated patterns.			
20. To sing two part harmony.			
24. To sing patriotic songs.			
28. To hear melodies based upon minor scales.			
30. To experiment with tone inversions.			

Responding The concern at this level goes beyond being attentive to a situation. At this stage or level, students are doing something with or about a stimulus. This reaction can vary from complying with a suggestion without fully accepting the need for doing so, to feeling satisfaction or enjoyment with it. Students are expected to respond with (1) compliance to a situation or

"Read each statement and place a checkmark on the line that indicates what you do."

Always	Sometimes	Never

1. ⊢————————⊥————————⊣
Read class assignments.

3. ⊢————————⊥————————⊣
Complete homework assignments.

7. ⊢————————⊥————————⊣
Submit assignments on time.

13. ⊢————————⊥————————⊣
Check my work before submitting it.

18. ⊢————————⊥————————⊣
Use library resources to complete my assignments.

20. ⊢————————⊥————————⊣
Tutor other students in their assignments.

task, (2) voluntary willingness to comply, or (3) satisfaction or enjoyment derived from completing the task.

Invite the students to brainstorm a list of free time activities. Afterwards, write the list on paper and ask them to indicate their choices by using the following letters.
A. I would like to build this into my life style; or, I have already added this to my way of life.
B. I would like to know more about this activity.
C. I would not like to participate in this activity.

_____ 1. Tutor students who are having reading problems.
_____ 2. Participate in singing duets or trios.
_____ 7. Coach Little League football.
_____10. Volunteer time at the school for mentally retarded children.
_____15. Participate in more intramural sports.
_____21. Attend a career day conference.
_____30. Earn a life-saving certificate.
_____42. Join a cycling club.

"Respond to the unfinished sentences as quickly as you can. Write in the blank spaces the first idea you think of."
The use of sound in John Huston's *The African Queen* suggests _____.
The satire in *The Man in the White Suit* makes me _____
_____ .

The silent comedies of Charlie Chaplin, Harold Lloyd, and Buster Keaton are
_____ .

In Michelangelo Antonioni's *L'Avventura*_____

_____.

The use of irony in Fred Zinnemann's *The Search* is _____

_____ .

Valuing Students' behavior at this level is consistent with and motivated by values. The influences for these values can exist outside the school as well as in the classroom. Valuing can vary from subscribing to the worth of an object or situation, to the willingness to be identified with a value, to displaying consistent commitment to a value and trying to convince others. Students' responses at this level range from (1) accepting a value (2) showing a preference for a value, and (3) demonstrating a commitment for a value.

> "Explain why, as a result of attending the city council meeting, you became convinced that city zoning is a problem."

> Place a check anywhere along the line toward the word that indicates how *YOU* feel about music."
>   Rock music is:
>   Ohhh _____•_____•_____•_____•_____•_____ ugh
>   Pop music is:
>   exciting _____•_____•_____•_____•_____•_____ noisy
>   Folk music is:
>   lively _____•_____•_____•_____•_____•_____ boring

> Ask students to react to different hypothetical situations, such as: "What would you do if you saw a man snatch a woman's purse in the parking lot of a neighborhood store?"

> Select editorials on the same subject. Ask the students to read the editorials and to identify the views with which they agree or disagree. After they have individually made this selection, invite them to defend their beliefs.

LEARNING TO DRAW WELL
"Describe any action you have taken on the following activities."

1. Practicing three-dimensional drawings.
3. Making realistic drawings.
5. Using geometric forms.
7. Making stylized drawings.
9. Showing contrast in form and color.
10. Adding animation to landscapes.

COMMITMENT TO PRACTICE

1. Demonstrate your change in backhand swing since last season.
2. Show how many successful serves out of 25 you can make.
3. Illustrate how you can place the backhand stroke in the area of the court you desire.
4. Tell how often you win the game.
5. Exhibit what you did to improve your forehand stroke.

Organization   At this level, students are required to organize their values in two ways. First, to reach a decision or make a judgment about a situation, students need to make abstractions and generalizations about a value they hold. Second, in situations where more than one value is relevant, students will find it necessary to organize their values by determining the interrelationships among the values and to identify those that are more dominant in their own behavior. This is a gradual process, and it can be modified as other values are intensified or as new values are incorporated into their intellectual schema. These response requirements range from conceptualizing values to organizing them into an ordered relationship.

> After studying the musical works of your favorite composers of pop music, select and record the melodies that recur throughout the work of the composer you like best."

> For an exercise in organization, present a complex issue, such as mining shale oil, to the class. Let the students seek further information and opinions about the issue. Ask them to write generalizations to support their values related to the issue in preparation for a group discussion.

> Research the impact the MX System will have on the region in which it is located in relation to job opportunities, environmental problems, and community changes. Determine which of these factors you consider to be the most and least important.

A higher level of thought within this category might be achieved by bringing together a complex of values into an ordered relationship. For example:

> "Weigh the pros and cons of offering immediate citizenship to all immigrants."

Characterization by a Value   At this level, the students' values are internalized and characterized by consistent behavior. Behavior characterization ranges from attitude clusters to a total philosophy of life. Behavior is related to the attitude clusters rather than to the subject or object of the attitude, and thus students' behavior is usually predictable. Seldom does a teacher have a direct role in developing this highest level of affective behavior. Responses to questions posed at this level only give indications of the overall outlook of students, rather than a precise characterization. Students' responses at this level reveal a consistency in their approaches to problems, as well as a total value system.

Social attitudes might be assessed by posing a realistic problem to the students.

> "Lani is a recent refugee in this country. The teacher has assigned her to sit by you. What will you do?"
> ———— Include her in your activities.

_____ Ignore her because she can't speak English very well and her mode of dress is strange.

_____ Ask your friends to be nice to her.

Ask students to review their reactions to a hypothetical meeting and think how they might help solve the problem. For example:

"The school principal called a meeting of the student council. He informed them that the younger students are being prevented from participating in group games. He asked them to come prepared the next morning to discuss ways of resolving the problem. How should the student council react to this request?"

"Cathy has been nominated as chairman of the school social committee. Jim plans not to involve himself in school activities because of his feelings about Cathy. What are your feelings about the matter?"

In helping students move toward characterization that might become a part of their philosophy of life, the teacher should ask questions that require them to probe their feelings about ideals and conscience. For example:

"Explain your goal in life."

"What is your relationship to your family? your friends?"

"What is your responsibility toward the community slogan of preventing litter?"

The figure below shows the sequences of the five categories of the affective domain question system. Each category subsumes the preceding levels and extends beyond the performance of each preceding category.

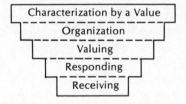

Sequence of the Affective Domain Question System

SUMMARY

Teachers ask far more fact or memory questions than higher cognitive questions. However, teachers' questions at higher cognitive levels can serve as an effective way of guiding students' responses toward similar levels of thinking. Affective questions are an integral part of value clarification and increasing comprehension in the content areas. Although in reality the cognitive and affective domains cannot be divided into isolated areas of learning, questions can serve to emphasize particular levels of thinking within both domains.

Systems for classifying questions into higher cognitive and affective levels were presented in this chapter. The use of such systems can improve teachers' questions, elicit higher level responses, and stimulate involvement by students.

Reinforcement Activities

1. Choose a section of a textbook and develop plans for improving the questioning strategies. Write the cognitive and affective questions that are necessary to supplement those listed in the textbook.

2. Plan a series of questions in the cognitive and affective domains to use in guiding a classroom discussion about a topic of interest.

References

ALLINGTON, RICHARD, and STRANGE, MICHAEL. *Learning Through Reading in the Content Areas*. Lexington, Massachusetts: D. C. Heath and Company, 1980.

AULS, MARK W. *Developmental and Remedial Reading in the Middle Grades*. Boston: Allyn and Bacon, Inc., 1978.

BLOOM, BENJAMIN, ed., ENGLEHART, M.D., FURST, E. J., HILL, W. H., and KRATHWOHL, D. R. *Taxonomy of Educational Objectives: The Classification of Educational Goals Handbook I: Cognitive Domain*. New York: Longmans, Green and Company, 1956.

CARIN, ARTHUR, and SUND, ROBERT B. *Creative Questioning and Sensitive Listening Techniques: A Self-Concept Approach*. Columbus, Ohio: Charles E. Merrill Publishing Company, 1978.

CUNNINGHAM, ROGER T. "Developing Question-Asking Skills." In *Developing Teacher Competencies*, edited by James E. Weigand. Englewood Cliffs, New Jersey: Prentice-Hall, Inc., 1971, 81–130.

DAVIS, O. L., and HUNKINS, FRANCIS P. "Textbook Questions: What Thinking Processes Do They Enter?" *Peabody Journal of Education* 43 (1966): 285–292.

DAVIS, O. L., and TINSLEY, D. C. "Cognitive Objectives Revealed by Classroom Questions Asked by Social Studies Student Teachers." *Peabody Journal of Education* 45 (1967): 21–26.

DUCKWORTH, ELEANOR. "Either We're Too Early and They Can't Learn It or We're Too Late and They Know it Already: The Dilemma of Applying Piaget." *Harvard Educational Review* 49 (1979): 297–312.

ELKIND, DAVID. *A Sympathetic Understanding of the Child: Birth to Sixteen*. Boston: Allyn and Bacon, Inc., 1974.

FLOYD, W. D. *An Analysis of the Oral Questioning Activity in Selected Colorado Primary Classrooms*. Doctoral Dissertation, Colorado State College. Ann Arbor, Michigan: University Microfilms, 1960, No. 60–6253.

GALL, MEREDITH D. "The Use of Questions in Teaching." *Review of Educational Research* 40 (1970): 707–721.

GALLAGHER, JAMES. "Expressive Thought by Gifted Children in the Classroom." *Elementary English* 42 (1965): 559–568.

GALLAGHER, JAMES, and ASCHNER, MARY JANE. "A Preliminary Report on Classroom Interaction." *Merrill-Palmer Quarterly of Behavior and Development* 9 (1963): 183–194.

GUSZAK, FRANK J. "Teachers' Questions and Levels of Reading Comprehension." In *Perspectives in Reading: The Evaluation of Children's Reading Achievement*, edited by Thomas C. Barrett. Newark, Delaware: International Reading Association, 1967, 97–109.

HOETKER, J. "Teaching Questioning Behavior in Nine Junior High School English Classes." *Research in the Teaching of English* 2 (1968): 106–109.

HOGG, JAMES H. "Development of Verbal Behavior through Cognitive Awareness Training." *Journal of Educational Research* 67 (1973): 9–12.

HONSTEAD, CAROLE. "The Developmental Theory of Jean Piaget." In *Early Childhood Education Rediscovered*, edited by Joe L. Frost. New York: Holt, Rinehart and Winston, Inc., 1968, 132–145.

HUNKINS, FRANCIS P. "The Influence of Analysis and Evaluation Questions on Achievement of Sixth Grade Social Studies." *Educational Leadership Journal, Research Supplement* 25 (1968): 326–332.

HUNKINS, FRANCIS P. *Questioning Strategies and Techniques*. Boston: Allyn and Bacon, Inc., 1972.

HUNKINS, FRANCIS P. "What to Ask and When." *Yearbook of the National Council on Social Studies* 44 (1974): 146–148.

KAPLAN, SANDRA N. "Language Arts and the Social Studies Curriculum in the Elementary School." In *The Gifted and the Talented*. Eighty-seventh Yearbook of the National Society for the Study of Education, edited by A. Harry Passow. Chicago: University of Chicago Press, 1979, 155–168.

KRATHWOHL, DAVID R., BLOOM, BENJAMIN, and MASIA, BERTRAM B. *Taxonomy of Educational Objectives: The Classification of Educational Goals. Handbook II: Affective Domain*. New York: David McKay Company, Inc., 1964.

LADD, GEORGE T., and ANDERSON, HANS O. "Determining the Level of Inquiry in Teachers' Questions." *Journal of Research in Science Teaching* 4 (1970): 395–400.

LANIER, RUBY J., and DAVIS, ANITA P. "Developing Comprehension through Teacher-Made Questions." *The Reading Teacher* 26 (1972) 153–157.

LUCKING, R. A. "A Study of a Hierarchically-Ordered Questioning Technique on Adolescents' Responses to Short Stories." *Research in the Teaching of English* 10 (1976): 269–276.

MEDLEY, DONALD M. *Teacher Competence and Teacher Effectiveness: A Review of Process-Procedure Research*. Washington, D.C.: American Association of Colleges for Teacher Education, 1977.

PARSON, THEODORE W., and SHAFTEL, FANNIE R. "Thinking and Inquiry: Some Critical Issues." In *Effective Thinking in the Social Studies*, Thirty-seventh Yearbook of the National Council for the Social Studies, edited by Jean Fair and Fannie R. Shaftel. Washington, D.C.: National Council for the Social Studies, 1967, 123–166.

PFEIFFER, L., and DAVIS, O. L. "Teacher-Made Examinations: What Kind of Thinking Do They Demand?" *National Association for Secondary School Principals Bulletin* 49 (1965): 1–10.

PIAGET, JEAN. *The Construction of Reality in the Child*. Translated by Margaret Cook. New York: Basic Books, 1954.

RUDDELL, THOMAS. *Reading-Language Instruction: Innovative Practices*. Englewood Cliffs, New Jersey: Prentice-Hall, Inc., 1974.

SANDERS, NORRIS M. *Classroom Questions: What Kinds?* New York: Harper and Row, 1966.

SCHAFER, PAUL J. "Effective Use of Questioning." *Reading World* 15 (1975): 226–229.

SCHREIBER, J. E. *Teachers' Question-Asking Techniques in Social Studies*. Doctoral Dissertation, University of Iowa. Ann Arbor, Michigan: University Microfilms, 1967, No. 67–9099.

SINGER, HARRY, and DONLAN, DAN. *Reading and Learning from Text*. Boston: Little, Brown and Company, 1980.

SLOAN, F. A., and PATE, R. T. "Teacher-Pupil Interaction in Two Approaches to Mathematics." *The Elementary School Journal* 67 (1966): 161–167.

SMITH, CHARLOTTE T. "Evaluating Answers to Comprehension Questions." *The Reading Teacher* 31 (1978): 896–900.

STEVENS, R. "The Question as a Measure of Efficiency in Instruction: A Critical Study of Classroom Practice." *Teachers College Contributions to Education* No. 48, 1912.

TABA, HILDA. "The Teaching of Thinking." *Elementary English* 42 (1965): 534–542.

TABA, HILDA. *Teacher's Handbook for Elementary Social Studies*. Palo Alto, California: Addison-Wesley Publishing Company, 1967.

TABA, HILDA, and ELZEY, F. F. "Teaching Strategies and Thought Processes." *Teachers College Record* 65 (1964): 524–534.

TURNER, THOMAS N. "Comprehension: Reading for Meaning." In *Teaching Reading*, edited by J. Estill Alexander. Boston: Little, Brown and Company, 1979, 132–148.

WADSWORTH, BARRY J. *Piaget for the Classroom Teacher*. New York: Longman, Inc., 1978.

Bibliography

ATHENY, IRENE. "Reading Research in the Affective Domain." In *Theoretical Models and Processes of Reading*, edited by Harry Singer and Robert B. Ruddell. Newark, Delaware: International Reading Association 1976, 352–380.

BARRETT, THOMAS C. "The Barrett Taxonomy: Cognitive and Affective Dimensions of Reading Comprehension." In *Innovation and Change in Reading Instruction*, edited by Helen M. Robinson. Sixty-seventh Yearbook of the National Society for the Study of Education, Part II. Chicago: The University of Chicago Press, 1968, 7-29.

BURNS, PAUL C., and ROE, BETTY D. *Teaching Reading in the Content Areas.* Chicago: Rand McNally, 1980, Chapter 4.

CROWELL, DORIS C. and AU, KATHRYN HU-PEI. "Using a Scale of Questions to Improve Listening Comprehension." *Language Arts.* 56 (1979): 38–43.

CROWELL, DORIS C., and AU, KATHRYN HU-PEI. "A Scale of Questions to Guide Comprehension Instruction." *The Reading Teacher.* 34 (1981): 389-393.

HAUPT, EDWARD J. "Writing and Using Literal Comprehension Questions." *The Reading Teacher.* 31 (1977): 193–199.

HERBER, HAROLD L., and NELSON, JOAN B. "Questioning is Not the Answer." *Journal of Reading.* 18 (1975): 512–517.

HILL, P. W., and McGRAW, B. "Testing the Simplex Assumption Underlying Bloom's Taxonomy," *American Educational Research Journal*, 18 (1981): 93–101.

OLMO, BARBARA. "Teaching Students to Ask Questions." *Language Arts.* 52 (1975): 1116–1119.

McGAW B., and GROTELEUSCHEN A. "Directions of the Effect of Questions in Prose Materials." *Journal of Educational Psychology.* 63 (1972): 580–588.

ROTHKOPF, E. Z., and BILLINGTON, M. J. "Indirect Review and Priming Through Questions." *Journal of Educational Psychology.* 66 (1974): 669–679.

VACCA, RICHARD. "Questions and Advance Organizers as Adjunct Aids: Implications for Reading Instruction in Secondary Schools." In *Secondary Reading: Theory and Application*, edited by C. Smith and L. Mikulecky. Bloomington, Indiana: School of Education, 1978, 47–77.

9 STRATEGIES FOR PROCESSING INFORMATION

OVERVIEW

In addition to teaching reading and studying skills, teachers can improve students' abilities to learn in the content areas by helping to sharpen other, related skills as well. This chapter is devoted to such instruction and includes materials dealing with questioning, discussing, listening, and group processing—each of which is shown to be critical to students' intellectual development. Useful suggestions for employing this instruction in the classroom are given.

READING STRATEGIES, an integral part of helping students learn the content of text materials, include: (1) questions to guide students' reading of a selection or chapter, (2) directed reading activities and study guides, (3) the involvement of students in asking their own questions, and (4) questions in classroom discussion. Some techniques are structured and teacher directed; others rely largely upon student creativity. The strategies are designed to teach students with varying abilities and readiness to learn from the same or different texts.

Why are reading strategies important?

The teacher has a responsibility to present meaningful reading assignments and to provide postreading activities. In addition to teacher directed lessons, active student involvement in posing questions is necessary if learning is to be meaningful. Attaining higher levels of thinking is fostered when students are guided in their reading and encouraged to develop skills in asking questions. It is also necessary to give them ample opportunities for dialogue with their peers and teachers to share, clarify, and extend ideas derived from reading content materials. The use of grouping patterns, a component of classroom management, will facilitate reading strategies to help students learn from text.

What are the teacher's responsibilities?

QUESTION TYPE AND PLACEMENT

Educators believe that higher level questions lead students to higher levels of thinking. Questions are considered to be instructional tools for helping students process textual information and for facilitating classroom discussions. However, the effects of questions on the learning are not fully known or understood.

What are the various types of questions, and how do their purposes differ?

Questions given to students before they read a passage are called prequestions. Questions inserted into the text are called adjunct questions, and postposed questions are questions that follow a passage. A study about the use of prequestioning procedures was conducted by Wiesendanger and Wollenburg (1978) with third grade students. According to their findings, third grade students scored lower in comprehension than students not provided with prequestions. However, among the students given prequestions, inferential type prequestions produced higher scores in reading comprehension than when factual questions were asked.

Higher order questions used as an adjunct instructional aid direct students' attention to additional pertinent information. Processing more information enables elementary, secondary, and college students who answer higher order questions to recall more on posttest performance. This direct attention effect was found in the studies conducted by Frase (1967), Frase, Patrick, and Schumer (1970), Rickards (1976), Rickards and DiVesta (1974), and Rickards and Hatcher (1977–1978). When students are given adjunct questions at the application level about concepts and principles, their ability to solve problems involving these concepts and principles is enhanced, whereas adjunct factual questions do not have this effect. Also, postposed questions lead students to review the passage, and, as a result, they recall additional information (Watts and Anderson 1971). According to Heller (1974) adjunct questions narrow the focus of attention, and when preposed and postposed questions are provided for the students, the focus of attention is even more sharply limited: students read or reread only to answer specific questions.

What is the value of placing questions throughout a selection?

Placing frequent questions throughout a selection tends to improve students' retention of relevant information. Koran and Koran (1975) explored differences in question placement. Three different patterns of question placement were used with college students enrolled in a teacher education course. Some questions were inserted after each page, some every four pages of the text, and some passages contained no questions. Posttest analysis showed that retention increased with question insertion. Rickards and DiVesta (1974) state that questions inserted after every two paragraphs led to a higher verbatim recall of the passage than when questions were asked after every four paragraphs. Higher level questions encourage students to read the passage more carefully, thereby resulting in greater recall.

McKenzie (1972) conducted a study related to weekly quizzes that required students to either recall information or make inferences about specific content. Eight weeks later the students took a posttest. The students given inferential quizzes did better than students provided with factual quizzes.

The effect of the types of questions asked on the immediate and delayed retention of text material by college students was investigated by Rickards (1976). Verbatim postquestions that required literal recall of specific information resulted in greater retention than prequestions. However, the higher level cognitive prequestions that required abstraction of the topic or of the overriding concept produced higher recall. The learning and recall generated by the conceptual prequestions deteriorated less over time than those engendered by verbatim postquestions. The conceptual prequestions apparently resulted in topically related materials becoming interrelated and organized around a structure of concepts or ideas. This technique aided long term retention of passage information.

In a similar study by Zeaman and House (1967), which dealt with the positioning of questions, adjunct or interspersed questions were presented at crucial points in the text, usually where a major topic concluded and a new topic was introduced. If necessary, information relevant to answering the questions could be reread, or the student could answer the questions and continue reading. These procedures were an improvement over simply asking factual prequestions or postquestions.

Andre (1979) suggests that students process information related to questions, and not other material. Only when questions lead the students to process information in ways they would not otherwise have done will questions influence their learning and retention of text materials. Andre contends that questions can influence students by changing their perceptions of a task and the strategies they need to use in completing the task.

Gall and associates (1978) found that a teacher's use of recitation or discussion is more significant than whether he or she used particular levels of higher cognitive questioning or the technique of probing or redirecting students' answers to questions. They also showed that recitation or discussion procedures used as a postreading activity stimulate better (1) acquisition and retention of content, (2) ability to listen and respond orally to higher level questions, and (3) ability to respond in writing to higher cognitive questions.

DIRECTED READING ACTIVITY

The Directed Reading Activity (DRA) is a lesson plan designed to help students successfully read basal readers and content materials at their instructional level rather than at the frustration or independent levels. The DRA usually consists of five steps that include pre- and postreading activities related to a particular assignment. These procedures familiarize students with the material before they actually read it, and opportunities are then provided for students to confirm or pursue ideas in follow-up activities. The DRA can be used with an individual student, a group of students, or an entire class.

The DRA is a structured and basic technique planned and guided by a teacher. In contrast to an unstructured assignment, in which students are asked to read a passage without a specific purpose, the teacher directs students how to read a selection. This systematic approach to instruction has five steps (Karlin 1975, pp. 259–262, and 1977, pp. 117–127; Dillner and Olson 1977, pp. 140–150; Burmeister 1978, pp. 94–100; Estes and Vaughn, Jr., 1978, pp. 140–142; Harris and Sipay 1979, pp. 79–81; and Singer and Donlan 1980, pp. 50–54.

How can the DRA help teachers in the content areas?

Preparation for Reading The first step is to prepare the students for reading an assignment, by (1) relating students' previous learning and past experiences to the topic of the passage or chapter, and (2) teaching key words that carry the concept load.

Presenting the key concept words and building students' backgrounds in relation to the topic are vital aspects of preparing for reading the assigned material. Preparing students for reading specific text material motivates and helps them to understand and retain what they read. Readiness is developed by using techniques such as word analysis, word meanings, lesson reviews, pictures, objects, and films.

Purposes for Reading Purposes, the second step, provide guidance in how and why to read a specific selection. This step uses the previewing technique of SQ3R or prequestions written by a teacher, or differentiates purposes according to the needs of students.

When a teacher has specific expectations of students, such as determining the relationship of ideas or the cause and effect of an action, or the explanation and use of a mathematical theorem, prequestions are posed as the purposes. With the previewing technique of SQ3R the teacher and students ascertain their own goals by using the process of prediction. Suggesting the rate at which to read the specific assignment is also appropriate.

Silent Reading   Silent reading of the selection is the third step. Students are to read the chapter after the completion of steps one and two, during subsequent class periods, or as a homework assignment for older students. Alternatively, the teacher can select appropriate places in the selection for oral reading and discussion by students between periods of silent reading.

Students are to read only after they have been prepared for the assignment. Students who lack the skills to read content material might, as an alternative, listen to a tape on which the text is recorded. Involvement in the readiness procedures and listening to the assignment prepares poor readers to participate in the discussion and follow-up activities.

Follow-Up Activities   After the students have read the assigned text, they are to react to the information, as the fourth step. The purposes for which the content were read serve as the focal point for their responses.

A useful way for students to respond to the content they have read for specific purposes is through discussion, which is an important postreading activity. During a discussion, students have opportunities to clarify and extend ideas and to become involved in convergent and divergent thinking. Students might clarify and verify their individual responses by reading orally from the text while others listen. Drawing pictures and diagrams or writing about the ideas read are other ways students might respond. It is important for a teacher to observe students' understandings of the material in follow-up activities. If it seems necessary, the teacher should provide further instructions and study.

Expansion Activities   The fifth step is to provide opportunities for students to expand their comprehension of the ideas learned. They might extend their understanding by doing further reading, research, an individual or group project, or creative activities related to the information read.

Expansion activities usually require students to engage in higher levels of thinking. Previous teacher instruction and activities in the DRA serve as a foundation for students to extend their learning. Students should have a choice of activities according to their interests, experiences, and abilities. In addition to the expansion activities planned by the teacher, students might make their own suggestions.

DIRECTED READING-THINKING ACTIVITY

The Directed Reading-Thinking Activity (DR-TA) was originated by Russell Stauffer (1969) as a method for directing students' questions and thinking about narrative and expository materials. The strength of this strategy is that students learn to set their own purposes for reading by utilizing the process of prediction. This opens the way for students to establish a dialogue between themselves and the author as they reason and prove or disprove their predictions while reading the text.

What are the benefits of the DR-TA?

An active search for meaning in the reading of expository materials is best fostered when students are encouraged to search for information to answer their own questions. Self-posed questions or purposes create a perplexity in the reader's mind which finding the answers resolves. It is through this process of seeking answers to their purposes that students improve their reading comprehension (Hoskisson 1973 and Stauffer and Harrell 1975).

The DR-TA is an effective way of teaching critical thinking skills to students of all ages. The DR-TA is used effectively with students whether their instructional levels in reading are above, at, or below a particular grade level. It's an effective method for above grade level readers (Petre 1970). The DR-TA may be used with individual students, small groups, or a whole class. Even without prior experience using the DR-TA, students tend to make responses that represent higher levels of thinking (Davidson 1970).

A critical reader needs to use three refined skills. First is the ability to ask relevant questions or to set a purpose for reading. The second skill is to read to process information. The third skill required is that of validating answers. These three objectives are the fundamentals of the DR-TA. The procedures to follow in achieving these objectives are those developed by Stauffer (1969, 1975, and 1980):

1. Students who have approximately the same reading level are grouped together for instruction.
2. Group sizes range from eight to twelve students in the elementary grades, to part of a class or a whole class at the secondary levels.
3. Students are to read the same material at the same time.
4. Purposes for the reading are to be established by the students.
5. Answers to questions must be discussed to be validated.
6. The teacher poses provocative questions and serves as a catalyst.
7. The teacher arranges an environment conducive to group interaction and cohesiveness.

Establishing Purposes Establishing purposes for reading is the most important part of the DR–TA. Individual or group questions or predictions serve as a reason for reading the unfamiliar material. A teacher facilitates this step by posing a question such as, "What do you think this chapter (article, story) with a title (pictures, illustrations, or diagrams) like this might be about?" Or, "Based on your knowledge of the subject, what information do you expect to find in this passage?"

The teacher's task is to elicit many diverse respones from students to serve as a foundation for their involvement. When students raise questions about a passage it keeps them on a progressive course as they read the material.

Processing Information   After the students formulate the initial questions or predictions, they silently read to a particular place in the material specified by the teacher. The material provides information for a dialogue about the questions and predictions previously set by the students. In addition to the dialogue, this process provides motivation, interest, and sufficient information for students to continue the process of posing questions and anticipating outcomes. They read to process information and to search for evidence to confirm or reject their earlier expectations.

A teacher selects appropriate places throughout the selection for students to stop their reading to continue the dialogue and to pose new questions. The teacher helps to facilitate this process by asking such questions as "What do you think now?" or "Why do you think that?" or "Have you ever experienced that before?"

Validating Answers   Proving or disproving predictions will challenge the readers to find proof or reasons to substantiate their ideas. The question "Why do you think so?" when asked by the teacher at strategic times in the dialogue affords students the opportunity to give proof or to alter their ideas. This is an opportune moment for teachers to have students reread orally passages that support their answers. This culminating step of the DR–TA helps students accept or reject a hypothesis based on available evidence rather than merely labeling an idea correct or incorrect.

Validating answers is a process of logical thinking. Students are to seek answers and find proof for their ideas. Dialogue is considered an important way to validate answers, and immediate feedback helps to develop a regard for authenticity. Proof that answers have been found in part or completely may be presented by oral or written reporting.

Advantages of DR–TA

When students use the DR–TA they are immediately involved in a discovery process because of their own purposes or questions. This procedure provides motivation for posing and seeking answers to questions, it focuses attention on the next event or concept, and it continually requires the students to reanalyze and synthesize the facts in order to hypothesize what will happen next. This frequent posing of and responding to higher level questions by students as they read encourages greater understanding of the material.

The DR–TA gives the teacher fewer guidelines to follow than the DRA.

The DR–TA is a flexible procedure that allows a teacher to accommodate the needs and interests of students. The teacher serves as a catalyst posing questions that extend beyond the literal level and helping motivate students to use divergent thinking.

A more structured version of the DR–TA questioning technique was utilized with learning disabled students by Schwartz and Sheff (1975) To start with, questions concentrated on one or two sentences at the beginning of a passage. The material covered was gradually increased from paragraph to paragraph as the students became more competent in asking and responding to questions. The students were guided in posing divergent questions and problems as they reasoned and read in the text to verify their ideas.

STUDY GUIDES

The wide range of reading levels and skills among students, and the heavy concept load contained in textual materials, are of concern to teachers. Study guides are written to help students deal with the acquisition of information from text. They may be written for individual or group instructional situations, for advanced readers, or for students with reading problems.

How can teachers use study guides to improve students' abilities to read?

A study guide is a plan for students to follow as they read a text. By providing a study guide, a teacher can direct students' attention to the important concepts explained in the selection and provide the purposes for a particular reading assignment. The guide is usually a typewritten copy of directions telling students what to read and the tasks to complete to help them process and comprehend the information. A guide can be designed to lead students to find facts, definitions, patterns, main ideas, and cause and effect relationships. A number of statements, questions, or problems can be posed for the students' reaction and completion; references on where to find the information may or may not be provided by the teacher, depending upon the reading and study skills of the students. In some instances, the students can be directed in surveying the information. Afterwards, they are to ask their own questions and read to answer them.

Before preparing a study guide, a teacher must read the text and decide what information is important, and what tasks students must complete to comprehend the selection. To be effective, a guide is written for a specific lesson and group of students. A teacher writes the guide to help students reach higher levels of thinking as they process their textual materials.

Study guides are part of a total lesson framework, and prereading preparation should precede the use of them. Building background, preteaching key concept words, and setting purposes prepares students to process information as they follow study guides. (Poor readers, of course, need more prereading instruction than good readers.) When the technique of using a study guide is new to students the teacher should guide the class through the completion of a guide. Instead of an individual student always working alone on a study guide, small groups of students can work together to complete the guide.

The length of the assignment should vary. Deciding how much structure to provide in a study guide requires that a teacher consider the competencies of the students, the purposes of the assignment, and the difficulty of the materials. Varying the amount of direction helps the students to complete an assignment successfully. This effect might be achieved by constructing a guide with questions and problems to answer that represent more than one level of comprehension, and by providing page and paragraph numbers as location aids.

Teachers may wish to use study guides in postreading activities. Class discussion serves as an important way for students to clarify and extend ideas gleaned through their independent study. Research, experiments, summary writing, small group discussion, individual or group projects, and additional reading are other postreading expansion activities.

Many types of study guides can be prepared to direct students as they read content materials. Singer and Donlan (1980, pp. 60–105) suggest that teachers prepare "reading guides and learning-from-text guides." The reading guides focus on reading skills. A plan that helps students understand new and difficult terms is an example of this type of study guide. Such a vocabulary guide would require students to define and apply the meaning of technical words as determined by context. Learning-from-text guides focus on the thinking skills. The model is a three level taxonomy. The authors suggest that the teacher construct the guide with the highest level statements first, and work backwards to the level of factual information. The facts are to support the inferences, interpretations, and generalizations. Other models usually follow a hierarchical order of working from the lower to higher levels of thinking.

Herber (1978, pp. 47–158) suggests developing guides that lead students from lower to higher levels of thinking, on the grounds that students need to master understanding at the lower level before proceeding to the next higher level. The teacher is to determine the concepts and level of understanding to be achieved by the students.

Two types of study guides are recommended by Tutolo (1977). One procedure includes statements that are at the literal, interpretive, and applicative levels of thinking. The questions at each level are grouped together and are not intermixed. The students are to answer the questions by proceeding from the lower to higher levels. The other type of guide does not include a hierarchical placement of statements. The students are not expected to sequence their thinking from lower to higher levels.

Another procedure, the Selective Reading Guide-O-Rama, was developed by Cunningham and Shablak (1975). The purposes of this study guide are to lead students step by step to ideas in a reading assignment that are considered important to the teacher, and to guide students in developing flexiblity of reading rate. The students are directed to look for specific information and what to do when found, such as to state the facts necessary to solve the problem. Guidance is given to help students develop flexibility of reading rate by telling them when to skim, scan or read carefully. For example, the students are told to read a passage quickly to get an overview of the information. Four sample study guides are presented. They are designed to help students increase their vocabulary and reach higher levels of thinking. Questions are used to direct students' attention to specific words, to make comparisons, determine cause and effect, make inferences, make applications, analyze situations, and to make judgments. This structured approach is more suited to students who need assistance in developing selected skills.

Study Guide
"The Sculptor's Funeral"

Directions: Read the story "The Sculptor's Funeral" by Willa Cather. Afterwards, respond to the questions below, and be prepared to justify your responses in a class discussion.

1. Notice the way Willa Cather relates ideas incidental to action in the story. Each element reinforces the other. List the ways a setting for the story is developed.
2. Reread the description of the Merrick house. How does the house reflect the reader's impression of the family and the town?
3. How did the characters of the Merrick family affect the life of Harvey Merrick?
4. Were you surprised that Jim Laird seemed to understand Merrick's aims in life? Why would he have been sympathetic to Merrick?
5. Do you feel the tongue-lashing delivered by Laird to the mourners was justified? Or was it as onesided as the mourners' comments about Merrick? Justify your answer.
6. In the story, Jim Laird states, "You hated Harvey Merrick more for winning out than you hated all the other boys who got under the wheels." Is this an expression typical of human nature? Be prepared to discuss the meaning of this statement as it relates to Merrick and to people you know.

Study Guide
"The Landlady"

Directions: On page 212 of the text is the short story "The Landlady," by Roald Dahl. Refer to the story for clues that will help you define the words listed below.

1. Word   Definition   Sentence in which word occurs
façades (p. 213)

dithering (p. 214)
compulsion (p. 216)
tantalizing (p. 221)

2. How did the author reveal the character of the landlady?
3. At what point in the story did you become aware of the landlady's intention? When did Billy become suspicious of the landlady?
4. How does Roald Dahl prepare the reader for the outcome of this story? Reread the story and list these clues.
5. Be prepared to discuss your opinion of Billy's fate, and whether the author's ending of the story was an advantage or disadvantage?

Study Guide
"Jacksonian Era"

Section A: Background

Directions: Chapter 12 deals with the Jacksonian period of early America. Many Americans joined organizations or movements for social and economic reforms. Although the Jacksonian period was idealistic, it was also practical. It was a period of expansion, economic opportunity, and drive for material gain. People moved about seeking a better advantage in industry, agriculture, transportation, communication, and land. Answer the following questions.

1. When did your ancestors come to the United States?
2. What was the reason your ancestors came to this land or moved west?
3. Did your early ancestors receive a public education in the United States?
4. What kind of work was available to your ancestors?
5. Did your ancestors seek to open new territory and to clear and own some of the land?
6. How do you think you might have felt about moving and coming to a strange land if you had lived at the time of your early ancestors?

Section B: Vocabulary

Directions: Look at the following words and write a one sentence meaning of each word as used in the text.

1. reformers (p. 276, col. 1, paragraphs 1 and 2)
2. free public schools (p. 268, col. 1, paragraphs 2 and 3)
3. feminists (p. 271, col. 1, paragraphs 1 and 2)
4. temperance movement (p. 274, col. 1, paragraph 1)
5. revivalist movement (p. 277, col. 1 paragraphs 2 and 3)
6. nationalism in American literature (p. 279, col. 2, paragraphs 1 and 2)

Section C: Patterns

Directions: After reading chapter 12, review the material to answer the following questions.

1. List the groups demanding and opposing free public schools for all
   people. In each case give the reasons for the demands.
2. What progress in education was achieved by 1860?
3. Explain why many women felt they were victims of political, social
   and economic discrimination during the Jacksonian period.
4. Compare the temperance movement with present state laws pertaining to this topic.
5. Provide examples of religious toleration and obstacles evident during
   the Jacksonian period.
6. Compare Americans today with Americans of the Jacksonian period
   in reference to their optimism about America and their practical
   spirit and progress.
7. Prove, by example, how Cooper stressed American scenes and themes
   in his novels.
8. Write a Chamber of Commerce brochure that could have been used
   by one of the larger cities to attract new citizens. Use research as a
   basis for the information.
9. Defend the need to make "America perfect" during Jackson's time.
10. Justify the contributions toward the building of America you consider
    were the most important during the Jacksonian period.

Study Guide
"The Consumer and Food Buying"

Directions: Answer the following questions as you read Chapter 8, "The Consumer and Food Buying."

1. Prices of fresh fruit change throughout the year. Examine the chart
   on page 98 and determine if there is a supply cycle that has a similar
   pattern each year. Where does a consumer find this information?
2. Why shouldn't shoppers consider everything in a food ad as a good
   buy?
3. List four ways menu planners might lower the food budget and still
   serve well-balanced meals.
4. Compare the kind of convenience foods that save both time and
   money with convenience foods that cost extra.
5. How can a family obtain needed protein and spend less money on
   meat?
6. Examine the labels of the three brands of canned stew on the table.
   Identify the ingredient that has the most weight in each brand.

7. Make a list of ten menu items that will reduce spending money on meat.

8. Examine the table on page 112 and determine which meat would cost the least per serving and the most per serving if all meats were selling for $1.00 per pound on tomorrow's special.

9. Check the food ads in today's newspaper for information on foods that are currently in plentiful supply and are good buys. Use this information to prepare menu plans for one day that (1) include as many of these items as possible, and (2) meet the nutritional needs of each of your family members.

INVOLVING STUDENTS IN QUESTIONING

How can students be better involved in questioning?

Students' readiness for and interest in an assignment help to determine what they will learn. Attaining higher levels of thinking is fostered when students are encouraged to develop the skill of asking their own questions and when they are given ample opportunities for dialogue with their classmates, as well as with teachers with whom they can share and clarify ideas derived from their reading.

In addition to questioning strategies to guide and manage what is learned and how it is learned, effective teachers help students ask and answer their own questions. Asking a question that gets a question in response is another way of involving students in asking questions (for example, showing a picture of a manned spaceship and asking the students what they would like to know about the model).

Although the questions teachers ask serve as models for students, students should receive specific instruction on how to ask their own questions. A question is the seed of inquiry, and students' learning is enhanced by becoming involved in the generation of questions that will help them process information, by emphasizing their purposes, and their interaction with the text (Singer 1980). Questioning models that include involvement and interaction between students and between the teacher and students can be used for this purpose. Each model differs in the amount of teacher direction and in the time required to complete the questioning and responding sequence.

Ortiz Model

Ortiz (1977), using herself as an experimental subject, determined through introspection that when she asked questions she really understood what she had read. She asked questions more frequently at the very opening of a book or passage than later on. Ortiz also discovered that when she had to read something of no initial interest to her, she acquired an interest by forcing herself to ask questions. And she asked better questions as she became aware of these processes. After reflecting on this information, Ortiz used various situations and activities to focus students' attention on the amount and variety of information they could learn by posing their own questions. The students also discovered that it was better to pose their own questions at the moment they found an idea obscure than to read to the end of the selection and not understand what they had read. The following activities, similar to those suggested by Ortiz, will help students learn to ask questions.

1. Write the first sentence of a short story, article, or chapter on the chalkboard. Have students ask or write at least ten questions (fewer for younger students) about the sentence. Afterwards, have them read the selection and be prepared to tell or write which, if any, of their questions were answered.

   Not all of the questions should be at the recall level. Posing many questions about one sentence almost guarantees that several higher cognitive level questions will be included. However, initial teacher modeling of the procedure will help students ask questions beyond recall level.

2. Choose a short nonfiction passage. Ask students to pose questions for the first sentence of every paragraph. Then have them write or give oral answers to the questions after reading each paragraph.

   It is important that students assess their understanding of each paragraph before they proceed with the task.

3. Select an exciting short story or a nonfiction article. Direct the students to read it silently; observe whether they ask questions and if so, the types of questions posed. Direct the students to place a checkmark (√) by the part they ask questions about. Let them react to the story.

   This procedure can be used with younger students. Read a selection to them. Let students ask questions as the story is read. Or stop reading in the middle of an exciting part and observe the students' questions.

4. Distribute to each student a comic strip or an editorial cartoon from which the words have been deleted. Ask them to determine the story or message by looking at the pictures and to pay particular attention to the things they ask themselves in the process. When they have finished, let them share their questions and the processes used in completing the task.

   The purpose of this activity is to center students' attention on asking questions and the pocesses they used in posing them.

5. Provide pictures or photographs for each student, or show a large picture, diagram, or chart to the entire class. Ask them to pose or write as many questions as they can about the object. Let students spend a few minutes sharing questions. Then let them write a description or story by using their questions as a basis for the activity.

   The focus in this exercise should be placed on the questions and how they lead to answers.

6. Instruct students to write as many questions as they can about a particular social issue or new scientific discovery. Afterwards, they are to answer their questions by writing a letter to the editor, an essay, or a research paper, or by preparing to debate the issue. They should consult a source other than themselves.

Using questions to obtain and share information that might influence the thinking of other people is the object of this exercise. This activity can be completed individually or as a group, and it can be done orally with younger students.

ReQuest Model

The ReQuest Questioning procedure was developed by Manzo (1969, 1979). The basic function of the procedure is to help students set their own purposes for reading after reacting intensively to the first sentences or paragraphs of a selection. The procedure uses reciprocal questioning between the teacher and students. The teacher listens to students' questions and builds on them until the students can set a purpose or prediction of what is going to happen in the remainder of the selection. This model can be used with one student in a conference or with a small group. It is suitable for use with students in kindergarten through college and with remedial reading students. The procedure can be used with either a reading passage or a picture.

Students are told that the purpose of the lesson is to improve their understanding of what they are to read. Then they are asked to read silently the first sentence. The students and teacher take turns asking questions about the first sentence and what it means. The students ask the first questions and are encouraged to ask questions a teacher might ask. The students are to ask as many questions as they wish while the teacher's book is closed. All questions are answered as fully as possible. If there is uncertainty about an answer, the responder should refer to the text. If questions are unclear, requests for rephrasing or clarification are permissible.

After the teacher has answered all the students' questions, the students close their books. The teacher asks as many questions as he or she deems necessary to add to the students' understanding of the content. Throughout this time the teacher is attempting to serve as a model for asking questions that are at the higher cognitive levels and are thus thought-provoking.

Having finished questioning students about the first sentence, the teacher may pose questions that integrate ideas with those expressed in prior passages or assignments. Students are encouraged to follow this same procedure.

ReQuest is continued until students can provide a reasonable answer to the questions. "What do you think is going to happen in the remainder of this selection?" "Why do you think that will happen?" "What have you read that allows you to think that?" After students respond to these questions, the teacher tells the students, "Read to the end of the paragraph (or selection) to see if your ideas were right." After the students have finished reading the designated material, the teacher should direct a very brief dialogue about the accuracy of their predictions. A teacher may select a follow-up activity related to the selection and to the needs and interests of the students.

Hunkins Model

A commonly asked question is, "How do I get my students involved in planning their questions to process information effectively?" Hunkins (1976) believes that this happens when teachers believe in the process, provide time, and present activities for students to develop the necessary skills. Hunkins has presented a model to involve students in questioning strategies.

Students are to plan questions, implement the plans, and assess the activities when they pose and answer questions. These operations are interrelated and facilitate the processing of information.

1. Planning consists of preparing for a particular situation. In this strategy it consists of:
   a. Determining the types of questions one should ask in an inquiry.
   b. Assessing the function of the questions.
   c. Developing a system for the use of questions in the inquiry.
2. Implementing refers to the ways the plan or activities are to be used. Students utilize their plans or question strategies to:
   a. Process information.
   b. Gain greater or new understanding of concepts.
   c. React to questions and responses as they read or in dialogue with classmates and the teacher.
   d. Generate additional questions for further inquiry when deemed necessary.
3. Assessing consists of students evaluating and judging the effectiveness of their own questions and procedures. Students assess their plans and activities by:
   a. Developing skills to assess their questions.
   b. Obtaining feedback on their effectiveness of processing of information.
   c. Evaluating or judging the accuracy or usefulness of the information learned.
   d. Deciding what changes, if any, need to be made in their plans or activities based on their utilization of the process.

Elementary and secondary students need to experience situations in which they plan, use, and assess their questions. It is important that students learn to deal with high level cognitive and affective questions. Within each category of a question taxonomy, the questions can range from easy to difficult. For example: An easy high level question might be, "Sample this food. Determine if it has been cooked sufficiently by using this criterion of taste." A more difficult lower cognitive level question might be: "State the procedures to be followed in the impeachment of a government official."

There is an array of ideas for providing students the opportunities for producing questions, using questions to gain information, and assessing the questioning activities. For example, Hunkins's suggestion of brainstorming question-types encourages students to produce a myriad of questions relating to a particular topic of a lesson. They are to list the queries that come to their minds without trying to decide if the questions are good or bad or to determine their cognitive level. After about ten or fifteen minutes the students share their questions about the topic. Questions can be organized by intent or by cognitive level. The teacher can guide this procedure without instructing students about details of the cognitive and affective levels of comprehension.

Checking question preference is another planning activity. To conduct this activity, the teacher provides time for students to generate ten questions they would like to ask about a particular topic. Then the students are asked to order the questions from the most important to the least important. After producing the questions, the students consider why they gave the ranking they did, and they judge whether such ordering was productive for formulating conclusions. After the students generate questions through brainstorming and ordering of questions from the most important to the least important, the next steps are the actual use of these questions in gaining information from textbooks and assessing the questions.

In addition to reading materials to answer questions, students might use questions to:

1. Ask a visiting resource person.
2. Investigate a key issue in mini-groups.
3. Create games to improve question and questioning skills.

Students might assess their use of questions by:

1. Evaluating their questions according to specified standards.
2. Developing a checklist to consider their affective responses to questions.
3. Analyzing the questions they pose in classroom and out-of-school activities.

DISCUSSION

What are the benefits of discussions?

Small group or whole class discussion is a way for students and teachers to share and exchange ideas from different points of view, focus on and clarify information, and solve problems in relation to a specific topic. This open minded search is based on questions posed by the students, a teacher, or both.

Student interaction is an important aspect of a discussion. Interaction occurs when students ask questions and take part in dialogue with classmates and/or the teacher about the questions they pose, and when the conclusions they derive from the information are evaluated. Student involvement in a discussion results in a higher proportion of higher cognitive and affective levels of thinking. Student led discussions create a higher proportion of student participation in asking questions and in divergent and analytic thinking. Furthermore, teacher or student led discussions allow the teacher to observe students' skills is posing and answering questions and whether they can seek and understand meanings of ideas at a variety of levels.

The core for interaction consists of the questions posed. Thus, understanding and using questioning strategies is fundamental for conducting an effective discussion. A teacher's questions during a discussion can stimulate concept learning. This experience is lost when a barrage of answers are provided for students who have not been involved in asking questions. When students prepare for discussions and ask questions, these problems are reduced. Small discussion groups provide for more interaction among the students. Any of the questioning strategies presented in this chapter might serve as the basis for small group or total class discussion. The initiating question might be posed by a student or by the teacher. There are two different approaches to using levels of questions in a discussion.

The method more often advocated is the hierarchical order of questioning. This strategy begins a discussion with lower cognitive level questions before proceeding to higher cognitive level questions. The purpose of this procedure is to provide a base of information upon which other questions and responses might be built and elaborated upon. This plan relies on an inductive approach to processing information and involving students in a productive discussion. Thus there will be many responses to some questions, and questions might be posed at the same classification level before other higher level questions are asked. Such questions should involve both the cognitive and affective domains.

What are some ways of generating discussions?

The second method of initiating a discussion can begin with any level question. A higher cognitive level question can be posed as a focusing question for discussion. When a higher level question is posed initially, it should be in reference to a situation with which the students are familiar. For example:

> "Willie was usually very careful in his dealings with people. Why do you think he threw away all caution when he agreed to let Steve take his car without any explanation?"

> "Explain what caused the water to run down the canyon and cause a flood of mud and debris in the upper valley."

The creative problem solving discussion probably uses the highest levels of thought and a high degree of diversity and creativity. The more unknowns in a problem, within reason, the greater the chance for creativity. Such a problem must not have a clear cut right or wrong answer. The creative problem solving type of discussion has no one best solution. The process is what is important. It is not necessary for the students to come to a consensus for every problem. Problem solving discussions should include the following six sequential steps:

1. Planning procedure
2. Clarifying problem
2. Suggesting hypotheses
4. Processing information
5. Selecting hypotheses
6. Evaluating hypotheses

Problem solving discussions are concerned with the steps and procedures rather than specific answers. The evaluation of ideas generated in a discussion is suspended until the steps in both a brainstorming session and creative problem solving are completed.

Four types of discussion are identified by Singer and Donlan (1980, pp. 11–122). Free discussion is classified as an unstructured process that demands little teacher control. Semicontrolled discussion is used when students read different texts to obtain information about a common topic. The teacher shapes the direction of the discussion with a broad question at the beginning. Students contribute to the dialogue, with little structure. A controlled discussion led by the teacher controls students' contributions to a planned sequence of hierarchical questions. Discussion clusters or small groups of students discuss a specific problem posed for them by the teacher. The selected leader of each group moderates the discussion and reports the group solutions to the whole class.

LISTENING

How will teaching listening skills facilitate learning in the content areas?

Listening skills are a crucial element of student involvement in a discussion. A share of the communication process is active listening to understand what is expressed by others; it is receiving a speaker's verbal and nonverbal message and reacting to the ideas expressed by others. Listening is an active mental process, involving the use of cognitive and affective skills and the honoring of ideas expressed by others.

Hearing and listening are not synonymous. Hearing is a physiological process, and listening is related to the intellectual and experiential aspects of learning. Background experiences can influence the quality and extent of students' listening. Students obtain little meaning when they listen to ideas that are unrelated to their linguistic and cognitive backgrounds and to their cultural experiences (Kean and Personke 1976, p. 165 and Lundsteen 1976,

p. 91). Poor listening habits can be traced to the experiences of the students (Robeck and Wilson 1974, p. 225). When cultural differences prevent students from listening to teachers and participating in discussion, teachers might use the nonverbal behaviors of eye and body movements and posture that communiate meaning (Lundsteen 1976, p. 91).

Comprehending printed materials and understanding spoken words involve similar processes, according to Lundsteen (1979, p. 9), Tinker and McCullough (1975, p. 199), and Singer and Donlan (1980, p. 487). Lundsteen (1977) states that although a relationship exists between reading and listening, speech and reading differ in conciseness, abstractness, and the visual skills required in reading. Donlan and Singer suggest that problems in listening may be more difficult than in reading because the thoughts of a speaker are usually heard only once, and the students therefore must rely on their memory and notes. Of all the factors involved in listening and reading comprehension, such as unusual vocabulary and complex syntax patterns, age is the most critical: age factors relate to the basic acquisition of skills and experiences necessary to processing information (Danks 1980).

The results of research over a period of many years indicate that listening skills can be improved with direct instruction (Devine 1978). Schneeberg (1977) found that students in grades one to six scored higher on standardized reading tests after participating in a program that included listening to texts while they read. Studies by Fawcett (1966) and Desousa and Cowles (1969) indicate that listening skills of middle school students can be improved through instruction. Lane and Miller (1972) found that listening instruction aided the reading of underachieving adolescents. By contrast, Hollingsworth (1964) and Brewster (1966) found that instruction does not improve listening skills signficantly; these researchers decided that teacher involvement is more important in encouraging students' growth in listening skills. Brooks and Wulftange (1964) found that interest in the topic and the personality of the speaker affect listening comprehension. Good listeners are better adjusted personally and socially, according to Kelly (1963) and Ross (1964). Swalm (1972) affirms that listening is more effective than reading for students who are below average in reading skills. Lundsteen (1966, 1979) feels both reading (visual) and listening (aural) instructional strategies are needed to foster learning.

Lundsteen (1979, p. 74) states that the more effective listener "is one who consistently, in the least time, and in the greatest variety of circumstances, most closely approximates the speaker's meaning in the widest variety of spoken material." Lundsteen (1976, pp. 78–79) reports that the speed of thought can be more rapid than the sound of speech. Thus, the listener has time or space to think during the reception of a speaker's message. Another component of listening is the background of the listener. If listeners lack the background to understand a message, they will not be able to listen with comprehension.

Critical listening demands a motive, a consciousness of purpose, if one is

What does critical listening involve?

to follow the thread of discussion. To obtain meaning from a message requires that students listen and concentrate on the message expressed by the speaker. In a discussion, a critical listener learns to anticipate what the speaker will say, identify main ideas, discriminate between fact and opinion, evaluate ideas in relation to evidence, and summarize main points. Often new ideas are added as the listener recapitulates what he has heard. Reacting to an idea or message is an important aspect of listening and can be accomplished and indicated to others by using both nonverbal or verbal communication. Factors that cause inattentive listening include too much teacher talk, poor motivation to hear a specific message, failure to anticipate content of the message, and excessive distractions (Otto, McMenemy, and Smith 1973).

Listening is a learned process, and so can be improved. In a discussion situation, the listening skills and involvement of students can be enhanced by:

1. Arranging the physical environment to make students comfortable in a face to face situation.
2. Providing a warm, accepting climate that encourages trust.
3. Increasing skills in relating to students.
4. Seating hard of hearing students where they can see and hear all communications made by the teacher and other students.
5. Serving as a model of one who actively listens to the ideas of others.
6. Accepting the ideas expressed by students.
7. Centering attention on the message of a speaker.
8. Recognizing when students want to share ideas.
9. Posing questions at strategic places to keep the flow of discussion meaningful and at a high level of thinking.
10. Teaching students to paraphrase ideas expressed by others.
11. Providing opportunities for students to correct their misunderstandings and errors.
12. Teaching students how to differ from one another without antagonism.

Research by Lundsteen (1979, pp. 59–61) identifies efficient general and critical listening skills that involve cognitive and affective processes. They include:

1. Remembering sequence of words and ideas.
2. Following sequence in character development.
3. Remembering relevant details.
4. Understanding meanings of words in context.
5. Understanding denotative and connotative meanings of words.
6. Answering questions.
7. Paraphrasing spoken messages.
8. Identifying main ideas.

9. Understanding interrelationships of ideas.
10. Appreciating artistry and felicity of phrasing.
11. Understanding cause and effect.
12. Distinguishing fact from fancy.
13. Comparing and contrasting ideas.
14. Recognizing devices speakers use to influence listeners.
15. Evaluating bias and prejudice.
16. Determining ways to apply ideas.
17. Judging logic and relevance of information.
18. Evaluating qualifications of a speaker.

TIME INTERVALS AND REWARDS FOR QUESTIONS AND ANSWERS

The time interval between questions and answers, and teacher rewards to students' responses to questions both affect questioning and listening. The postreading activity of discussion provides opportunities for these interaction skills of wait-time and rewards to be learned and used.

The average teacher's "wait-time" is approximately one second between asking a question and calling on students to answer. After students make a response, a teacher generally waits less than one second to repeat what was said, to rephrase, or to ask another question (Arnold, Atwood, and Rogers 1973 and 1974; Rowe 1974; and Atwood and Stevens 1976). Such teacher domination prevents students from becoming involved in a discussion, encourages lower level questions and responses, and hinders the development of listening skills.

A fast pace of asking postreading questions is suited to some purposes, such as the review of facts, or memorizing basic information for skill building in mathematics. However, according to Rowe, an increase to five seconds or longer in the interval between the question and a student's response is more conducive to productive answers on higher thinking levels. During the longer wait-time, the students organize more complete answers rather than responding with "I don't know," or with a very short or incomplete answer, or with silence or a shrug of the shoulders. When the wait-times are very short there is little flexibility in the responses accepted by teachers. In contrast, when students are informed that a more difficult question is going to be asked and that they are to take time to think about it, their responses are more complete and more satisfying to them and their teachers.

Rowe (1969) found that when the time interval between the asking of a question and the response was increased the following changes occur in students' responses:

1. The length of student responses increases.
2. The sentence length increases.

3. Confidence, as expressed by voice tone, is higher.
4. Speculative thinking is evident.
5. Evidence is quoted to support ideas.
6. The number of questions asked by students increases.
7. The number of explanatory statements increases.
8. The number of suggested activities increases.
9. The interaction is greater among students as they share ideas.
10. The students rated as slow answer more questions.

Rowe and her associates also note that teachers who prepared through participation in an inservice program prolong wait-time change in their classroom behavior by:

1. Listening more carefully to student responses.
2. Showing a greater variation in the kinds of questions they ask.
3. Posing more higher cognitive level questions.
4. Modifying expectations for student performance.

Student involvement in a classroom discussion declines, and the positive influence of a longer wait-time is diminished, when teachers use positive verbal rewards generously. When teachers change their behavior over a period of a few weeks and stop giving positive verbal rewards, students react in the following ways, according to Rowe (1974):

1. There is more student interaction.
2. A greater number of academically less able students participate in discussions.
3. The students' task persistence is greater.
4. The spontaneous sharing of ideas between students is greater.
5. The number of alternative explanations offered is greater.
6. More suggestions for new activities are made.

Conversely, effective student involvement in classroom discussion is obstructed by verbal rewards from the teacher. Student behaviors that result include:

1. The number of alternative explanations offered markedly declines.
2. Task persistence decreases.
3. Teacher approval is sought by the use of speech and eye movements.
4. Problem solving efficiency is lowered.
5. Students tend to ignore information supplied by other students.

When high verbal reward systems operate in the classroom, the following teacher behaviors are observable:

1. The verbal rewards constitute up to one fourth of the teacher's total speech output.

2. The less achieving students receive more rewards that are ambiguous and less obvious.
3. The less achieving students are rewarded for trying rather than for accomplishing specific tasks.
4. The less achieving students receive more negative sanctions from teachers than the high achieving students.
5. The students judged to be bright by the teacher receive more smiles and eye contact.

Students participate more, become more self-directive, and more diverse in their responses to questions when teachers use verbal rewards sparingly or even withdraw them during a discussion. The purpose of not rewarding students is to obtain more student involvement and speculative and critical thinking during discussions. There is the possibility that when students are participating in a difficult task, verbal rewards given by the teacher may interfere with logical thought processes and increase the need to repeat steps.

For discussions to be of maximum value, the students must be active participants in asking and responding to questions. The teacher serves as a catalyst, which means responding in some way to students' ideas and posing questions at strategic places. A teacher may nod while students are responding to indicate his understanding of their communications. Eye contact and facial expressions can invite further student responses. General statements such as "Good thinking," "I like that," or "Fine" might be replaced with more directive language, for example, "That explanation of why the cost of living continues to climb provides us with a different idea to consider," or "That is a good way to conserve energy," or "What other ideas do you have?"

But of course, even if teachers should be sparing of verbal rewards during class discussion, they must find other ways to praise the students' accomplishment or contribution. Students' knowledge of their achievement in specific skills and their teacher's genuine liking and concern for them are essential to continuing progress in the academic area.

GROUPING PATTERNS

Grouping is an organizational plan for placing students who have similar needs or interests together, to improve instruction and enhance their achievement. Patterns of grouping should be flexible, and all students should have an opportunity to work in a variety of groups. The teacher will serve as a model discussion leader.

What are grouping patterns used for?

Reading differences among students are marked, and become greater at each higher grade level. Teachers use a variety of grouping patterns to cope with these differences. The size of groups may vary, from one individual to a whole class. The students may be grouped according to needs in specific skills, interests, and task or problem solving assignments. The purpose for the group determines its size and type. The number of groups depends upon the needs of the students, and the teacher's skill in classroom management (Burmeister 1978, pp. 90–91; Dillner and Olson, 1977, pp. 380–381; Harris and Sipay 1979, pp. 151–155; Karlin 1977, pp. 291–299; and Singer and Donlan 1980, pp. 123–130).

The use of groups helps a teacher to individualize instruction by modifying the purposes for instruction, the assigned task, the amount of practice time, the materials, and the follow-up activities. The difficulty of the instruction and task is adjusted to meet the needs of the students and purpose of the group.

There are times when all students in the class will benefit from the same instruction or activities. When a new chapter or unit of study is introduced or a filmstrip is used to provide background, for example, the whole class should meet as one group. But class instruction is not equally profitable for all students. Assessment of students' skills, such as using the card catalog or understanding basic concepts, serves as a basis for temporarily placing students with similar needs into a subgroup to receive the necessary instruction and practice. While the teacher provides instruction to a needs group, other groups of students work independently to complete assigned tasks. Not every group needs to do the same type of activity at the same time.

Students who share analogous interests can be formed into groups regardless of their reading abilities. Several of these heterogenous groups may function at the same time. Membership in interest groups may be voluntary. Interest groups may form to share experiences with a particular book or to work on a common project, disbanding when they complete their plans.

Discussion as a postreading activity may be accomplished in small groups or as a whole class. A total class activity may lead into small group activities, or small group work can precede a whole class endeavor. Students can be assigned to small groups to discuss a problem and find solutions. The discussion leader of each group might share the convergent or divergent solutions in a panel discussion. Fader (1976) suggests that students be assigned to a regular group of three to assist each other. In this group pattern, the students are to review and correct their assignments before submitting them to the teacher. As students work together on common assignments and problems, they reinforce their understandings, they interact, and they develop cohesiveness and continuing interrelationships. This pattern of grouping also provides time for a teacher to hold conferences with individuals and to instruct small groups of students.

Sometimes it is desirable to let students form groups on the basis of friendship and mutual interests. This procedure provides the teacher an opportunity to observe group behavior. Other small group formations might be achieved by:

1. Assigning numbers on a random basis, having students with the same number form a group.

2. Using geographical room locations, having students seated in the same small area work together as a group.

A minimum of three and a maximum of eight students are recommended for working together in small groups. Group processes improve when one student serves as an observer and reports his or her perceptions to the group.

Successful group activities in the content areas are based on many factors. These components are:

1. Using flexible grouping patterns.
2. Maintaining a warm, accepting climate in the classroom.
3. Arranging the physical facilities of the room to accommodate different groups.
4. Establishing the purposes and procedures for the groups to follow.
5. Evaluating the processes of groups.
6. Assessing the work of students in the various groups.
7. Keeping records of group formations and activities.
8. Planning ways to improve students' participation in group activities.

When students understand group processes and have been given guidance, they learn to plan and work together to meet group goals.

SUMMARY

Question type and placement in textual material functions to guide the students' expectancies concerning what might be critical to learn from content. Preposed, adjunct, and postposed questions stimulate students to search and process specific information. Directed reading activity and study guides are considered as ways to help students process information deemed important by the teacher. The directed reading-thinking activity and similar models involve students in directing their own reading by asking questions and establishing purposes.

Discussion, a postreading activity, provides students the opportunity to listen with understanding and to clarify and extend their understandings. This interaction process is improved when a teacher increases wait-time for answers to questions, and omits verbal rewards for correct answers.

Different patterns of grouping can be used to manage the reading differences among students by providing instruction and assignments to meet their assessed needs. Patterns of grouping students together should be flexible, and can vary in size from one individual to a whole class. The physical environment of the classroom should be organized to facilitate the seating arrangements and work of students as they participate in various group activities.

Reinforcement Activities

1. Plan and conduct both a Directed Reading Activity and a Directed Reading-Thinking Activity. Observe the different processes involved and note the strengths of each technique.

2. Select a chapter from a text. Design a study guide to help students process the information you consider important. Develop a guide that uses different types and placement of questions and uses questions in either a hierarchical or mixed order.

3. Examine the physical arrangement of your classroom. Could any changes be made to facilitate the involvement of students in a discussion? Record or videotape group and class discussions. Afterwards, listen to the recording and analyze your wait-time and verbal reward and feedback system, your use of question types, placing and pacing, and the amount of student involvement in asking questions. Devise a plan to follow in making any changes you deem necessary to improve the behaviors you analyzed. Put your plan into action and record the discussion. Evaluate and practice until you have reached your goal.

4. Listen to a speaker. Afterwards, write the main ideas and relevant details of the message.

5. Divide students into small groups to discuss solutions to a common problem. Provide time for the group leaders to share the solutions with the entire class. Afterwards, analyze the students' participation and understandings. Make plans to increase their learning and participation.

References

ANDRE, THOMAS. "Does Answering Higher-Level Questions While Reading Facilitate Productive Learning?" *Review of Educational Research* 49 (1979): 208–318.

ARNOLD, D. S., ATWOOD, R. K., and ROGERS, V. M. "An Investigation of Relationships among Question Level, Response Level and Lapse Time." *School Science and Mathematics* 73 (1973): 591–594.

ARNOLD, D. S., ATWOOD, R. K., and ROGERS, V. M. "Questions and Response Levels and Lapse Time Intervals." *Journal of Experimental Education* 43 (1974): 11–15.

ATWOOD, R. K., and STEVENS, J. T. "Relationships among Question Level, Response Level and Lapse Time: Secondary Science." *School Science and Mathematics* 76 (1976): 249–254.

BREWSTER, LAWRENCE W. "Effect of a Brief Training Program in Listening Improvement." *Speech Teacher* 15 (1966): 8–10.

BROOKS, KEITH, and WULFTANGE, SISTER J. MARIE. "Listener Response to Oral Interpretation." *Speech Monographs* 31 (1964): 73–79.

BURMEISTER, LOU E. *Reading Strategies for Middle and Secondary School Teachers.* 2nd ed. Reading, Massachusetts: Addison-Wesley Publishing Company, 1978.

CUNNINGHAM, DICK, and SHABLAK, SCOTT L. "Selective Reading Guide-O-Rama: The Content Teacher's Best Friends." *Journal of Reading* 18 (1975): 380–382.

DANKS, JOSEPH. "Comprehension in Listening and Reading: Same or Different? In *Reading and Understand-*

ing, edited by Frank B. Murray. Newark, Delaware: International Reading Association, 1980, 1–39.

DAVIDSON, JANE L. *The Quantity, Quality, and Variety of Teachers' Questions and Pupils' Responses during an Open-Communication Structured Group Directed Reading-Thinking Activity and a Closed-Communication Structured Group Directed Reading Activity.* Doctoral Dissertation, University of Michigan, 1970.

DESOUSA, ALBERT M., and COWLES, MILLY. "An Experimental Study to Determine the Efficacy of Specific Training in Listening." *Elementary English* 46 (1969): 512.

DEVINE, THOMAS G. "Listening: What Do We Know after Fifty Years of Research and Theorizing?" *Journal of Reading* 21 (1978): 296–304.

DILLNER, MARTHA H., and OLSON, JOANNE P. *Personalizing Reading Instruction in Middle, Junior, and Senior High Schools.* New York: Macmillan Publishing Co., Inc., 1977.

ESTES, THOMAS H., and VAUGHN, JR., JOSEPH L. *Reading and Learning in the Content Classroom.* Boston: Allyn and Bacon, Inc., 1978.

FADER, DANIEL N. *The New Hooked on Books.* New York: Berkley Medallion Books, 1976.

FAWCETT, ANNABEL E. "Training in Listening." *Elementary English* 43 (1966): 473–476.

FRASE, L. T. "Learning from Prose Material: Length of Passage, Knowledge of Results, and Position of Questions." *Journal of Educational Psychology.* 58 (1967): 266–272.

FRASE, L. T., PATRICK, E., and SCHUMER, H. "Effects of Question Position and Frequency upon Learning from Text under Different Levels of Incentive." *Journal of Educational Psychology* 61 (1970): 52–56.

GALL, MEREDITH D., et al. "Effects of Questioning Techniques and Recitation on Student Learning." *American Educational Research Journal* 15 (1978): 175–199.

HARRIS, ALBERT J., and SIPAY, EDWARD R. *How to Teach Reading.* New York: Longman, Inc., 1979.

HELLER, JACK H. "Learning From Prose Text: Effects of Readability Level, Inserted Questions, Difficulty and Individual Differences." *Journal of Educational Psychology* 66 (1974): 202–211.

HERBER, HAROLD. *Teaching Reading in Content Areas.* 2nd ed. Englewood Cliffs, New Jersey: Prentice-Hall, 1978.

HOLLINGSWORTH, PAUL M. "Effect of Two Listening Programs on Reading and Listening." *Journal of Communications* 14 (1964): 19–21.

HOSKISSON, KENNETH. "False Questions and Right Answers." *The Reading Teacher* 27 (1973): 159–162.

HUNKINS, FRANCIS P. *Involving Students in Questioning.* Boston: Allyn and Bacon, Inc., 1976.

KARLIN, ROBERT. *Teaching Elementary Reading.* 2nd ed. New York: Harcourt Brace Jovanovich, Inc., 1975.

KARLIN, ROBERT. *Teaching Reading in High School: Improving Reading in Content Areas.* 3rd ed. Indianapolis: Bobbs-Merrill Educational Publishing Company, 1977.

KEAN, JOHN M., and PERSONKE, CARL. *The Language Arts: Teaching and Learning in the Elementary School.* New York: St. Martin's Press, 1976.

KELLY, CHARLES M., "Mental Ability and Personality Factors in Listening." *Quarterly Journal of Speech* 49 (1963): 152–156.

KORAN, MARY LOU, and KORAN, JR., JOHN J. "Interaction of Learner Aptitudes with Question Pacing in Learning Prose." *Journal of Educational Psychology* 67 (1975): 76–82.

LANE, P. K., and MILLER, M. S. "Listening: Learning for Underachieving Adolescents." *Journal of Reading* 15 (1972): 488–491.

LUNDSTEEN, SARA W. "Critical Listening: An Experiment." *Elementary English* 66 (1966): 311–315.

LUNDSTEEN, SARA W. *Children Learn to Communicate.* Englewood Cliffs, New Jersey: Prentice-Hall, Inc., 1976.

LUNDSTEEN, SARA W. "On Developmental Relations Between Language-Learning and Reading." *The Elementary School Journal* 77 (1977): 192–203.

LUNDSTEEN, SARA W. *Listening: Its Impact at All Levels on Reading and the Other Language Arts.* Rev. ed. Urbana, Illinois: National Council of Teachers of English, 1979.

MANZO, ANTHONY V. "The ReQuest Procedure." *Journal of Reading* 2 (1969): 123–126.

MANZO, ANTHONY V. "The ReQuest Procedure." In *Reading Comprehension at Four Linguistic Levels*, edited by Clifford Pennock. Newark, Delaware: International Reading Association, 1979, 57–61.

MCKENZIE, G. R. "Some Effects of Frequent Quizzes on Inferential Thinking." *American Educational Research Journal* 9 (1972): 231–240.

ORTIZ, ROSE KATZ. "Using Questions as a Tool in Reading." *Journal of Reading* 2 (1977): 109–114.

OTTO, WAYNE, MCMENEMY, RICHARD, and SMITH, RICHARD. *Corrective and Remedial Teaching.* 2nd ed. Boston: Houghton Mifflin Co., 1973.

PETRE, RICHARD M. *Quantity, Quality and Variety of*

Pupil Responses During an Open-Communication Structured Group Directed Reading-Thinking Activity and a Closed-Communication Structured Group Directed Reading Activity. Doctoral Dissertation, University of Delaware, 1970.

RICKARDS, JOHN P., and DiVISTA, FRANCIS J. "Type and Frequency of Questions in Processing Textual Material." *Journal of Educational Psychology* 66 (1974): 354–362.

RICKARDS, JOHN P. "Interaction of Position and Conceptual Levels of Adjunct Questions on Immediate and Delayed Retention of Text." *Journal of Educational Psychology* 68 (1976): 210–217.

RICKARDS, JOHN P., and HATCHER, CATHERINE W. "Interspersed Meaningful Learning Questions as Semantic Cues for Poor Comprehenders." *Reading Research Quarterly* 4 (1977–1978): 538–553.

ROBECK, MILDRED C., and WILSON, JOHN A. R. *Psychology of Reading.* New York: John Wiley and Sons, Inc., 1974.

ROSS, RAMON. "A Look at Listeners." *Elementary School Journal* 64 (1964): 369–372.

ROWE, MARY BUDD. "Science, Silence, and Sanctions." *Science and Children* 6 (1969): 11–13.

ROWE, MARY BUDD. "Wait-Times and Rewards as Instructional Variables: Their Influence on Language, Logic and Fate Control: Part I. Wait-Time." *Journal of Research in Science Teaching* 11 (1974): 81–94.

ROWE, MARY BUDD. "Relation of Wait-Time and Rewards to the Development of Language, Logic, and Fate Control: Part II. Rewards." *Journal of Research in Science Teaching* 11 (1974): 291–308.

SCHNEEBERG HELEN. "Listening While Reading: A Four Year Study." *The Reading Teacher* 30 (1977): 629–635.

SCHWARTZ, ELAINE, and SHEFF, ALICE. "Student Involvement in Questioning for Comprehension." *The Reading Teacher* 2 (1975): 150–154.

SINGER, HARRY. "Active Comprehension: From Answering to Asking Questions." In *Inchworm, Inchworm: Persistent Problems in Reading Instruction,* edited by Constance M. McCullough. Newark, Delaware: International Reading Association, 1980, 222–232.

SINGER, HARRY, and DONLAN, DAN. *Reading and Learning from Text.* Boston: Little, Brown and Company, 1980.

STAUFFER, RUSSELL G. *Directing Reading Maturity as a Cognitive Process.* New York: Harper and Row, Publishers, 1969.

STAUFFER, RUSSELL G. *Directing the Reading-Thinking Process.* New York: Harper and Row, Publishers, 1975.

STAUFFER, RUSSELL G. *The Language-Experience Approach to the Teaching of Reading.* 2nd ed. New York: Harper and Row, Publishers, 1980.

STAUFFER, RUSSELL G., and HARRELL, MAX M. "Individualizing Reading-Thinking Activities." *The Reading Teacher* 28 (1975): 765–769.

SWALM, JAMES E. "A Comparison of Oral Reading, Silent Reading, and Listening Comprehension." *Education* 92 (1972): 111–115.

TINKER, MILES, and McCULLOUGH, CONSTANCE. *Teaching Elementary Reading.* 4th ed. Englewood Cliffs, New Jersey: Prentice-Hall, Inc., 1975.

TUTOLO, DANIEL J. "The Study Guide—Types, Purposes and Value." *Journal of Reading* 20 (1977): 503–507.

WATTS, G. H., and ANDERSON, R. C. "Effects of Three Types of Inserted Questions on Learning from Prose." *Journal of Educational Psychology* 62 (1971): 387–394.

WIESENDANGER, KATHERINE D., and WOLLENBERG, JOHN P. "Prequestioning Inhibits Third Graders' Reading Comprehension." *The Reading Teacher* 31 (1978): 892–895.

ZEAMAN, D., and HOUSE, B. J. "The Relation of I.Q. and Learning." In *Learning and Individual Differences,* edited by Robert M. Gagné. Columbus, Ohio: Bobbs-Merrill, 1967, 192–212.

Bibliography

ALEXANDER, J. ESTILL, and FILLER, RONALD C. "Group Cohesiveness and Reading Instruction." *The Reading Teacher.* 27 (1974): 446–450.

AMIDON, EWARD, and HOUGH, JOHN, eds. *Interaction Analysis: Theory, Research and Application.* Reading, Mass.: Addison-Wesley, 1967.

BROPHY, JENE. "Teacher Praise: A Functional Analysis." *Review of Educational Research.* 51 (1981): 5–32.

BUSH, CLIFFORD L., and HUEBNER, MILDRED H. *Strategies for Reading in the Elementary School.* New York: Macmillan Publishing Company, Inc., 1979.

ESTES, THOMAS, and VAUGHN, JOSEPH JR. *Reading and Learning in the Content Classroom.* Boston: Allyn and Bacon, Inc., 1978.

GRAVES, MICHAEL F., and CLARK, DONNA L. "The Effect of Adjunct Questions on High School Low Achievers' Reading Comprehension." *Reading Improvement.* 18 (1981): 8–13.

MILES, MATTHEW. *Learning to Work in Groups.* New York: Teachers College Press, 1973.

MOFFETT, JAMES, and WAGNER, BETTY JANE. *Student-Centered Language Arts and Reading, K-13.* Boston: Houghton Mifflin, 1976.

MANZO, ANTHONY. "Guided Reading Procedure." *Journal of Reading.* 18 (1975): 287–291.

SEFKOW, SUSAN B., and MYERS, JEROME. "Review Effects of Inserted Questions on Learning Prose." *American Educational Research Journal.* 17 (1981): 435–447.

SHAVELSON, RICHARD J., BERLINER, DAVID C., RAVITCH, MICHAEL M., and LOEDING, DAVID. "Effects of Position and Type of Question on Learning Prose Material: Interaction of Treatments with Individual Differences." *Journal of Educational Psychology.* 66 (1974): 40–48.

SMITH, CARL, SMITH, SHARON, and MIKULECKY, LARRY. *Teaching Reading in Secondary School Content Subjects: A Bookthinking Process.* New York: Holt, Rinehart, and Winston, 1978.

WAYNANT, LOUISE, and WILSON, ROBERT. *Learning Centers—A Guide for Effective Use.* New York: McGraw-Hill, 1974.

SUBJECT INDEX

A
Abbreviations, in homemaking reading, 36–37
Adjunct questions, 177–79
Advance organizer, 102
Allegory, 129
Analysis, questioning for, 164–65
Affective questioning, 167–72
Antonyms, 123–25
Art, reading skills for, 29–30
Assessment
  of readability, 42–65
  of study skills, 71–85

B
Basc clauses, effect of on readability, 47
Bibliographic and note cards, teaching use of, 94–96
Book classification systems, 93–94
Buros Mental Measurement Yearbook, 73
Buros Reading Tests and Reviews, 73
Business, reading skills for, 27–29

C
Card catalogue, teaching use of, 92–93
Character analysis, as component of comprehension, 21–22
Classification, as comprehension skill, 16
Cloze procedure, 51–55
Cognitive questioning, 159–67
Comprehension. *See also* Readability
  cloze procedure and, 52–53
  depth of meaning as part of, 21
  factors influencing, 3–4
  improvement of, in content areas, 8–9. *See also specific content areas*
  informal test of, 59
  open textbook inventory for, 59
  overview of, 1–4
  questioning for, 164
Concept development, 118–21

Conceptualization of time and space, 12
Conclusion, signals of, 128
Content areas
  comprehension in, 8–9. *See also specific content areas*
  concept development and, 120
Context clues, 123–31
  assessment of use of, 83
Criterion-referenced tests, 75

D
Dale-Chall Readability Formula, 44, 49, 50
Data, description and application of in science reading, 17
Definitional paragraphs, 131
Depth of meaning, reading for, 21. *See also* Comprehension
Descriptive paragraphs, 132
Diagrams and charts
  interpretation of, for art reading, 29
  interpretation of, for homemaking reading, 36
  interpretation of, for physical education and health reading, 34
Dictionary
  assessment of use of, 82–83
  usage of, 134–35
Directed Reading Activity (DRA), 179–80
Directed Reading-Thinking Activity (DR-TA), 181–83
Discussion, 192–94
Drama, reading skills required for, 24–27

E
Educational Resources Information Center/Clearinghouse for the Retrieval of Information and Evaluation on Reading (ERIC/CRIER), 73

English, reading skills required for, 20–24
Euphemism, 129–30
Evaluation, questioning for, 65–66
Explanatory paragraphs, 132
Expository writing, 9
Eye movements, in reading, 143–46

F
Facts
  determining significant, 19, 28
  differentiating from opinion, 12
Figures of speech, 129–31
Flesch Formula, 44
Flexible reading, 141–42
Fog Formula, 44
Following directions, 28, 30, 110–12
  in homemaking reading, 36
  in physical education and health reading, 33–34
Formulas, scientific, 13, 16
Fry Readability Formula, 44, 49, 50
Fry Readability Graph, 45–47

G
Glossary, teaching use of, 91
Grammar, effect of on readability, 47
Graphic information, 2
Graphic materials
  teaching correct use of, 112–14
  use of, in science books, 13–15
  use of, in social studies books, 10
Graphic post organizer, 104
Graphic symbols. *See* Words
Grouping patterns, 199–201
Group reading inventories, 56–57, 60–62

H
Harris-Jacobson Readability Formulas, 44
Hidden thoughts, discovery of, 84

NAME INDEX